BOU BOUSTEAD; H. SIR.

THE WIND OF MORNING

511527

D1610849

THE WIND OF MORNING

THE WIND
OF MORNING

The autobiography of
HUGH BOUSTEAD

*Once in the wind of morning
I ranged the thymy wold;
The world-wide air was azure
And all the brooks ran gold.*
A SHROPSHIRE LAD

1971
CHATTO & WINDUS
LONDON

Published by
Chatto and Windus Ltd
40 William IV Street
London WC2

*

Clarke, Irwin and Co Ltd
Toronto

ISBN 07011 1314 6

Copyright © Hugh Boustead 1971
Printed in Great Britain by
Butler & Tanner Ltd, Frome and London

FOREWORD

WITHOUT the expert editorial assistance of Mr Peter Cochrane this personal story would never have appeared in print. I am deeply indebted to him, not only for his skill and judgement in editing the manuscript, but also for his kindness and patience throughout its preparation.

In its original form the manuscript was dictated by me: the Sudanese and Ethiopian chapters to Sudanese clerks immediately after the Ethiopian Campaign and the Border Force operations ended in 1945; the rest, twenty years later, to Mr Ronald Kilgour in Tangier, where I worked on it with his help for nearly a year. I am greatly indebted to him for his help and advice.

The only diaries I ever kept were during the Russian Civil War on the Don in 1919, the Ethiopian Campaign of 1940–41, and on Everest and Kangchenjunga. But for the period of the First World War I have been able to draw on the long letters I wrote to my parents from France. For the rest, I have trusted to a very vivid (though quite possibly inaccurate) memory, and like Disraeli may well have 'remembered more than I have seen'.

H. B.

CONTENTS

ILLUSTRATIONS

MAPS

Chapter One

CADET AND MIDSHIPMAN

When I would muse in boyhood
The wild green woods among,
And nurse resolves and fancies
Because the world was young.

A. E. HOUSMAN

MY grandfather, John Boustead, came of an old Cumberland family. He was born in Ceylon in 1820 where his father owned extensive coffee estates which he had purchased between 1810 and 1840 while Army Agent to the British regiments in Ceylon. John Boustead studied for the engineering profession but entered his father's coffee business which by 1850 had reached large proportions, and for thirty years he devoted himself energetically to its cultivation and extension.

In 1879 the leaf blight on coffee plants created a crisis in the industry, culminating in the total failure of the coffee crop throughout the island. However, his foresight and resource proved equal to the occasion and his energetic leadership as one of the influential owners and agents in Ceylon was instrumental in securing the adoption of tea in place of coffee, which led to the ultimate recovery of the island from economic disaster.

My father, who was at Harrow when the coffee crash came, abandoned his intention of going into the Indian Civil Service and after a year in my grandfather's London office went out to Ceylon to spend the next twenty-five years tea planting. The family by this time had had nearly a hundred years' connection with the island.

During a holiday in England he met my mother who was the third daughter of Jameson Alers Hankey, and they were married two years later. Jameson Hankey, my grandfather, went into the Indian Civil Service. He had a large income, retired from the I.C.S. after five years, and spent much of his life cruising in his yacht.

I myself was born in 1895 on a tea estate in Ceylon, and have the most vivid memories of the island. My father was in charge of probably the most beautiful tea estate in Ceylon, above Nuwara Eliya at a height of 8,000 feet. There were about seven acres of garden round the house, which looked across a lake on to forested mountains. The family was blissfully happy in these lovely surroundings and it was a paradise for children.

It was about 1904, when I was nine, that my parents decided to come home permanently, for their children's education, and settled in Wimbledon. After a year at a private school, my brother and I were sent to boarding school at Horton Hall, in Bedfordshire. We were enormously happy there, but I was determined to get into the Navy and got the idea in my head that the school would not prepare me properly for entrance to Osborne, the naval cadet College. I badgered my parents to send me to Cheam School on the grounds that it was a preparatory naval school with a high record of success, and eventually got my way. I was booked to come up before the Board of Admirals in the autumn of 1907, and if successful would join Osborne College as a naval cadet in the Easter term of 1908. Walking in before the Board, dressed in a green Norfolk suit, I was asked by some old Admiral, 'That's a very nice suit you've got on, my boy, what's it made of?' The answer, 'Lovat tweed, sir,' brought a nod of approval; I remember little else of the various questions except that they asked me whether I had any relations in the Navy. I have no doubt that my answer that Admiral of the Fleet Sir Algernon Lyons was a great uncle assisted their decision. Lord Fisher is recorded as having said, 'a bit of healthy nepotism is one of the keys to efficiency'.

It was a cold day in early February when the 1908 Drake Term, which was our batch, crossed to Cowes in the ferry boat, all very self-conscious in our new cadet uniforms. We were all about twelve and a half years old and had two years to run at Osborne before going on to Dartmouth. The discipline was strict; you ran everywhere at all times. You jumped into a cold plunge first thing in the morning, and into a hot one after games, which, alternating with runs, beagling, boxing or rowing, were compulsory every day. Discipline was maintained by the dormitory Cadet Captain who had a knotted white bell rope which rang the gong by his bed and served as a 'tickler' for cadets who were late out of bed on their way down to the plunge.

Archer Shee (the Winslow Boy) was in the next bed to me. It was about half-way through our first term that the poor lad was accused by the postmistress of having forged a postal order belonging to Terence Back who camped on the other side of the dormitory. The boy was expelled, and it was several years before he was cleared by Lord Carson's persistence and personal faith in the boy's rectitude. It entailed the passing of a Bill through both Houses to enable Major Archer Shee to sue the Crown, and in doing so he was virtually ruined, even though he had been a rich man and eventually

won his case. At some late stage in the trial the postmistress admitted that she had been mistaken. Lord Carson was said to have refused the Woolsack in order to clear the boy. Young Archer Shee was sent to Stonyhurst, later joined the Guards at the beginning of the War and was killed in action at Neuve Chapelle in 1915.

Once at Osborne I went steadily down the term and was very near the bottom. Languages, English, History and Seamanship I enjoyed, but Mathematics, Science and Engineering I positively disliked. It was customary for the bottom two or three boys in each term to be sacked before they could go on to Dartmouth. I evaded this, I think partly by having had the good fortune to take up boxing at Cheam and showing a certain aptitude for it.

I loved the life at Dartmouth College, above all for its setting in some of the finest countryside in England. My most vivid memory of the place is of the rain blowing over the wooded Kingswear Hills across the River Dart.

But I remained very low down the term throughout my time there, for exactly the same causes, and continued to hate Engineering and Science. For English and History I was lucky to have Mallory of Everest fame and another master who was a keen Alpine climber, whose name I have now forgotten. They both used to end their lessons by reading and discussing mountaineering stories and showing us pictures of the High Alps. They soon set us alight to follow in their steps. Fourteen years later Mallory was killed on Everest and in 1933, when I was a member of Ruttledge's Expedition, we found his ice axe above Camp Five. The mystery as to whether he ever reached the summit, or perished in the first attempt, remains unsolved.

On whole holidays during the winter and easter terms, the boys were allowed to hire horses and to follow the beagles which were hunted by Buller, the Commander. We invariably had a tremendous run. I enjoyed it so much that I spent my winter holidays hunting with the Garth hounds in a country which has long since been spoiled by motor cars and buildings. Riding and hunting had now become an obsession only equalled by dreams of service with a cavalry regiment on the North West Frontier.

In February 1911 the Drake Term reported at Plymouth on board H.M.S. *Cornwall* for a six months' cruise in the West Indies, thence to Bermuda, Halifax, Nova Scotia, and Newfoundland. It was an idyllic cruise in the Caribbean; Halifax was bitterly cold in contrast. I will never forget having to raise steam in the picket boat at 5.30 a.m. whilst she was lying at the boom in harbour tossing about in the troubled waters. I went over the lower boom, tremulously hanging on to the safety wire, and dropped down, frozen in a canvas overall too tight to wear warm underclothes, seasick and wretched, trying to make the boilers get up steam. The combination of cold, seasickness and the smell of oil was a torment and made me increasingly dislike the engineering side of the Navy. By this time I had come to loathe the heated constriction of the enforced tours of duty in the engine room so much that I decided I had better break away at the end of this cruise and go to a profession where I could ride horses to my heart's content and live under the open skies away from the claustrophobia of marine engineering.

The cruise was followed by manœuvres in the North Sea. We then had to sit our examinations before going on leave pending our appointments as midshipmen. I had planned to fail in the engineering exam and turned out papers which were calculated to ensure it. My parents were shocked when the results came out. However, to their surprise, the Admiralty letter informing me that I had failed in engineering stated that 'by their Lordships' pleasure' I was posted to the Blake Term to accompany them in H.M.S. *Cumberland* on the second part of their cruise to the Mediterranean.

My parents' reaction was that I was singularly fortunate and blessed by some unseen power to have been given another opportunity to take the examinations. I told them that I disliked the engineering so much that I would prefer Sandhurst and a military career; but they persuaded me to persist in my naval career and to take the next engineering exam in earnest.

It was winter in the Mediterranean when I joined the *Cumberland* but still very pleasant weather as we visited the principal Mediterranean ports east to Alexandria. As a result of my parents' admonitions I successfully passed all the exams, felt extremely virtuous and had a very happy family Christmas at Ascot, with a few weeks of fox hunting.

The New Year brought great excitement with the news that I was appointed to join H.M.S. *Hyacinth* in Portsmouth on 6th February. She was to be the Flagship on the Cape Station. The *Hyacinth* was an old cruiser with many years' service in the East Indies. The new junior midshipmen were very frightened when we joined on a freezing February morning in 1913, and we tossed up to settle who should go on board first and report to the Commander, Kemble Lambert, who was commissioning the ship alongside the quay at Portsmouth. Kemble Lambert, though still only thirty-seven, had snow-white hair over a very handsome face with striking blue eyes. Most of us were terrified of him and I remember I used to run anywhere to avoid him, or appear to be doing something when he approached.

Hyacinth carried a ship's company of some 800 men. The midshipmen's quarters were very cramped and uncomfortable. The Gun Room was a narrow passage, just wide enough to take a long table with a settee on one side and a bench on the other. It was above the engine room, and just outside the engine room door, so we enjoyed the smells and noise of the machinery whenever the door was open. We slept in hammocks either down below or up on the quarter deck. There were two Sub Lieutenants in charge of the Gun Room, and its eight midshipmen; and in those days Gun Room discipline was strict. We were beaten for our sins of omission and commission, in addition to the risk of being mast-headed by the Commander.

I did not enjoy our first cruise very much until we reached calm seas, for it was the junior midshipmen's job to carry out 'scuttle drill' which consisted of opening and closing the scuttles between rolls, to aerate the Gun Room. But once on station at the Cape I began to enjoy life. The Cape Squadron covered the Atlantic and west coast of Africa up to Sierra Leone, including the islands of Ascension and St Helena. On the east, the station covered the Indian Ocean north to Mombasa and the Seychelles, and to the south as far as Tristan da Cunha. Our base was the lovely harbour of Simonstown, below the hills which dominate False Bay. We were to spend about half the year at Simonstown, and the other half cruising to the ports and islands in our area.

The Cape station was a 'plum', and we all felt fortunate to be there. The cruises were a delight, apart from the torture of having to spend a total of three months a year working in the engine and boiler rooms, a steaming hot prison in which one was deafened by the old reciprocating engines. The people of the Cape were very hospitable; we were invited to stay for weekend leave at houses and farms where we could ride, or go to the races, or play rugger, or swim in the gigantic surf at Muizenburg. When we were cruising, we could get shore leave to go shooting, and to see something of the territories we visited.

A feature of the Cape summers was the east wind which blows with tremendous force across False Bay. The Commander was a keen sailor, and to make the midshipmen good at handling boats he encouraged us to use the ship's sailing boats to fetch stores or carry the liberty men to and from Simonstown. The largest of these boats were the sailing launches, which could take about fifty men and in a smart breeze moved through the water at a great pace.

I have a very vivid memory of leaving Simonstown pier in a near gale, as midshipman of a sailing launch full of liberty men bemused with beer from the local pubs. We scudded the mile or so to the ship at tremendous speed and when the final moment came to put the helm down to bring her bow up into the wind to come alongside, I left it a second or so too late. We tore ahead into the Admiral's gangway, carrying away the lower half, and with the weight we were carrying shot ahead so that the mast went through the bottom of the starboard cutter which was hanging in davits over the ship's side. Whilst this performance was going on, the Commander stood on the gangway roaring at me through a megaphone. I think this helped to unnerve me sufficiently to impair my judgement. Anyway, it was 'up the masthead till told to come down', which would normally be at sunset. It was now about 4 p.m. Shortly afterwards, the Commander slipped ashore where he and his wife had a very pleasant house. He would return in the morning at 5.40 sharp in the whaler and, as the crew pulled him off, would eye the ship with loving care to see that the yards were square and all was trim.

It was cold on the foretop, particularly in a midshipman's round jacket, and after dusk I came down surrepetitiously and got the quartermaster to give me cocoa and biscuits and some blankets under one of the ladders. Before first light I was up again sitting expectantly on the topmast. As the Commander pulled off he quickly spotted a figure aloft; he was startled and spurred the boat's crew to pull hard. He sent the side boy straight up to call me down. I was already very cold, and pretended not to feel the side boy's hand on my foot as he stretched up from the rigging below to shake my leg. Eventually after some minutes I moved down very slowly. The Commander, who had forgotten to leave an order for me to come down, was clearly shaken and said, 'Been up all night, boy? Go down to the Gun Room and get some cocoa and warm up.'

Our last peace time cruise, which I spent on loan to H.M.S. *Pegasus*, was to Mauritius and then Madagascar, where we had our first news of the seriousness of the situation in Europe. We were told by the Admiralty to clear all ships for action, and to be ready to return to war stations. I was recalled to the Flagship, and we steamed to Zanzibar, which has always seemed to me an epitome of the east – palm trees and cloves, coral shores and calm blue seas, smells of spices and Arab food.

A German light cruiser, the *Königsberg*, was known to be off the East African Coast and it was not difficult to guess that her war task was to harry British shipping in the Indian Ocean. On the night of 3rd–4th August, as we steamed south from Zanzibar, we passed her steaming north. Both sides had darkened ship and were ready for action, but there were still a few hours to go before the ultimatum to Germany ran out; we passed in silence. Those few hours were costly, for in the next month or so the *Königsberg* sank a lot of merchant ships, and early one morning caught the *Pegasus* taking

1b. Private soldier,
South African Scottish
1915

2. Sudan 1930: Camel Corps on trek

on rations in Zanzibar Harbour, sinking her with many casualties. She then went up the Rufiji River in German East Africa.

Our first task as a squadron was to escort a fleet of transports taking British troops back home from South Africa. It was an uneventful voyage for us, but soon after we handed the convoy over to the cruisers *Crecy*, *Hogue* and *Aboukir*, a German submarine attack was mounted, and all three were sunk with all hands. About twenty Osborne cadets, only fourteen years old, were drowned in the sinking.

In late November 1914 we were ordered west to the Falkland Islands. Admiral von Spee, commanding the *Scharnhorst* and *Gneisenau*, had crossed the Pacific from China waters, and almost annihilated Admiral Craddock's squadron at Coronel, off the west coast of South America. A counter force was rapidly built up, but our presence was unnecessary since Admiral Sturdee destroyed both battle cruisers a few days before we reached the Falklands. Christmas found us covering the landing of South African troops at Luderitzbucht and Walfisch Bay for the assault on German South West Africa.

From the time war was declared my night action station at sea was the foretop of the *Hyacinth*, situated half way up the mast and only slightly above the tops of the funnels. There were six of us who slept on this circular platform on gym mats. It was surrounded by a circular metal sheet, shoulder high, and above that a canvas cover. At this height whenever the ship rolled the foretop travelled about four times the distance. When she pitched and came down in a heavy sea the whole mast reverberated on the descent. If the wind was astern the coal and cinders from the funnel would blow in through the awning cover, and we would climb down after 'stand to' in the morning looking like chimney sweeps. This situation intensified my seasickness and for the first three days each successive time we went out I kept a bucket in the foretop and would be sick into it, sometimes seven times an hour. We took it in turn to look out, one seaman and one officer on watch at a time. The nights on those voyages through the Southern Ocean to the Falklands were some of the most trying I ever experienced; we were moving perpetually through huge seas.

Early in 1915 the *Hyacinth* returned to Zanzibar, which for the next few months was our base for the blockade of the Rufiji River, where we had to keep the *Königsberg* bottled up. Our forward base was Mafia Island, off the river mouth, but we returned to Zanzibar every week or ten days to refuel and give the men a run ashore.

Three of us midshipmen, McCall, Pasmore and I, planned an operation to blow up the *Königsberg* with underwater charges. The

plan involved floating into the Rufiji River on a raft covered with
leaves, paddling up by night and fastening charges to the hull of
the *Königsberg* below water. The plan was eventually turned down
by Admiral King-Hall as too dangerous, and there is no doubt
that the risks of both crocodiles and malaria would have been considerable, quite apart from the Germans. The entry to the mouth
of the river was guarded by machine guns and light guns from the
Königsberg.

During these days of watching, the Captain received a coded
signal from the Admiralty telling us that on the following morning
at 6 a.m. a cargo ship, flying the Norwegian flag and with a cargo
of timber, would be at a certain latitude and longitude in the Indian
Ocean. The signal continued: 'Underneath the timber are arms and
ammunition for the German troops in East Africa. Intercept and
capture her.' There was considerable excitement on board and
shortly before 6 a.m. we were waiting with the Admiral and the
Captain, the Commander and the Navigator, all anxiously surveying
the horizon from the bridge.

No wisp of smoke, no sign of a mast or a hull appeared. By 6.30
a.m. the Navigator became agitated and started anxiously checking
his position as worked out by star sights. To his horror he discovered
that we were some twenty or thirty sea miles south of the latitude
given by the Admiralty. We dared not look at the Admiral or the
Captain when this appalling blunder was disclosed. The Navigator,
who saw his whole professional future dissolve, looked as though he
would faint, and the Captain was beyond speech. We steamed north
till we reached the proper position but no ship was in sight. The
Admiralty were informed by cable and came straight back with a
reply that at six o'clock the next morning we would find the ship
off Mansa Bay and about to enter it.

At six the following morning, there she was. On sighting us she
steamed full speed along the tongue of land which encloses the
harbour and at the end of which is the entrance. It was decided to
follow her in and, keeping as near as possible in her wake to avoid
any mines, we entered the harbour with the six-inch guns trained
forward. The crew had already made off in the boats for the shore
and a machine gun opened up on the *Hyacinth* from the mainland,
about a quarter of a mile away. I spent the next hour or so at the
direction control in the foretop with the Gunnery Lieutenant, while
we exercised the six-inch guns at point-blank range, and watched
the masts and the poop fly out of the ship as the shells raked her.
A boarding party was sent off but returned to report that she was
burning furiously. We did not wait long in Mansa Bay, but the
interlude was a lively one for the ship's company.

In June 1915 the monitors *Severn* and *Mersey* arrived from England to attack the *Königsberg* in the Rufiji River. These ships were specially designed for actions in shallow waters. We covered their entrance to the Rufiji River by bombarding the Boche gun emplacements at the mouth with six-inch shells from the *Hyacinth*. They steamed in and during the subsequent action that day the *Königsberg* guns caught one of the monitors, destroying a gun and its crew. The action continued well into the afternoon with the *Königsberg* still firing. They returned next day and continued the action until all the *Königsberg's* guns were silenced and the aeroplanes overhead reported her out of action.

After this final action on the 6th July 1915, with the seas cleared of enemy ships, it was apparent that we would be filling a purely routine security role on the Cape station for the rest of the war.

I was thoroughly unsettled, and determined somehow to get into an area of active service; the war seemed very far away from the pleasant life of the Cape station. Just before the Rufiji River action, I had received a telegram from my parents telling me of my brother Clive's death. He was with the Dublin Fusiliers, and had been killed in the Gully Ravine at Gallipoli.

There was a chance of volunteering for the newly formed Royal Naval Air Service, but the Admiral turned down my application. Then in July 1915 all the other midshipmen except me were recalled to the Home Fleet. We had a tremendous party to celebrate their sailing orders, and the day after it I went riding at Muizenberg. There I saw a poster announcing that a South African Brigade was being raised at Potchefstroom in the Transvaal for service in France. I decided that this was my way out.

Chapter Two

PRIVATE SOLDIER

Clay lies still, but blood's a rover;
Breath's a ware that will not keep.
Up, lad: when the journey's over
There'll be time enough to sleep.

A. E. HOUSMAN

MY plan was soon made. I took into my confidence my greatest friend on board, Dennis Pasmore, then paymaster sub. Two days later on 4th August 1915 I left the *Hyacinth* for Capetown and travelled by the afternoon train from Simonstown carrying a bag containing civilian clothes; we were not allowed ashore except in uniform. In Capetown I changed in a public lavatory at the station and put the bag containing my uniform into the cloakroom.

The city was crowded, and after two years on and off at the Cape going ashore and meeting a large number of people, I was afraid of being recognized. I had chosen the name of McLaren as my pseudonym and decided to join the South African Scottish, newly forming from the Transvaal Scottish and Cape Town Highlanders. I gave Springfield Farm near Pietermaritzburg as the place where I was serving my apprenticeship as a young farmer. I did not pretend to be South African born but said I was a public school boy from home proposing to settle in Natal.

I got through the initial attestation easily enough and there were no queries about the existence of a Springfield Farm in Natal. The real difficulty came when I went in for the medical examination. We had to strip to the buff and to my horror the doctor in front of whom I appeared was none other than Sir John Hewitt who had been dining as the principal guest of the Gun Room only a few days before. He took one look at me and said, 'What are you doing here, my boy?' I looked at him blankly, feeling at a great disadvantage in my nakedness, and replied, 'I'm down from Natal.' He said, 'But you are a sailor.' I said, 'I don't understand you, sir – I am a farmer in Natal,' and stared at him brazenly, my whole flesh going redder and redder under his gaze. However, he had other people waiting, so I got away with it.

Once on board again (the ship was in dry dock) my next problem was to get leave for the 22nd August, when I had told the army authorities I would be back from Natal. It was fortunate that I had already spent two memorable and enjoyable leaves staying on Lord de Villiers's lovely fruit farm at Stellenbosch below the Drakenstein Mountains, shooting in the hills with him, and had made friends with the family. The Admiral and Flag Captain had both enjoyed his hospitality and I had no difficulty in obtaining official permission to go there again.

I was very worried that something would stop this leave and behaved in the most careful fashion during the next three weeks. The Navigator, in particular, to whom I had been 'tanky' (that is, assistant navigator) for some months, was not a friend, and I was always afraid that he would cancel my leave as he had done on various occasions previously.

But all went well. The 22nd came round, we were still in dry dock and I adopted the same routine as on the first journey up to Capetown to enlist, except that I was now carrying an extra bag for clothing for the journey across the High Veldt to Potchefstroom, about 1,000 miles away and four nights on the train. Again I changed in the loo at the Capetown station but this time gave the bag containing my uniform to a coloured boy with instructions to bring me the ticket for it. This he did, and I went off to the Recruiting Hall. From there I marched in fours with a thousand or more young men all heading for the waiting troop train. I carefully put myself in the inner group of fours, hoping that I would not meet friends en route. Once in the train I sat with my back to the platform in a corner seat reading a paper, with my Burberry turned well up and the hat turned well down.

It was winter on the High Veldt and the journey across the Karoo Desert to Potchefstroom was extremely cold – so indeed were the barracks there on our arrival. We slept on hard floors and I think we had two blankets, but every night I woke up shivering in the early hours. There was a hard ground frost at night, and it was very much colder than the Cape. We fell into the normal routine life of a soldier very quickly; of course a large number of these young men had come from the German South West campaign and were consequently already in uniform. I carefully joined the Transvaal Company of the South African Scottish, to reduce the risk of meeting friends from the Cape.

I found that my main difficulty was answering to a strange name. We would be sitting round talking or having a meal or playing cards between parades, when the orderly sergeant would appear and call out, 'Private McLaren, Private McLaren,' and there would be no answer until someone would give me a dig and say, 'Hi, Jock, aren't you McLaren?' and I would reply, 'Oh, my God, yes I am,' and would get up blushing and feeling rather awkward.

The 26th August came round and Midshipman Boustead did not appear on H.M.S. *Hyacinth*. It was assumed on the first day that he had sprained his ankle or something whilst shooting, but on the second day when he was still absent a telephone call was put through to Rustenburg Farm. Lord de Villiers said that he had been expecting me but that as I had not turned up for leave he imagined some service matter had intervened. There remained only twenty-four hours before the ship was due to sail for the East Coast. Then the wires were really set humming and messages were sent out to police stations and notices put up in the ports and railway stations describing a missing midshipman. The only part of the description I remember was that 'he has a very brown face and very blue eyes'. The ship sailed after informing the Admiralty of my disappearance and suggesting that I might possibly be with the South African Brigade but had probably taken ship to Australia to join the Australian Forces bound for the Middle East.

After a few weeks drilling and weapon training at Potchefstroom we took the long journey back by rail down to Capetown to embark in the *Balmoral Castle*. Boarding the ship and the subsequent wait before she sailed were the most anxious moments that I had until our arrival in Bordon Camp in England. After what seemed like an eternity we pulled out to sea and I had the restful feeling of being away from all inquisitors on land.

It must have been some time in late September that we arrived with the convoy in Plymouth Harbour. The leaves were turning russet as our train came through the apple orchards and coombes of the Devon countryside which I had not seen for two and a half years. It was a marvellous feeling to be back after this first spell abroad, mainly in the brown and violet countries of Africa.

To prevent my parents worrying too much, I had asked Pasmore to write to them saying that all was well, and that I hoped to see them before very long. Unfortunately his letters were censored on board and he had no opportunity to send one home without giving me away, so nothing reached my parents and they were naturally troubled and anxious. About this period the fates must have stepped in; the Admiralty appear to have had a shrewd idea that I was with the Brigade and passed this information to my parents. They acted quickly; they came down on our first Sunday to Bordon Camp and started to investigate.

Whilst walking up between the lines somewhere outside Quebec Barracks, they saw a young officer of the Natal Regiment and said to him, 'We are looking for somebody, I wonder whether you could help.' He was so fresh and frank that my father immediately took to him and said, 'Well, look here, we don't know what regiment

my son is in.' So the young officer asked, 'What name?' And my
father realized he would have to tell him the story in confidence and
explained the situation frankly. This lad was very sympathetic and
said, 'Well, I am interested, and I think he's probably with the
South African Scottish in Quebec Barracks.'

That first Sunday afternoon I was out striding through the fields
with a friend; I had been planning to take advantage of the following
weekend to see my parents. I returned, I remember, about five
o'clock, to be greeted by our platoon sergeant, one Ainslie, who
was a relic of the Boer War, an ex-Sergeant of the Seaforth Highlanders with a big moustache and a strong grizzled face, bushy
eyebrows and fierce, deep-set blue eyes. He looked at me alarmingly
and said, 'Private McLaren, you're wanted in the orderly room –
there's been folk to see you. Aye, a man and a woman and they're
in black.' And he looked at me curiously again. I could have fallen
over as I realized that they must be my parents.

Major Browne, the adjutant, was sitting by his desk and looked
at me hard. He said, 'Private McLaren, what is your real name?'
And forsaking all subterfuge I answered, 'Boustead.' He then said,
'Well now, don't be too alarmed, just sit down on that chair and
wait. Your father and mother have come down to see you and are
now having tea in the officers' mess. But tell me, what made you
join the South African Scottish?' I said, 'An overwhelming desire to
serve in France with the Army.' And so he nodded sympathetically
and said, 'Well, the Colonel knows and is most sympathetic. So
I wouldn't worry too much. Your father and mother will be along
presently.' They turned up at the orderly room and we were
reunited after two and a half years.

We went out together for the remainder of that Sunday evening.
I found that my father had aged very considerably. His moustache
had gone completely white and his face was heavily lined. This
was due to my brother's death in Gallipoli.

During our meeting, I discovered what had happened inside the
orderly room. My father had taken the card of the young officer
they had met to the adjutant of the South African Scottish, who
himself had been immediately sympathetic, and anxious to help.
The adjutant, after hearing the story, sent through to the orderly
room for the nominal roll of C company, which was the Transvaal
Company of the regiment, saying, 'These are the most likely chaps
for your son to join up with.' He began going through the papers
one by one until they came to the one marked McLaren. My father
immediately noticed that the school shown was Charterhouse and
that the home address was stated as Armathwaite Hall in Cumberland, my father's old home and long since sold. Reflecting, my

father said to the adjutant, 'You know, it's very odd but my father's gamekeeper on the estate was called McLaren – but I'm sure he's never had a son who went to Charterhouse.'

Now at this time, shortly after the battle of Loos, casualties were mounting steadily on the Western Front and the idea of my going out as a private soldier to France was one which my father and mother regarded with real horror. My mother asked me what would be my feeling about going back to the Navy, if I were allowed to do so without any loss of service or blemish on my character. I told her that I thought it was far too late, and that I had shot my bolt.

However, we parted that evening with the position unsettled, and the adjutant said to my parents, 'Well, he must have the whole of next weekend at home.' I must say I didn't look forward to it; I felt it was going to be a real struggle with my parents, anxious to get me back into the Navy which I had now left for good as far as I was concerned.

During that week there arrived a letter from my mother's first cousin, Sir Maurice Hankey, Secretary of the Imperial Defence Committee, of the War Cabinet, and of the Privy Council. He was to hold these three vital posts for the next 25 years, and had a hand in influencing the whole of the strategy of the war in the west. He wrote me a very severe letter. I must return to the Navy, it was my duty to do so, I had committed a most inconsiderate and thoughtless act, doubtless meant with the best intentions of getting on active service, but quite beyond the pale. He added that he had spoken with their Lordships and that they were prepared to take a lenient view, on account of my youth.

The next weekend was not easy. My parents were staying in Kensington and I was committed to go and meet my formidable cousin in his office in Whitehall Gardens. Looking back on it later, I wondered how he found the time, with all his responsibilities, to write me a four-page letter or to interview me as if he had no worries at all.

He put me at my ease immediately in his charming way. None of the severity of his letter was apparent on his face or in his words. He said, 'Hugo, you've had my letter and I want to know what you have decided to do.' I replied directly, 'Cousin Maurice, it's quite out of the question for me to go back to the Navy unless I am forced to. I took this action with my eyes open, and with my eyes open I want to see it through. I wish to go to the front and I have no other desire.' He asked, 'Do you really mean this?' I replied, 'Yes, I not only mean to but insist that I must.' He seemed somehow relieved and said, 'Well, you have made your bed and you will have to lie on it, but we must get you under your right name.' And so I said, 'But isn't that difficult?' He replied, 'No, it will not be difficult – it can be arranged. And no stigma will appear in the Gazette or otherwise; should you be fortunate enough to get a commission you will not be gazetted as having been passed out of the Navy.' My parents, needless to say, were terribly disappointed and upset at this decision, but I felt that I could do nothing else. Looking back on it later and realizing after reading Vera Brittain's *Testament of Youth* exactly what parents had to suffer in that First War, I felt remorse at the appalling anxiety that I was to inflict on them in the coming years.

However, at the time I was full of glee at having won what I considered a very difficult tussle, and returned at the end of the weekend to the regiment. The Colonel said to me, in a somewhat inscrutable way, 'I believe there's been some trouble with the Admiralty and that you are anxious to alter your name. A soldier can have as many names as he likes. What name do you want to be under?' I told him that I wished to be known as Private John Edmund Hugh Boustead, so he laughed and told the adjutant to put it in orders.

My most vivid memories of those days in Bordon Camp are of walking across the Hampshire countryside in the long autumn evenings when parades were over. I do not think that England has ever appeared more beautiful to me. I had come by chance on a copy of the *English Review* containing John Masefield's lately published poem 'August 1914':

> An endless quiet valley reaches out
> Past the blue hills into the evening sky.
> Over the stubble, cawing, goes a rout
> Of rooks from harvest, flagging as they fly.

> So beautiful it is, I never saw
> So great a beauty on these English fields,
> Touched by the twilight's coming into awe,
> Ripe to the soul and rich with summer's yields.

Whenever I recall that poem now I associate it with the Selborne countryside in the glowing autumn of 1915.

My next weekend leave was a singularly difficult one for me and no doubt for my parents; however, they seemed to be reconciled to my decision. In many ways it was an intense relief when our orders to move came, very suddenly, just before Christmas. My parents had just time to come down and to wave goodbye from the platform at Alton as we entrained for Plymouth. It was generally assumed – I don't know how – that we were going to Egypt and not to the French front.

On arrival at Plymouth we were taken out to a ship called the *Oriana* and lay there in the Sound for two or three days waiting for various members of an Australian contingent, who had been wounded in Gallipoli, to turn up. They made their presence felt in no small measure. I can remember waking up when the sailors came round with a hosepipe. It was bitterly cold and a strong tide was running in Plymouth Sound. A six-foot-four Australian turned over as the sailor came nearer shouting, 'Heave out, heave out – the sun is scorching your eyelids.' The Australian drawled, 'You bring that hosepipe one foot nearer me and I'll chuck you in the Sound.' The sailor, I suppose, felt in a stronger position with his companions at hand, so he approached the bed of another sleeping Australian. The next thing we knew was that the sailor was caught by the slack of his pants and the neck of his sweater by this huge, sturdy man and there was a plosh and all the hooters were blowing. Boats were lowered and the dripping seaman was fished out cold and miserable, no doubt regretting his rashness. The Australian turned back into bed again, he had not even bothered to look.

Eventually we left in a convoy zigzagging down across the Bay of Biscay, cold and wet, swaying and surging in the winter gale, until we turned east into the warm Mediterranean. We had become accustomed to this transport life in the *Balmoral Castle*; as then, I took up station on deck and slept in the open air to guard against seasickness. The flats down below were unbelievably smelly and the latrines nauseating.

When we arrived in Egypt and disembarked at Alexandria to make camp, the Western Desert campaign against the Senussi and the Turks was just beginning. After a period of desert training in the sandhills and dunes to the west of Alexandria, we were bundled suddenly late one afternoon into trawlers in Alexandria Harbour and sailed west to Mersah Matruh. That night journey I shall never forget – it was a torture to all of us. I remember lying in a kilt under the winch of the trawler, the sea washing over me all night, soaked through, very cold and very wet, and utterly seasick. Most of my companions were suffering in the same way. Some were so ill when they got ashore in the calm, lovely harbour of Mersah Matruh on the following day that they could hardly stagger ashore. However, we had time to recuperate in Mersah Matruh camp and to spend some days retraining there before we set out for the Western Desert campaign.

We marched about 180 miles from Mersah Matruh to Solum carrying on our backs ninety-four pounds in weight, which included two days' rations, our overcoats and all our clothes, in addition to a rifle and one hundred rounds of ammunition. We moved off daily at 5.30 a.m., marched till noon, bathed and lunched and marched on at one o'clock till sunset. Though the enemy were reported at various stages along our route they never appeared. At the time I remember feeling that the load was sometimes unbearable – we covered twenty-eight miles a day in desert formation, walking across country over the scrub of the Libyan Desert. It was considered a disgrace to fall out, and nobody would accept a ride on the transport wagons if they could possibly avoid it. The merciful feature of that march was a daily bathe at noon when there was a brief halt for lunch; we all threw off our packs and rushed naked into the sea, the blue and gold sea of that lovely coast in the winter sunshine.

It was about this time that I first met a remarkable lad whose name and memory has lived with me ever since. His name was Veitch, but we naturally called him Yank; he was a young American boy, only seventeen. He came of a wealthy Boston family but was very wild, and had determined to go to the front in France and see the fighting. He had come over to join the French Army first, but he was pushed back on board again and was not allowed to stay with them. I think they thought that he was too young to be a soldier. Anyway, he managed to get into the South African Scottish draft in Capetown and arrived in Alexandria while we were there.

We were in the same section. The first thing that struck me on that march was the extraordinary selflessness of his behaviour. If any man was limping or absolutely whacked, he would immediately take his rifle from him without a word and carry it himself. He would share his rations, and he would share his last drop of water with a comrade. Never had I seen anyone who bore the marks of utter selflessness more unconcernedly and more naturally. He aroused the admiration of all the young South Africans who met him and knew him. And his selflessness was only excelled by his valour in the field later in the Somme Battle.

The main features of that little-known and long forgotten campaign were the extreme shortages of water and our consequent thirst, the marching, and above all the weight of our packs. The Duke of Westminster's armoured cars had been patrolling ahead of us. We came up with them one evening and were so thirsty that we drank with relish the water out of their radiators. Another night I can well remember paying the Egyptian camel drivers no less than sixteen shillings for half a water bottle. Under the bright enormous moon, with all the camels round, came the camel drivers with their skins bargaining for money. They made enormous profits.

In the meanwhile a Yeomanry charge at Agagia had more or less finished off the campaign and the Turkish leaders were captured. For us the campaign ended at Solum, where we were immediately set to work making a road from the coast up to the plateau while we waited for the trawlers to take us back again to Alexandria. So hideous was the memory of the voyage to Mersah Matruh that most of us would rather have marched. Fortunately the sea was far calmer on the return journey and we eventually fetched up in Alexandria, to look forward to the next stage in the campaign in France, for we knew that this would be our destination in the spring.

Later it transpired that the authorities, requiring troops for the Senussi campaign in the Western Desert, hit on the idea of sending the South Africans out there to avoid the English winter. It was a saying among the British troops in Bordon before we left, 'If you want to pass the afternoon, go round to Quebec Barracks and hear the South Africans cough.' They were certainly at first very affected by the damp English climate. However, by the end of the desert campaign everybody was in strapping condition and ready for the journey to France.

Chapter Three

THE WESTERN FRONT

Here dead lie we because we did not choose
To live and shame the land from which we sprung.
Life, to be sure, is nothing much to lose;
But young men think it is, and we were young.

A. E. HOUSMAN

IT was April 1916 when the South African Scottish arrived at Marseilles. We were greeted at the dock gates by a magnificent regiment of mounted Chasseurs d'Afrique in most colourful uniforms, complete with a mounted band. For a short spell we were camped on the farm of St Valentine, some miles outside Marseilles, among flowing streams with milk, eggs, red wine, French bread, and French girls, all available. Then the regiment left for the north.

It was a six or seven mile march to the station and we stepped out boldly with the pipes skirling, the Colonel and the field officers riding, and all the young South African Scots cheerful as sand boys. It would seem that no kilted regiment had visited Marseilles since the war began, judging by the ardour of the Marseilles girls who thrust into the ranks, so that by the time we reached the station the fours had been broken into single file, and each Jock had great difficulty in seeing the next one ahead of him for the mass of girls in between. Fruit and flowers and red wine and champagne were thrust on us, while the Colonel and the mounted officers were presented with huge bouquets. Each Scottish soldier was hugged by about fourteen girls during his passage.

The journey north, sitting tightly packed in second and third class carriages, was unspeakably uncomfortable and lasted two full days and nights. We slept in turns on the racks and on the floor of the carriages.

In mid-April the Brigade joined the 9th Scottish Division and immediately occupied the trenches of Ploeg Street Wood in a salient between Armentières and Lille. This lies in the flat lands of Flanders and the parapets of the trenches had to be built up above the ground. During this early spring of 1916 it was considered a quiet sector and a good one in which to break fresh troops in to trench warfare.

Whizbangs and snipers were our main problem and caused most

of the casualties. The sound of the whizbangs came with the shell, giving no warning. German snipers lay out in the grass among the wild flowers which grew in abundance that spring between the trenches, or were cleverly hidden in pollarded poplars above the dykes that intersect the Flanders countryside. They would lie up all day on the watch for some casual passer-by raising his head above the communication trench or lingering in a gap to watch the spring scene. A crack and the passer-by would lie stretched on the duck-boards with a hole through his head. They were skilled performers with their telescopic sights, and we lost some very fine N.C.O.s and senior officers.

About this time I myself became a sniper and joined Yank Veitch. Our main purpose was to lie up between the lines to spot and shoot the German snipers. They were wonderfully concealed, and it was not easy. I remember early one morning climbing into a pollarded poplar beside a dyke; after one or two shots a whizbang shot away the poplar next door to me, some five yards off, and I found it was time to drop into the grass and crawl elsewhere. But the fields and flowers between the lines provided a far more refreshing atmosphere than the close confines of a trench, and at night I found patrols in no-man's-land in the open under the stars and star-shells more exhilarating than the closed walls of the parapet and parados of the fire-trench.

In early June the whole battalion set off by train for the south. There were wild rumours of an impending advance in which the 9th Scottish Division were to take part. This Division consisted of the Highland Brigade, the Lowland Brigade and the South African Brigade. During our spell in Ploeg Street Wood, Winston Churchill was one of our neighbours in the Lowland Brigade, commanding the Royal Scots Fusiliers. I saw him one evening outside Armentières; the previous time had been some three years before on board H.M.S. *Cornwall*, when he was wearing a top-hat as the First Lord.

We disembarked from the train one morning in a country of folded hills and rivers, the plains of Picardy, which was to be the scene of our training and our fighting for the next three months until the battalion was decimated. In May and June the countryside was splendid after Flanders; rolling wheat lands interspersed with orchards, and great rivers like the Somme flowing down valleys filled with poplars. The farms, where we slept in the hay, held everything we wanted; the peasants were kind and hospitable and only too ready to sell us eggs, milk and chickens in abundance, and wine.

The training was very strenuous. We would march out some nine miles in the morning carrying a heavy pack, lunch from the field-cookers, and after training all day march back nine miles in the evening to the sheds where we slept. The whole battalion was splendidly fit, enjoyed the country life and surroundings and was inspired by the thought of the battle which lay ahead. Our superiors had murmured that it was destined to end the war. After some weeks we moved down to a beautiful downland country of woods and cornfields sloping down to the Somme River, near Albert. Our training was now complete. We waited for the battle in days of late June sunlight, swimming down the Somme with the current and returning sun-warmed on the barges steaming upstream. It was delightful.

Over the horizon we could hear the perpetual thunder of the guns, increasing daily as new guns registered; at night the horizon was picked out by their flashes and by the coloured star-shells over the lines.

The young soldiers of Kitchener's Army were like hounds held back on the leash; but for all our confidence, we had some notion of what lay ahead, and knew that this idyllic life in a beautiful, un-marked countryside had to be savoured for the enchanting interlude that it was. I suppose that if we had been individuals confronting alone the agony of the Somme, we should have run away; but we were tied inextricably to one another by our training and our shared experience. No other endurance except great danger at sea or on the mountains could bring about the same link of comradeship. We were bound to one another, men on the same rope.

This is an aspect of war too often recognized only by the soldiers. It was wonderfully expressed by Vera Brittain in *Testament of Youth*:

'The causes of war are always falsely represented, its honour dishonest and its glory meretricious, but the challenge to spiritual endurance, the intense vitalizing consciousness of common peril for a common end, remain to allure those boys and girls who have just reached the age when love and friendship and adventure call more persistently than at any later time. . . . While it lasts no emotion known to man seems to have quite the compelling power of this enlarged vitality. . . . I do not believe that a League of Nations or a Kellogg Conference or any disarmament conference will ever rescue our poor remnant of civilization from the threatening forces of destruction, until we can somehow impart to the rational processes of constructive thought and experiment that element of sanctified loveliness which, like superb sunshine breaking through the dark clouds, from time to time glorifies war.'

These words were written in 1933 by one who had herself undergone intense sorrow and anguish of spirit, illness, hardship and personal bereavement in the war of 1914–18; who had lost her fiance, her only brother and her two best friends, who as a V.A.D. had nursed for two years the torn bodies and blinded eyes of men returning from battle. If a sensitive woman of an unemotional and civilized race whose cardinal virtue is sound commonsense can be conscious of this aspect of war, how much more it must affect the primitive races of the world, who need no schooling to look on horror and brutality with indifference.

I have seen too much of what men do to one another – the torturing and mutilating of the Whites by the Red Army in Russia, savagery in Africa and in Arabia, above all the butchery on the Western Front. This is evident to anyone who thinks about war; what is less obvious is 'the compelling power of this enlarged vitality'. That constitutes indeed the real problem of any League or United Nations.

On 1st July 1916 the battle broke. In the afternoon the first German prisoners came pouring down into the cages below our hillside camp. All the young Highlanders, Seaforths, Gordons, Camerons, Argylls and South African Scottish, seemed to have heard simultaneously of their arrival, and swept down through the cornfields in a galaxy of different tartan kilts to assure themselves of the extent of our gains. After the terrific thundering which we had heard for the past few days the jauntiness and self-confidence of many of the prisoners came as something of a surprise.

The next day we left for the Happy Valley. The battalion bivouacked on a hillside in immediate reserve, whilst the drum fire of a gigantic barrage rolled across the hills and valleys of Picardy. At daybreak a regiment of Canadian Cavalry appeared suddenly out of the morning mist and rain in the valley below our bivouac. With them were two squadrons of Bengal Lancers. Steel helmeted, on shining horses with jingling harness, they presented a superb picture as they rode past with a cheer. A stir of rising excitement swept us; we had visions of a break through into the open plains of Picardy.

> *And down the distance they*
> *With dying note and swelling*
> *Walk the resounding way*
> *To the still dwelling.*

The call came that afternoon. The division moved up to Bernafay and Trônes Wood in preparation for the attack on Delville Wood. Our brigade crossed the scarred fields through the stricken squadrons. Dead and dying horses split by shellfire, with bursting

Forming a defensive square

The last parade before mechanization:
Sir Stewart Symes, Governor General,
and the author

4a. Baggara girl on trek

4b. Kordofan family *en route* to new grazing

entrails and torn limbs, lay astride the road that led to battle. Their fallen riders stared into the weeping skies. In front, steady bursts of machine gun fire vibrated on the air. Caught by a barrage, these brave men and fine horses had been literally swept from the Longueval road.

The South African Scottish spent the night in the support lines; I was called by the Colonel as a runner to his H.Q. The next days we spent in a trench called Dublin Trench after my brother's regiment, a battalion of which had been in action here, and I had to move about from company to company with messages from H.Q. It was a bad day. Colonel Jones, the kindest of men and the most loved of commanding officers, was killed by a shell in the support trenches that same evening, just after he had sent me down with a message. The following morning in Dublin Trench we heard of Lord Kitchener's death in the North Sea. It is an astonishing thing but here among the South Africans and among all Kitchener's Army it came as a devastating personal shock and a grave setback to the war. Whatever may have been written of Kitchener by politicians, the troops looked on him with nothing short of hero-worship. We could talk of little else for days, even in the midst of the battle.

About two o'clock that afternoon the Boche guns opened up on a battery position at one end of Dublin Trench. The gunners were fully occupied replying and didn't notice that some oily waste lying on top of a tarpaulin on the cordite dump had caught fire. At this particular moment young Veitch happened to be passing, spotted it immediately and without hesitation went over and pulled the whole blazing tarpaulin off the cordite. Yank then walked on down the trench as if nothing had happened. The Battery commander had seen him, however, and rushed over to find out who was the kilted soldier who had saved the battery. Yank merely laughed and shrugged his shoulders: 'Say, that's nothing.' He was recommended by the Battery commander for an award for his cool and courageous conduct.

There followed two nights of wiring parties in Trônes Wood which was still partly occupied by the Germans. With the intense fire which went on all night and the stream of flares pouring into the sky from both sides, it seemed to me impossible that any of us could survive the wiring parties. Every time the lights went up, we had to freeze where we stood, and the wiring took all night in consequence. The chatter of machine guns and the bursting of bombs all round kept us all keyed up. On the third afternoon we moved up from Dublin Trench to Montauban Alley. German balloons were up all over Montauban and Delville Wood and it looked as though they were watching our every movement.

Our guides led us into a broken-down fire trench where the original parados which was to form our parapet had been blown in by our guns while the Germans were holding it. The trench offered little shelter. The balloons continued to watch us and presently a salvo of 5·9 inch shells pitched over us, quickly followed by a short bracket. I thought immediately, 'The next one will be ours.' And it was. Although a shell pitched practically in the middle of the section, the three of us in the centre escaped any hurt other than a tremendous shock and blast which blew the equipment off our shoulders, our steel hats away, and poured tear gas in great clouds all over the trench. Coughing and spitting and weeping and blinded by the tear gas we could hear those of our comrades who were wounded moaning under the debris. Six of the section, three on either side of us, were utterly destroyed, torn to pieces, and six more were wounded.

Yank was the first up; he jumped up to the parados immediately shouting for a stretcher. None appeared, so we went over to get one and started to carry the wounded through the mist of tear gas down to a clearing station half a mile back. It was already getting dark and the mist and our tear blindness made the going very difficult. It must have been midnight before we had got the remaining casualties cleared and searched ineffectively for our equipment and rifles.

The proper identification of the dead was nearly impossible. Four years later I received a letter from the War Office asking me if I could throw any light on the grave of Number 5100, Private Hugh Boustead of the South African Scottish, the cross of which had been erected in Montauban Alley in 1916 during the Somme Battle.

Our move to Montauban Alley was a preliminary step for the main advance of the South African Brigade on to Delville Wood next morning. Without a doubt the balloons had picked us up and it was clearly a mistake to have moved up before dark into a trench with no adequate shelter. Late that night we collected rifles and equipment off the dead and lay down exhausted, sleeping fitfully, waiting for the signal to move before first light.

It was still dark when we reached the outskirts of Longueval which was to form the pivot of the next four days' fierce fighting for Delville Wood. After tea in the Longueval Road we were given our platoon objectives in the wood. Ours ran through an orchard. The wood was the first I had seen in the front line which was still unscathed with its trees green and branches unshattered by shell fire. The Germans had stocked it with snipers, their hands and faces painted green, and leaves and branches over their head and shoulders. We could hear the continual crack of rifles but could see nothing.

It was uncanny. We moved forward through an orchard in single file led by the platoon officer. Smith, the Second Lieutenant, got through but the next seven who followed him were shot dead in a circle of a few yards, picked off by clean shooting without a murmur.

I was not an N.C.O., but to follow these seven seemed madness, so I led the remainder round the edge of the orchard to the rise we were told to occupy. We dug for dear life with our entrenching tools, making as little movement as possible. The crack of snipers' rifles went on continually and the gaps increased in the lines of chaps digging themselves in. We had with us the bare iron rations we were carrying and a water bottle and when night fell those of us who had not been picked off were both hungry and thirsty.

It was impossible to get food or water up in day time, so under cover of darkness two of us went back to bring up tins of bully beef and cans of water. I passed a young South African boy, sixteen years old, lying in a fox hole, wounded in the stomach. He begged for water and I urged him not to have a drink as it would be fatal and said we would try and get him help. The journey through the wood was eerie, with the flares shining on the leaves and branches of the trees. In the meantime the German soldiers ahead of us started to attack our lines at intervals. It must have been some three hours later when we got back from Longueval with the bully beef and water cans for the remainder of the now decimated platoon. The jerry cans had not been cleaned out properly and the water was nauseating, tasting of petrol. For the next four days this horrible taste and smell lived with us, and you had to hold your nose to drink.

The night battles went on ceaselessly. The German officers seemed to us to be very brave and led their men well in advance and with great courage. It was clear that they had reinforced the wood now, but still there was little shelling except into Longueval and outside it. On the second night we nearly suffered complete annihilation from our own 'steel footballs' – circular bombs with a long stick on which the charge is propelled. They went on pitching among us for hours on end, curiously causing no casualties, but they added to our terror. By the third night we were practically worn out through lack of sleep. We had been living on biscuits, cold bully beef and petrol-water under continuous fire by day from snipers and by night from attacking Germans. Reliefs came in and we moved to the edge of Longueval to sleep in some trenches outside the wood. The day following I was sent up with a party of snipers to try and stop Germans moving from Waterlot Farm, which lay outside Delville Wood, into the wood to the west. Three of us spent the afternoon there. There were already six South African Scottish lying dead in their firing places ahead of us, but we were able to effect quite a good shoot on the Germans moving from Waterlot and after a number of hits they stopped.

When night fell I moved into one of our trenches on the edge of Delville Wood when suddenly a heavy shrapnel barrage opened on the trench. It was a deep trench with safe dug-outs on the sides where I had hoped to get some sleep after a meal. The last thing I remember was a tremendous bang on the head. I was woken in the early morning by a South African Scottish sergeant standing on me. He was an enormous man called Maclean, weighing about fifteen stone, and this apparently brought me to. My head was throbbing considerably and my hair was covered in blood from a cut in my skull. My steel helmet which was lying beside me was caved in on top, evidently by shrapnel. Maclean picked me up and I had the head treated at the dressing station, and after some aspirin was O.K.

I rejoined my platoon which was back beyond the orchard trench again, only to come out that evening for a rest in the Longueval Road, lying in holes cut in the bank and hoping for the best. By now the shelling was almost incessant, but the snipers had done the main work and the toll of death among the South African Brigade was very heavy. On the morning of the 18th there was a a sudden alarm and dropping with sleep we fell in on the road after daylight, with orders to go back to the orchard and the woods. A barrage came down at that moment and of the thirty men now left out of the original two hundred and fifty in my company, four were wounded straight away. I was blown across the road, and went back to the Bernafay dressing station with a hole through my kilt and thigh. At the dressing station I asked to go back to the line since the wound was clearly a light one, but the doctors said the wound was poisoned and this meant Etaples at least and possibly England.

The operation in Delville Wood finished on that day for the South African Brigade. The South African Scottish alone had lost over nine hundred soldiers killed or wounded out of a thousand in a matter of four days. During those nights in the wood bomb and bayonet had been used continuously. Delville Wood was later presented as a war memorial to the South Africans.

My main relief at being hit was the chance to get some sleep. For five days and nights we had hardly slept at all and at times I was conscious of a longing to get hit anywhere to be able to sleep. It was now late July and within the next week I found myself back in the London General Hospital with hundreds of others wounded in the Somme streaming in daily. After ten days in hospital I was given leave and stayed with my parents at Ashtead in Surrey where they had taken a house outside what was then a country village.

Only a week or two of my leave had passed before I was told that I had been commissioned in the field and would report at Bordon Camp as a Second Lieutenant in the South African Scottish. My father and mother were delighted at my commission, but the shadow of my return to the front must have lain heavily upon them. The life of a Second Lieutenant in France in those days was estimated at three weeks.

The Somme battle, which we had thought was to be the last, continued on a vast scale and the papers were daily filled with the appalling casualties. Maurice Hankey's brother Donald was killed, to my mother's great grief. He had written to me at the front reminding me of his own time as a private soldier. I had now been a private for a year including some of the toughest fighting, and I found, as Donald Hankey had, how very comfortable it was to be an officer after having been a private. It soon became clear that to have responsibility for men under your command immediately removed that concentration on your own self which could greatly increase your fear in battle. Really the whole of Donald Hankey's theme in his *Letters of a Student in Arms* was that personal happiness entirely depended on being able to step outside of yourself.

It was late September when I returned to Bordon as an officer for a few weeks before returning to the front. October had come round when I was drafted out to France to the Bull Ring at Rouen. This was a training staging post where drill sergeants exercised ferocious discipline while they freshened up new recruits, and officers and men returning to the front.

The South African Scottish were now occupying a sector north of the Scarpe River and east of Arras, with some distinctive features. In no-man's-land there were four great mine craters blown at an earlier stage of the war and known to the troops as Claude, Cuthbert, Clarence and Katie. The lines were mainly far apart and patrolling between them was continuous.

I reported my arrival at the battalion H.Q. to a new Colonel, Christian, the third since the battle of the Somme started. He had come to us from the Natal Regiment, having served like nearly all the South African commanding officers as a regular officer in the British Army; he was very popular with everyone and much respected. The weather was already extremely cold. This was to be the coldest winter France had known for some thirty or forty years. From November onwards about seven feet of snow lay on the trenches and over the hills and valleys of the Arras countryside, and remained until the end of April. The South African Brigade now thrived on it and I remember General Lukin, the South African Divisional Commander, remarking that most of the young South African lads at that time in France had complexions their sisters would envy.

Looking back on it now I can hardly believe my indifference to the cold. I had a horror of getting lousy and used to change my vest daily to stop lice breeding, and every morning would rub myself all over with snow in the trench. I remember one very Scotch South African coming round the bay of a trench whilst I was stripped and rubbing myself with snow, stepping back to a friend behind him and whispering, 'Aye, Jock, yon's mad.' During the whole of that winter I never wore an overcoat night or day and in fact prided myself on not doing so.

The High Command were at all times in search of information and identification of enemy units, which meant raids on the enemy line. In February 1917 I was sent for by the Colonel and told to prepare a night raid on a sector of the German front line. We were to go over with revolvers, and clubs, daggers and bombs, to obtain sufficient identification for the Command. This was my personal responsibility and I was much elated by it.

The cost of the barrage was considerable – I was told about £40,000. It would be put down on their front line and then lifted onto a box round the support trenches to prevent reinforcements coming up. I spent some ten days out of the line with a specially selected raiding party rehearsing the whole operation on taped trenches on the ground.

We returned to take over our trench section the day before the raid was planned to take place. That afternoon from 4 p.m. till 9.30 or 10 p.m. the Germans bombarded our line with Minenwerfer bombs – huge tanks of ammonal fired into the air from a mortar. 'Mini guards' were put out to signal the line of their descent to enable the unfortunate troops being fired at to avoid them. One whistle meant 'the mini is coming straight at me', two blasts 'it is coming to the right,' and three blasts 'it is coming to the left'. One mini bomb would blow in a hole the size of a large room.

By the evening most of the trench had been blown in and it was quite unrecognizable, but thanks to the skill of the sentries and the avoiding action of the company there were no casualties. The men were very much shaken and exhausted by the noise and concussion and movement, for they were forced to move above ground under enemy machine gun fire as the trench was blown in. I was the officer on duty all that afternoon and the next morning before daylight.

With the first streak of light I watched green German star-shells go up and knew immediately that this was a signal for a bombardment. A 5·9 barrage came down like an avalanche on our already battered front line and as I walked quickly up and down the broken line to see the men were taking up firing positions, I felt that each moment was my last. After some ten minutes or so the orange flares appeared with their inevitable connotation that the barrage was lifting to block off the support trenches.

Fortunately we had saps out (trenches at right angles to the main trench, running well out into no-man's-land) which were manned with Lewis gun teams. These enfiladed our wire. As the barrage lifted the grey wave of Germans came in. There was a dense fog off the Scarpe River and figures could only be made out at very close quarters. A German officer got through the wire but was shot by Lieutenant Wallace, who had come up from the Company H.Q. dug-out in response to my message that a raid was on. For the rest, the sap-heads caught them and those who were not killed on the wire withdrew in the mist to their own lines.

At 10 a.m. the General came up looking very smart and red-hatted, and congratulated us on having held the raid. He said to me, 'There is no point now in putting in your raid for further identification, but I would like you to bring in what is on the wire tonight.' We spent all day trying to dig out the broken-in trench, and that night I went out on the wire to bring in identification. The German raiding party, all very young, smelt strongly of rum and had evidently been over-primed before they left their trenches.

Next day we moved out of the line for relief. The men were desperately tired after these two intense bombardments which had caused six deaths in the company, although my own platoon had escaped without casualties. The strain did not end until we had got back to our rest camp well behind Arras. All the way down the communication trenches there was a danger of snipers, and the Boche would put down barrages when they thought reliefs were on the move. There was a terrifying one that night on the cobbled road that led to our rest camp from the Arras gate, with horses and men being killed by monster shells plunging into the road.

I have referred earlier to the tremendous tie between men who have undergone dangers together in war. These long days and nights in the trenches, interrupted by violent bombardments in which all the men were called to 'stand to' to await an attack, were a bond between all of us, and particularly between a platoon officer and the men whom he had to encourage and lead.

We returned to the front-line trenches all too soon. One morning with the duck-boards covered in ice and the snow frozen over the trenches I saw a short figure stepping briskly up the communications trench where I was on duty. This was young Jack Hinton, the head of snipers' intelligence, with whom I had become great friends. He and his twenty-five snipers used to do the day observations and a great deal of the night patrolling, an arduous and attractive job, and a tricky one requiring good judgement and the capacity to know when and where to take risks. He said, 'Have you seen Major Clarke?' I said, 'No.' 'He will be coming along presently,' said Jack, 'please tell him I've gone down to Claude Crater Observation Post, to watch the Royal Scots putting over a daylight raid.'

Some minutes later Major Clarke, the second-in-command, came stalking up the duck-boards; he was a fine-looking Australian who had lost an arm from an assegai wound in 1906 in the last Zulu War. He said, 'Young fellow, have you seen Jack Hinton?' I explained what was happening and asked if I might accompany him to the observation post. He said, 'Of course you can come, but you will probably have to find room on the ladder leading up to the post.' We got there and stood for some time, myself on the ladder below them, examining the great sweep of white ground which fell away to the neighbouring battalion area on our left. It was now about lunch time and we could see the smoke coming up from the cook-houses in the German trenches. Presently the raiding party, who had chosen this quiet noon-day hour when food was imminent, could be seen moving over in the snow apparently unobserved, all in white. A barrage would have given them away. Presently I heard a German machine gun stutter and up went a line of green lights from the German line – a signal to put down a barrage. Jack Hinton was jumping about with excitement and presently he said, 'By God, they're through the wire,' and handed his large glasses to Major Clarke. At that moment a salvo came down all along the Royal Scots line and extended to the trench where we were standing. A 5·9 burst on the parados and a strip of shell caught Jack Hinton full in the chest. Obviously mortally wounded, he was taken down to St Pol, and he died that same night.

An orange flare then went up from the Germans, to withdraw the barrage into no-man's-land, and attempt to cut off the raiding party as it came back from the German lines. We watched the Royal Scots lads returning with their prisoners in spite of the German barrage. The raiding party had come as a total surprise to the Boche and was completely successful.

When we next came out of the line I was sent for by the Colonel and told to take over Hinton's snipers and intelligence chaps, which meant leaving my platoon and 'B' Company where I had now made great friends with the officers and the men. I felt leaving the

Company very badly after all we had been through together, but I found myself commanding a picked crowd of men, and the work was fascinating. As the battle of Arras approached (it was due to begin on 9th April, although of course none of us knew this) identification raids became more frequent and the night patrols and observation work of the sniper section absorbed all my time.

Two nights before the battle the Colonel sent for me and said, 'I want you to lay out tapes in no-man's-land from which the two leading companies will advance at zero hour when the barrage starts. These can only be laid out early in the night and then I want you to lead the companies on to them.' As soon as dusk fell I was out with the snipers with the tape and by about ten o'clock we had the line laid. Then I had to get the two companies into their positions, followed by a re-check right down the line before reporting to the Colonel.

On reaching the left-hand post which I had put out first I began to question them in a whisper asking if all was well. There was no reply, though they were all lying exactly as I had left them. I shook one or two and thought they were all heavily asleep. I found the Section Commander and shook him but no answer. It was very dark apart from the flares. I thought this was strange and began to examine the corporal with a small torch. He was quite dead from a shrapnel shell which had burst straight over the shell-hole they were occupying. His whole section had been killed by the same burst and were lying as I had left them. This was a nasty start. Fortunately there were no more incidents during the night. The Colonel was greatly relieved when I reported. He said, 'There's three quarters of an hour to go; have a cup of hot coffee and lie down.' I can see his face now, tense with the rising anxiety of the coming battle in front of him. He felt terribly the loss of his men. He said, 'I want you to stay with my H.Q. during the action.' I pleaded to be allowed to take the snipers forward, since we might be useful if there was any hold up. He eventually gave way, and as the barrage broke I moved with my men over the parapet with the left-hand leading company which was led by Captain Brown, an ex-regular officer.

The barrage was quite indescribable. I believe there were more guns wheel to wheel covering the area of advance than at any time during the 1914–18 war. General Carton de Wiart confirms this in his *Happy Odyssey*. The shells flew like a tornado of steel and sounded only a few feet over our heads. They seemed to lift us out of the world and gave one an indescribable feeling of excitement without fear. Every now and then a short would drop among our advancing line of soldiers and throw a man high into the sky.

After we had advanced some way over the first line of enemy trenches the German troops came pouring through with their hands up and with a look of intense fear on their faces.

The objective of that day, a high railway embankment with a cutting in it which was called Blue Line, presented a most formidable obstacle to our advance. The German machine gunners kept up a steady fire from this dominating position in spite of the barrage. Presently I saw Brown fall, shot in one knee, and as I passed him he said, 'I'm afraid I can't get on.' I had already passed one of his Second Lieutenants, a man of about thirty-five, shot in the spine, his eyes already glazing. It was clear that the left-hand company must push on quickly if we were to make the objective and take full advantage of the barrage. I moved the snipers round to where some form of covered approach gave us a chance to get forward on to the left of the enemy machine guns. The German gunners were so engaged that only their officer noticed us. I suddenly saw by my side an officer of the Royal Scots with his pistol raised, but the German officer got him first, and I in turn got the German officer with my pistol at some thirty yards. In the meantime the snipers with me had got two of Brown's Lewis gunners forward where we were able to enfilade the vital German machine guns holding up the attack. Presently the whole line came forward and the Blue Line, the great railway cutting, was ours, with God knows how many prisoners. I sent a signal back to the Colonel with a runner immediately and we pushed our patrols ahead in case of counter attack.

The troops were delighted with the success of the day and the huge number of prisoners captured, and it seemed as if the war was going our way. Little did we know what was coming to us three days later.

In the meanwhile the snow fell that afternoon and the cold was intense. For two days we lay, 'resting', on this high ridge with the snow falling in a bleak wind while the battle passed beyond us in a white world.

It was on the third day, the 12th April, about 11 a.m. that we were sent for by the Colonel to describe our next move. It appeared that the Germans had rallied at the chemical works at Roeux which lies north of the Scarpe River and was on our right front. Here they were alleged to be holding a strong position with heavy machine guns covering their whole front. We gathered that the High Command had ordered that the attack must go forward on this front although there would be no adequate barrage. The Colonels of the South African Brigade had all protested but without effect. Colonel Christian looked terribly upset.

At two o'clock that afternoon we left the railway cutting with orders to assemble in the village of Fampoux by the Scarpe River at four. I remember just as we were moving off a big chap called Hill whom I didn't know particularly well came up and shook me by the hand and said, 'Goodbye, I will not come through this.' He was the first man to be killed that afternoon.

Again I asked the Colonel if I could go forward with the snipers and after some discussion he agreed. As we moved into Fampoux in platoon groups I saw two eight-inch shells land in the middle of one of the platoons of another South African battalion, blowing them to pieces in the cobbled street. The German O.P.s had clearly spotted the assembly line and from then on a concentration of shells was turned on the village.

I led my snipers out behind the leading company, who had deployed outside the village and were moving in extended order across an open plain with their rifles at the port. We moved out in file, taking advantage of a low wall and the last of the houses for cover.

It was then I felt a bang on the outside of my left thigh as if it had been hit by a log of wood. I fell into a shell hole full of icy water and snow. Alongside, as chance happened, was a young medical student, Hugh Leith, one of the brightest of my snipers. As sniping officer, because of perpetual night patrols, I was not wearing the kilt, but breeches, and I could feel them filling with blood inside. On taking them down I saw the blood spurting out of the main artery as from a pump. Leith immediately opened my field dressing and applied it as a tourniquet to the wound; had he not done so I would have died within a few minutes. We lay together in the shell hole, shivering with cold, our feet in the icy water, while the eight-inch shells poured round us. In the meantime I told my sergeant to take the snipers on, and lay watching in anguish while the German machine guns from the chemical works kept up a heavy fire which cut the advance company down like swathes of corn under a sickle. I felt that it was ghastly and hopeless to attack across an open plain against fire like that.

Presently streams of wounded began to come back. The flow of enemy shells became so terrifying that we crawled into a nearby house to try to get some feeling of security. However when the roof of the next room was smashed in we crawled back to the shell-hole. It was eight in the evening when the firing started to abate. All the stretcher bearers had been killed and the only wounded who could get back were those who could walk.

I got hold of a stout South African from the Cape Regiment who had been hit in the arm and could support me with his other arm. We moved back together to a place called the Candle Factory, some mile or so down the Scarpe River, which was the nearest dressing station. It took us about an hour and a half. The doctor looked at my wound and asked me how I got back to the dressing station. When I told him I had walked he would not believe it.

Here at the dressing station there was a road head and the doctor put me into the front of a lorry. The open back was crowded with wounded. The night was unusually cold and we jogged endlessly over cobbled roads, my thigh aching at every bump. It was already light by the time we reached St Pol, a casualty clearing station for the Arras front. The subsequent hospital train and a bed in the Duchess of Westminster's hospital at Le Touquet were another world in which for the first few days and nights one slept and slept, making up for nights of sleepless exhaustion.

After an operation I was labelled for England and found myself on a Channel boat with a nurse in charge who happened to be a first cousin. We were both equally surprised. I was taken from Victoria to Richmond Park where the South African Hospital had been built; as far as I was concerned it might have been put up specially for me. Spring was breaking; the first buds were coming on the chestnut and beech trees which stood around our building; the weather was magnificent, and the authorities kindly agreed to let me have my bed in the Park all day long – the wards ran out into the open. Visitors were plentiful and the rules were not strict. Many of the young chaps in with me were personal friends, and as soon as we began to recover from the strain of the past weeks the wards were full of laughter and practical jokes. I had one serious operation at an early stage to arrange for the blood to flow through veins where the artery was severed. This produced a major aneurism which seemed to give the doctors a tremendous kick. Medical students and others used to come in droves and listen to it with stethoscopes, which caused us all much amusement.

The Colonel came two or three times, and told me that he had put me in for an immediate award of the M.C., which I received from King George V some weeks later at an investiture at Buckingham Palace. It was, I remember, July before I was allowed home to convalesce in my father's house at Ashtead tucked below the North Downs. As I improved we were able to play golf together at Woodcote.

Officers and other ranks from the South African Scottish came to visit me and I began to grow restless to get back. However, in September 1917, when I was recovered from the wound, I was posted to the 4th Gurkhas, Indian Army, and told that I would be joining the Second Battalion, fighting on the Tigris in the Mesopotamia campaign.

Chapter Four

FIGHTING IN RUSSIA

On acres of the seeded grasses
The changing burnish heaves;
Or marshalled under moons of harvest
Stand still all night the sheaves.

A. E. HOUSMAN

IT was late September 1917 when I sailed for India via the Cape to report to the 4th Gurkhas depot in Bakloh in the Western Himalayas. During the coming months, the fighting in Mesopotamia ended with the fall of Baghdad; serious opposition was practically over and it appeared that the 4th Gurkhas had plenty of officers.

In the meanwhile in France the great March retreat of 1918 had taken place. The South African Brigade losses had been enormous for the fourth or fifth time. It was more than I could stand to remain for the rest of the war peacefully on a mountain top in the Himalayas, whilst my friends at home were falling daily at the front.

So I went down to Delhi to press for an early posting back to the South African Brigade in France, and after a frustrating few months of waiting for permission, I was successful in obtaining my posting. During this period I entered for the All India Boxing Championships and won the lightweight event.

When I reached France in late September the Brigade were moving on to Le Cateau, the scene of one of the earliest battles of the B.E.F. in 1914. The whole front had taken on a completely different complexion; the Germans had been falling back and we were well clear of any scenes of previous trench warfare, and were advancing almost daily.

Again we had a new C.O., Colonel Browne, who as adjutant had confronted my parents at Bordon. Many of the officers had come up from the ranks of the South African Scottish where I had known them previously as a private soldier: my Company Commander was a dour Scot called Cameron, an ex-Cameron Highlander.

It was now open fighting in the fields, woods and orchards that led up through Dompierre to the Belgian border. The Germans were really on the run though still fighting hard; there was every scope for enterprise by junior leaders. Casualties were on the whole few on the Brigade front and the nearest that we came to total destruction was the night before the Armistice. We had marched into a village in the late afternoon and I had gone down to look for billets for the company whilst they were waiting in the square. As I stepped out of one house I saw the whole of the side of the street opposite me framed in a blazing light from the sky, lean forwards towards me as if it were going to fall on top of us, and then rock back again. This was immediately followed by the noise of a tremendous explosion. It turned out to be the destruction of two German ammunition trains by accurate night bombing. The cavalry guard on the station were blown to pieces.

This time it was the end of the 1914 War, for at eleven o'clock next morning we had news of the signing of the armistice. There were feelings of a sort of dim uncertainty and stupefaction and almost unbelief that peace had really come. In no time we were on the move again to take up our armistice stations. It was not now a matter of advancing in diamond or square formation through the fields and orchards to overcome pockets of German resistance, but a peacetime march in column of route with the pipes and drums going full blast and all the panoply that we could muster.

The country around us was beautiful upland with wide green pastures stocked with Belgian cattle. At Marche, on the edge of the Ardennes forests, we spent the next few months mainly engaged in one form of sport or another. The South African Brigade played the New Zealanders at rugby – intense excitement. We boxed against the Army on the Rhine in Bonn, we steeplechased and hunted wild boar in the Ardennes. Leave parties went home through Brussels, where there was a continuous scene of gorgeous and erotic excitement over the Armistice. The hotels were filled with young officers from all the allied armies out for a splendid time, and they were crowded with girls from Paris and Brussels.

In late December we moved down to Huy on the Meuse. I remember bathing in the river on New Year's Day at about eight o'clock after a fantastic hogmanay in the South African Scottish Mess. The Meuse was frozen and it makes me blanch even to think of it now.

That very jolly evening ended badly for Doctor Lawrence who had that day received the news of the award of a Military Cross for his gallantry at Le Cateau. He was delighted and celebrated tremendously. He was billeted in a farmhouse outside Huy and his friends, who were in no fit state to take care of him, insisted on seeing him safely to bed. But they took him to the wrong house and put him into a large double bed where an old farmer's wife was lying huddled in a corner of the bed in the dark, too terrified to speak or move. As it happened the farmer was also celebrating and came home even later to find a strange man in bed with his wife. He couldn't have helped noticing that he was tight and quite impotent, but picked him up and put him on the doorstep outside for the night where the poor doctor quickly took a very bad go of pneumonia.

As the months passed and release from anxiety and strain brought new vitality into the minds of the young men who formed the Brigade, our thoughts were turning to what we would do in the future. Places were being offered at Oxford and other universities for forestry, agriculture, medicine, and so on, and I thought seriously of forestry as an alternative to staying in the peacetime army. Having cast aside the Indian Army, I was unsure that peacetime soldiering would be in my line, if indeed I were to be selected for it.

Suddenly out of the blue an officer called Pougnet, a regular staff officer in the South African Defence Force who was serving with the Brigade, told me that the Brigade had requests for officers to go out to a mission in Russia to assist the White Armies in their campaign against the Bolsheviks. He had the forms with him and said that it appeared that the applicants might go to either North or South Russia according to the need.

I told Pougnet that he could send in my application straight away. I had found the ardours and endurances and dangers of the past years, shared in company with men whom I admired, greatly stimulating in spite of the horrors of the Western Front. So the idea of riding across the steppes of the Don or Ukraine with a Cossack brigade fired my imagination; all thoughts of Oxford or the forest service vanished into the background.

By March we were in England in Shoreham camp preparing to disband for home. The War Office sent for me, and I found myself, with Dennis Pasmore who had come up to meet me, drawing a shuba – a huge Russian coat lined with fur – and fur boots and a fur hat from the Tower of London, where for some obscure reason these articles were stored.

I said goodbye to the Colonel and to all my friends, and embarked at Southampton in late March for a journey across France and Italy to Taranto, where we picked up a boat for Salonika.

At Salonika I had a few days to wait for a ship to Constantinople. Luckily the boat had to make a twenty-four hour stop in the Dardanelles, so I seized the chance to go down to Gully Ravine to look for my brother's grave. I was lent a horse and a guide by the Graves Registration Unit, and we rode straight down to Helles from the top of Achibaba, which dominates the southern end of the peninsula and gives a superb view of the fields of Troy across the Narrows, and of Tenedos and other Aegean islands to the south.

They stood out like amber gems in the violet light of the spring morning. The rusting hulk of the *River Clyde* still lay nosed into the beach, and from the shore, the graves clustered thickly, mostly of men of the immortal 29th Division to which my brother's regiment belonged. Up the Gully Ravine, past one group of graves and another, we reached the Bluff which had been the scene of my brother's last fight on 29th June 1915. The wild flowers, of every colour, flowed down the hillsides. I picked some for my parents, and took a few photographs; and then rode hard to get back to the ship before she sailed.

The next morning we steamed into Constantinople, a breath-taking panorama which I was to know very well in years to come. But now there was no time to explore the city; after a couple of days we sailed in a tramp steamer across the Black Sea to Novorossisk.

Novorossisk lies at the north-east corner of the Black Sea, where the Caucasus runs down to the coast. The harbour is surrounded by ranges of well-forested hills; it is attractive and warm, much frequented in happier days as a seaside resort. No doubt it is a resort once again.

There was a British cruiser in the harbour and a British railway transport officer and port officer to arrange accommodation and to give us instructions.

The British Military Mission under General Holman to which I was accredited had been formed under the aegis of Winston Churchill, then Secretary of State for War. He arranged to send out a million pounds' worth or more of surplus stores including clothing, Vickers and Lewis guns and ammunition, which were desperately needed by the White Armies who were trying to reconquer their country.

The Mission itself was primarily a training and advisory one and was not supposed to take any active part in a campaign which was in itself a civil war. The weapons were new to the Russians and the first object was to teach the Russian instructors. The clothing was needed as badly as the arms. It was commonly said that a great part of this unused British Army clothing was sold by General Sidorian's staff to the Jews in Rostov. Certainly I saw little sign of it at the front and at the bases it was mostly worn by the officers.

At this period of the civil war three separate White Armies were trying to converge on the Red forces. Admiral Kolchak was advancing from Siberia, whilst in the north General Yudenich was operating from Estonia and the British were supplying General Miller from Murmansk and Archangel. General Denikin, to whom

General Holman's mission was attached, was striking north from the area of the Black Sea with his headquarters in Ekaterinodar.

Denikin's army had been raised at the time of the Revolution by General Kornilov. Based on a nucleus of eighty followers, it had grown to a force of nearly 200,000 men, based on the northern coast of the Black Sea. He had brought his army successfully through a winter campaign in the Kuban in spite of unspeakable suffering, and was on the point of seeing the provinces of Southern Russia in his hands when he was killed in action. Denikin took over command, and although he lacked the magic of Kornilov's name, he was energetically trying to set up an organised government, and to hold the ground that had been gained.

One of his difficulties was the bands of brigands – the so-called Green Army – who infested the territory in the rear of his forces, cutting his communications and plundering town and countryside. Denikin could not spare the troops from the hard-pressed front line to suppress these bands, whose marauding did enormous damage to the distressed country and to the White cause.

After a train journey across the Kuban steppe I reported to General Holman at Ekaterinodar; he was a big man, full of vigour and always cheerful. His Senior Naval Liaison Officer was Captain Fremantle, R.N., 'Old Mossyface', immediately collared me when he heard that, despite my army rank, I had been a midshipman. So my first job was to go to Rostov-on-Don, interview the Russian admiral and report on the suitability of some gunboats in the dockyard there for operations on the Volga in support of Denikin. The admiral was a little taken aback at being asked technical naval questions by a young army officer wearing the kilt, but he was courteous and helpful, and exceedingly hospitable to me and my interpreter, Prince Obolenski. This trip was my introduction to vodka and its unnerving delayed-action effect.

In a day or two I was posted to Novocherkask, a sort of Cheltenham set in the steppe above the Donetz River, with a society consisting largely of retired officers, and the site of a military college. The town itself was distinguished by its cathedral with many golden domes, a miniature version of the Kremlin.

The Russians had a machine gun school in the town, where I spent a fortnight before taking on the training of the Lewis gunners of an infantry brigade which was to leave very shortly for the front. The next three weeks were very hard work. I used to ride out from Novocherkask nine miles to the village where the Don Plastun Brigade was stationed (unwittingly I earned good marks by asking for a horse instead of insisting, like my predecessor, on the use of one of the very few motor cars). I would start work at seven, with three

D

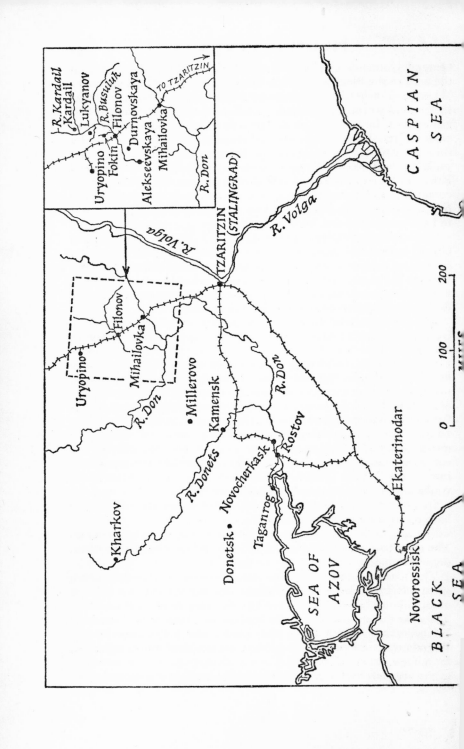

officer instructors and several N.C.O.s from the Machine Gun School as my assistants; the cool mornings beside the Gruschefskaya River were spent in instruction on the Lewis gun, followed by hours in the blazing sun on the ranges, with a mirage dancing in front of the targets. We had no elaborate targets, and could not do any training in indirect fire on the Vickers guns, for few of the Russian soldiers could read and hence use the necessary instruments. But the Cossacks were surprisingly quick at picking up the mechanical knowledge necessary to understand the eccentricities of the guns.

General Karpov was in charge of the Brigade's training. He was one of the most likeable men I met in Russia, thick-set, with blue eyes in a red face, and bristling with energy. He was a remarkable figure in a Tommy's khaki uniform, a D.S.O. ribbon and a Russian colonel's shoulder straps. He was a complete contrast to the colonel in charge of the Machine Gun School; when I had reported to him, he sent for coffee and launched into a lengthy conversation in French. After several unsuccessful attempts to get away, I finally excused myself and said I would report to the senior instructor. 'Work is not a bear,' he replied, and when I looked puzzled, explained, 'it won't run away into the woods. It will still be here tomorrow.'

General Karpov was extremely strict on duty, but full of happy geniality when he was 'off parade'. He insisted on my lunching with him every day at the priest's house where he was billetted. The old priest was a keen bee keeper, and would give us the most delicious honey with our tea from the samovar. Karpov was a professional through and through, and our conversations at lunch were nearly always on soldiering, and on the civil war. His French was execrable, his only tense being the past, so that I had to guess from the general flow of his talk whether he was speaking of the future or the present, or indeed of the past. 'Mon Capitain,' he would say, 'j'ai allé à le Rostov.' When I asked, rather cautiously, 'when', the reply might well be 'après demain'.

His infectious enthusiasm turned out the best brigade of soldiers in South Russia. He could talk to officers and men in an earnest yet very taking way, pointing his remarks from the rich treasury of Russian proverbs. The Russian soldier would not understand a silent, un-communicative commander. He was accustomed to being addressed collectively as 'my children', being severely blamed for doing badly and extravagantly praised for doing well. When the brigade was on parade, the commander would say, 'Health to you, Plastunis,' to which as one man the parade would shout, 'Welcome to you, our Commander.'

Training the soldiers was delightful since they were so gentle and straightforward, and at the same time maddening because they were forgetful and lazy. Their interest was intense for a short time, and then quite suddenly they would say to themselves, 'I know it all now,' and nothing but firm driving or bitter experience at the front would make them learn more. In any event, the time we had for training gunners was far too brief, because the brigade was under orders for the front.

Before we set off, we were inspected by the Commander in Chief, General Sidorian. On one of the hottest July afternoons the battalions marched past singing as only Russians can. The leading sections of four start the first line and the columns take up the chorus in strong, clear, ringing voices. The effect is wonderful, and no band or pipe music can approach the inspiring effect of these songs on long marches.

After the march past, the men were inspected. No British officer could see the condition of their clothing and their lack of equipment without pity. From General down to Plastuni, the dress order of the day was sacking, small caps which gave no protection from the sun and, for at least half the men, no boots. Even the sacking tunics did not meet across their chests, and they wore no underclothing. They had fought through a Russian winter in this state, and more awful hardships lay ahead of them.

After the parade, we carried out machine gun firing exercises and then fell out, the troops back to their billets, the officers to the celebration that usually ended up any big occasion. Toasts were proposed and returned, a somewhat laborious procedure through the medium of an interpreter, and the officers of the brigade got down to serious drinking. The Russian idea of a good evening differs from ours. He doesn't drink to be good company, or to make himself more amusing, or even as an incidental to good conversation; he drinks with the firm determination of putting himself and his friends under the table before the night is out.

We set off for the campaign on 1st August, on a train journey that lasted over a fortnight to Tzaritzin, now Stalingrad, and then on to Filonov, a village on one of the tributaries of the Don. I travelled in a cattle truck with my interpreter, Mr Highton, and the Brigade M.O., and an officer and his wife who could both speak a little English. In the next truck were the General with his chief of staff and staff captain: to our intense regret, we had lost General Karpov, promoted to be Inspector of Infantry, and his replacement was a General Popov, a typical Don Cossack and a subject of the Ataman of the Don, who in pre-war days had almost as much authority as the Czar himself in the province.

The Chief of Staff was a large, silent man; the Staff Captain,

Smelietov, was an engineer from Petrograd with a loud and cheerful voice and an insistent thirst. The first afternoon of the trip, I invited General Popov and the staff officers to tea in my truck. It proved a great success from the moment the Chief of Staff sat on my camp bed, which collapsed under his weight, to the time when I handed round the last of my whisky. Mr Highton – a bank clerk in peace-time – was an excellent interpreter and a very good fellow.

It was thanks to his enthusiastic display of the shotguns which were in our baggage that the train journey became an extended shooting party. For the General was also a keen shot, with the happy result that the three of us spent each day of the journey on foot, walking up partridge, grouse and hare, and on occasion flighting geese and duck. It was possible to do this because the single track line wandered over the steppe in huge curves, and the train was in no hurry. Coal was scarce, since the Bolsheviks had destroyed the machinery at the Donetz pits, and thirty miles a day was a good run for a wood-burning engine.

The Don country in summer was very beautiful. The wheat all round was golden, the folds in the steppe were wooded and the many little winding rivers were banked by thickets of silver birch. Over us was the turquoise sky, with white drifts of cloud blown by the soft steppe wind. It is only when you cross a trackless country, where people are few and far between and the only noise is the wind stirring in the corn, that you realize how long a day can be.

Those peasants who were not fighting with one side or the other spent their lives in the fields at this time of year. The whole family would leave their village, with sour milk and water melons loaded into a cart, and move across their own steppe, cutting and binding the corn as they went. They rose with the dawn at three, and worked until they fell asleep under the stars at dusk. After the long, weary toil of the harvest, they had before them the prospect of being cooped up in their village huts by the frost and blizzards which grip this smiling steppe in the winter. It must have been a more fear-some prospect than normal, for the peasants were almost destitute of clothing and fuel.

But in the summer, winter seems far away, at least to the Cossack children taking the horses down to the river in the evening – naked infants of three and four, galloping down to the water with several horses abreast, and plunging in, still mounted, to take their bathe with the animals. The village elders would sit and talk with us while we ate our supper of eggs and sour milk, waiting for the train to come along. It would puff its way up the line, we would climb into the General's truck, weary after a fifteen-mile walk and a swim in every river we crossed; and we ended the delightful day by singing Cossack songs in chorus far into the night.

Only once did our expeditions miscarry, and that was the last stage to Tzaritzin. A Russian officer and I left the train at a wayside halt to try and get a view of the Volga; to our dismay, the train set off and left us no alternative but to walk after it, twenty-five miles to Tzaritzin. It was the hottest day I remember in South Russia. By good luck, we came on a train in a siding, and were greeted by an R.A.F. officer saying, 'Hi, Jock, come in and have a drink.' I could hardly believe my eyes: but it seemed that No. 47 Squadron was operating from this base in support of the Caucasian Army under Baron Wrangel. Our good Samaritan gave us iced beer, an excellent lunch and a lift up the line in a tender to Tzaritzin, where the General roared with laughter at our pursuit of the train.

From Tzaritzin we marched across the steppe to what became our headquarters, the village of Filonov. The delightful holiday of our journey was over, and henceforward the brigade experienced little but hard times. The Plastunis dreamed that we would go on northwards to Moscow; we little realized that the catastrophe of a great defeat was so nearly upon us.

Filonov is one of a group of villages in a saucer-shaped hollow of the steppe; the regiments of the brigade were billetted in the neighbouring villages, ten or twelve versts apart (the verst is about four-fifths of a mile). I spent the day after our arrival, 8th August 1919, in sorting out the machine guns and their gunners; I was discouraged to find that of the 130 men I had trained at Novocherkask, no more than twenty were present. The rest had fallen sick with typhus or cholera.

The Russian word *bolnoi* covers every form of illness, from an ordinary stomach ache to the death throes of cholera. Luckily the cholera was not the deadly Asiatic type but a much milder form resulting in a week or two of sickness. The Plastuni thought nothing of drinking from the river where they had bathed and watered their horses; they would eat unwashed cherries from the tree, and wash them down with unboiled milk. The typhus was more dangerous. The soldiers had only their one sacking uniform, and since the louse which carries typhus infests clothing, it was not surprising that they went down with it. There were few comforts for the sick, so at least half of those who contracted it died.

The machine gun and Lewis gun training had to be re-started with great urgency, because at any moment we were likely to be moved to the front from our reserve position at Filonov. At this time I got to know the colonels of the four battalions well, officers of very different types. There was Gilensky, a charming old regular army officer, lazy as a summer's day and full of promises which he would never keep. Efanov was the exact opposite, a fierce Siberian Cossack who was a born leader of men and always at loggerheads with his commanders. He was both extravagantly brave and packed with common sense, and devoted to his men.

Kustrekov was an old cavalry officer, brave, fat and popular. He took immense pains over his personal appearance, which hardly justified his efforts. The fourth colonel, Stefanov, was a gay and spirited adventurer, who had travelled all over Russia. Although he was not a Cossack, he could perform their mounted games with marvellous skill. These games are called *jigitovka*, and are hair-raising exhibitions of horsemanship. Most of them involved the use of the vertical wooden handpiece on the pommel and cantle of the Cossack saddle – springing into the saddle, picking a piece of melon off the ground, turning in the saddle and sitting backwards, standing in the saddle; and all done at full gallop.

We had a company of cavalry allotted to us, under the command of a Cossack officer whose mother was American; he spoke Russian with a strong American accent. He was very friendly, and I enjoyed having supper with him. His men were old Cossacks, who had learnt after years of soldiering to scrounge for themselves and their horses; they produced a supper of wild goose, honey and cream. He had been leading his cavalry scouts for six successive months, and was tanned nearly black by the sun and wind of the steppe, and looked exhausted by the strain. The scouts ran constant risk of capture, and for an officer capture meant death. He was good enough to give me a fine chestnut horse which carried me well during the campaign.

Our cavalry was not good. The Reds had driven off the best of the horses in 1918 before they had been pushed out of the Don and Kuban steppes; and they had, too, some of the young and most venturesome Cossacks on their side. The Cossacks tended to follow their headman, and one in particular, Miranov, who had joined the Reds in the hope of becoming Ataman of the Don, had attracted a considerable following.

The Red forces were a curious mixture. The hard core consisted of officers and men imbued with Bolshevik ideals, and therefore – like the Whites – fighting for a cause. The commisars were of course particularly virulent, or idealistic; their role appeared to be that of surveillance over the officers or generals who might be thought lukewarm. The commisars were detested, and blamed for the torture and death of captured White officers, whose mutilated bodies I saw on several occasions; and so a captured commisar was shot. At Filonov a most unpleasant female commisar was taken prisoner; she looked more like a wild beast than a woman, and boasted in my hearing that she herself had shot a hundred officers in Odessa.

Then, as I suppose in every army, there were the pressed men, who would desert to Denikin's army at the first opportunity. Finally, there were the Chinese, who had originally been in the Labour Corps during the 'German' war, and fought for the Reds for food and clothing. At this time a great proportion of the infantry opposing us on the 2nd Corps front were Chinese. They were not very good at attacking because they could barely understand the orders of their commisars, but they were brave and resolute.

The war was entirely one of movement. To occupy the steppe was pointless: instead, both sides aimed at seizing the few vital points like river crossings and railway bridges, to gain the power of movement and thus isolate and bring to battle the enemy forces. There was no front as such, and villages far behind the 'line' might well be in the other side's hands. Communications were extremely bad, and one never knew whether a village was in Red hands or our own until the cavalry scouts had been in to investigate.

At dawn on 20th August we marched from the Filonov area to take up position some thirty versts to the north. We looked like a mob of prisoners captured after months in the trenches; most men were without boots, and their sacking uniform was even more threadbare. As we marched, the field kitchens cooked the mid-day meal, which consisted of the thinnest of thin soup and badly cooked black bread. The villages we passed could offer little more; many armies had crossed and re-crossed this poor district, each hungrier than the last.

On the march I usually rode with Brigade Headquarters, which signalled its whereabouts by carrying a large red flag. This led to misunderstandings; at one village, where the people thought we were Reds, they opened fire on us, fortunately with no casualties. With me went Mr Highton, my interpreter, and an admirable Cossack orderly who had been allotted to me. Vasili Topolskov (who is living in England now) saved my life on two occasions, and became a valued friend. He had the gift of conjuring up a piece of bread from somewhere or other when I thought we would die of hunger, he looked after the horses in the worst of the campaign, and he was quite fearless.

Chapter Five

DEFEAT OF THE DON ARMY

THE brigade took up position on a ridge between two villages, some fifteen versts apart. One of the numerous little rivers of the Don country ran through the valley where these villages lay. And yet valley is not the word, for on the southern bank of the river the country was quite flat, and then across the river it rose literally like a great step up to a higher plane.

I lunched with Colonel Gilensky at his headquarters. As we left to ride up to the forward position, one of my American friend's scouts rode in with his arm bleeding profusely, and his horse ridden to a standstill. He had had a near thing with the enemy cavalry; six of them had ridden at him as he was returning from Popov, a village six miles to the north. He seemed very unconcerned as he handed the Colonel a message that two battalions of Red infantry were occupying positions to the east of Popov.

As we rode round to the left flank of the brigade, we had our first view of the Red cavalry. The steppe ran down to the north west, and there, on the slope of a far rise, were three Red squadrons. The village we were looking at, which was apparently behind our left flank, was in enemy hands.

The Plastunis were all dug in on the ridge. The weather was warm, and they were keen for a fight, and very cheerful. They were trying to catch up on their sleep: at night the cold dew of the steppe kept them fitfully dozing. They had neither overcoats nor blankets.

After leaving Colonel Gilensky in the evening, I rode back to Brigade Headquarters, which were whenever possible located in some village midway between the Regimental Headquarters. The General ordered the 1st Regiment to occupy the village of Schakin at daybreak. This village, which was some six miles away, was reported by our cavalry to be unoccupied.

I wanted to emphasize some points about carrying the Lewis guns while on the march, so I rode out to the 1st Regiment while it was still dark and went the round of the battalion gun teams before they moved off. We approached the village at first light down a long slope. At the foot was the usual river, with a green forest bordering its banks. Beyond the forest on the right was a wooden church, which like every village church in Russia was a large white wooden building with a grey dome.

I was riding at the time with the left-hand company, who were marching through breast-high grass. We were still some eight hundred yards from the wood when the scouts came running back. Before the company had time to deploy, three squadrons of Red cavalry burst from the fringe of the forest, with sabres already drawn, and it looked as though we were trapped.

It was a very bad moment, but Sergeant Sultricov, a very intelligent Roumanian Lewis gunner, saved the situation. Rushing his two gun teams to the left of the column, which had had no time to extend, he fired the guns from the men's shoulders, one man supporting each gun on his shoulder. Owing to the high grass, this was the only effective way of working the Lewis gun.

This was the first cavalry charge that I had seen, and it was the first action for most of these young Plastunis. It looked at one moment as if nothing could stop the dense mass of horsemen, and the effect of their determined rush with flashing sabres and cheering shouts was enough to cause an intense state of 'wind up', even amongst old soldiers. The line of cavalry looked as if they were almost on top of us. But the effect of the Lewis gun fire was devastating. Sabres flew, and horses reared and fell on their riders; through a cloud of dust the screaming of the horses and the shouts of their riders were loud in our ears.

The enemy line melted under the fire at this range. As those in the rear turned and fled, they were followed by bursts from the other two machine guns that had by now opened up.

The Plastunis could hardly believe their eyes. Hardly a man had fired a shot from his rifle. It was all over in two minutes, and each individual man should have thanked Sergeant Sultricov for his life. The confidence which this action inspired in the Lewis guns was most fortunate. One stoppage at so short a range would have been fatal, but as they were Sultricov's guns, the stoppage did not occur.

It taught us that when we were in wheat or high grass, we must fire the guns from the shoulder of the second number, which was not too pleasant for him because the guns became so hot. So in future the No. 2 was provided with old pieces of sacking to wear on his right shoulder as a protection. It had to be the right shoulder, since the gun ejected to the right; I once saw an unfortunate No. 2, in a hurry, supporting his gun on the left shoulder, and nearly swallowing the empty cases as they flew out, hot and oily.

By this time both our battalions were deployed into line, and they continued to advance in two waves towards Schakin. The Red cavalry, seeing that we intended an occupation of the village, retired. All this happened between 6 and 8 a.m. About ten o'clock orders came from Brigade to evacuate Schakin and fall back on a ridge about four thousand yards south of the river.

As we fell back, the reason for the order was apparent. Three regiments of Red cavalry had worked past our right flank, and endeavoured to close with us as we retired. The 21st and 24th Don Cavalry, in their turn, endeavoured to envelop these regiments from their left flank.

As the retirement was completed, I went to the top of a haystack with Colonel Efanov, where we could see for miles. We watched the enemy scouts, also on haystacks, with their horses hidden behind, firing on our scouts as they advanced.

We sent for a Lewis gun, and kept up a heavy fire on them. We could see them jumping from the top of the haystack into the saddle, and galloping away when the fire became too hot for them.

Noon brought bad news. One of the companies, No. 4, was missing. They had been on the outskirts of the village, and it was believed they were cut off by Miranov's squadrons when retirement was ordered.

About 4 p.m. the Chief of Staff rode up with orders. Colonel Efanov's regiment would attack Schakin forthwith. One gun of the battery attached to brigade would assist the attack. The little field gun turned up at 8 p.m. and fired a few small shells at the village, and then we advanced again over the same ground as in the morning. It was dark before the scouts came back and reported the village clear of the Reds, and we rode in with Colonel Efanov at the head of the column.

The villagers told us that the lost company of the morning had indeed been cut off by the Reds and the officers, poor fellows, tortured and then killed. As we rode past the northern outskirts of Schakin, we saw their three bodies, stripped naked and mutilated, lying in the moonlight.

At daybreak came orders for the brigade to assemble at Lukyanov, a village ten versts from Schakin. The next three days were to give me some idea of the extraordinary distances that the Russian soldier can march on a minimum of food. We followed the river valley, a delightful ride for those of us who were mounted, but for the men thirty versts of long, dry, dusty steppe.

I rode with Colonel Stefanov in the scout line. He told me that this was Miranov's district, and the villagers were likely to prove liars and Bolsheviks. Towards evening we reached the day's objective, a village called Nikolaev, and asked an old woman, tilling the fields on the outskirts, where the Reds were.

She said they never came there or worried them. She was full of questions as to the strength of the brigade, and who we were.

We did not answer her, but moved on. Stefanov remarked that 'the women are worse than the men when they turn Bolshevik'. Later that evening the scouts brought back news that the Bolshevik outposts were in the next villages, to the north and east. We posted picquets to the north and east of Nikolaev that night and waited for orders from Division.

When the orders came, they were disconcerting; only later did I learn that the Divisional Commander had pushed our brigade too far north, and we were in serious danger of being cut off by the enemy. To enable the brigade to retreat along the long, dusty road we had covered the previous afternoon, the 2nd Battalion and a Volunteer Regiment under Colonel Smelietov were ordered to make a feint attack on the village of Kardail.

We marched forward with the forced gaiety and uneasy anticipation that precedes any battle, little knowing that bad staff work had led to the Volunteer Regiment's attacking before we arrived. They were easily beaten off, and the Red defenders of the village were ready to concentrate their forces on us. We had two six pounders in support of our attack, with some cavalry protecting our right flank. Our Vickers machine guns were carried in small carts drawn by ponies; their ammunition, and that for the Lewis guns, was also carried in carts.

There was of course no element of surprise as we moved over open ground in full view of the village towards a ridge in the shelter of which we formed up for the attack. The Red artillery secured a number of direct hits on the column, knocking out one of the Vickers guns and killing the team. Once behind the ridge, Colonel Efanov formed up his men, ordering two companies to lead the attack and two to follow up and prevent our flank being turned by the brave and well-handled Red cavalry.

I left Mr Highton and Vasili with the horses and ammunition cart, and went forward with the right hand company. As we crossed the ridge, a hail of fire swept over our heads; like all partially trained troops, the Red infantry was firing too high. But the shrapnel barrage was effective enough, and as we advanced and closed the range, the enemy rifle and automatic fire was too intense to go forward. All three company officers were hit, two being killed outright. Then I saw a cloud of dust moving to our right flank – three enemy squadrons making the first outflanking move. The two Lewis guns were having stoppages because the gunners were excited and hurried, and the position looked bad.

Mr Highton came forward to me over the ridge, and I was able to send him off with a message to Colonel Efanov that the company had to retreat or be surrounded. I gave the order myself, since there was no Russian officer left; miraculously the stoppages cleared and our gunners opened up a devastating fire on the cavalry who had been confidently advancing in close formation.

We managed to get back across the ridge, to see a long line of enemy infantry advancing towards us from Kardail. They drove us from the front, halting to fire as they came, while the cavalry, on both flanks now, herded us like sheep dogs. I had no idea which way to direct the retreat, and could only pray for Colonel Efanov to appear.

The men had been splendid up till now, but the sight of the enemy in superior numbers and further salvoes of accurate artillery fire demoralized them. In the nick of time the Colonel galloped up with Mr Highton behind him; fierce and relentless, he shouted his orders over the din, pointing the way with his sword. We had to keep the line extended, and all would be well. The immediate crisis was over; we were in touch again with the left hand company, and if we could maintain a steady retreat and steady fire, darkness would save us.

We made a halt at a line of haystacks. From their tops we had a fine field of fire covering the retreat of the left flank. I got some guns into action, cursing in my few words of Russian the gun teams who had left their magazines where they had used them instead of bringing them in to be re-filled. Vasili spotted an ammunition cart slipping away and galloped after them with my revolver, to drive them back to the line.

The stand at the haystacks inflicted a vital check on the enemy advance. The battle round them was fierce; at its height a Russian sister in her white dress walked calmly up and down the line of soldiers, tending the wounded despite being hit in the arm by a bullet. She organized the placing of the wounded men in the machine gun and ammunition carts, their only chance of escape. Already our doctor and the two ambulance carts, with ninety-six men and eight officers, had been cut of by Miranov's Cossacks and the Chinese. Their fate was too horrible to think about.

The retreat continued, with a final determined cavalry charge just being beaten off as a heavy rain storm gave us a cloak. On we went, the wounded lying groaning in the carts, the Colonel riding up and down the line to prevent its closing up into a huddled mass, the Vickers gunners shooting from their carts as they frantically drove their ponies to the rear, and the Red bullets singing in the air and kicking up the ground. And then the sun went down behind a purple bank of cloud, a golden glorious sunset of deliverance from the immediate danger. We formed up behind a field of sunflowers in full bloom, to march back to the brigade we had been trying to protect. Our cavalry, whom we had needed so much all day, at last joined us and formed a protective screen behind us, their long lances standing high above the sunflowers.

The great autumn retreat of the Don Army had begun. Denikin's advance guards entered Orel, only two hundred miles from Moscow; but Russian campaigns are fought on lines of communication, not on front lines. Denikin's thrust was bound to fail with his vital rail and river links so often disrupted and sometimes permanently occupied by partisans and the Red cavalry.

We fell back to Lukyanov, and then to Fokin, and to our bewilderment crossed the Filonov railway line and pushed west into the steppe. This entailed long marches in bitter cold nights, although it was still August. The men were soaked, exhausted and hungry, but the Lewis guns were clean and in good order. It was clear the men had begun to realize how they must rely on them. But we were very short of magazines and spare parts for the Lewis guns and of belts for the Vickers, and no one seemed to have signalled to base for them. The Brigade Commander agreed that I must set off at once for Novocherkask and fetch the spares.

That was a nightmare journey for Mr Highton, Vasili and me. We rode off on 27th August, and reached Novocherkask on 6th September. Our first objective was the railway: we heard that Filonov had been taken by the Reds, so rode south west to Alekseevskaya. Filonov was recaptured, so our weary horses were driven hard to Durnovskaya, and on to Filonov. But the last train had left the day before, the Reds were attacking in force, and the division was in retreat. Back to Durnovskaya and west across the steppe; fresh horses, new guides, on and on.

At Novocherkask I said goodbye to Mr Highton who had driven himself to the point of complete exhaustion. It was remarkable that a man in his forties, whose life had been spent working in a bank, could endure all that he had done. I went to the arsenal and made arrangements for all the spare parts for the guns to be looked out and got ready, and the same night left for Taganrog, on the Sea of Azov, where General Holman's Mission H.Q. was now situated. It was long past midnight when I arrived, and walked into Colonel Julius, my immediate superior. 'Good God,' he said, 'I thought I'd seen a ghost – you were reported captured and killed weeks ago.'

I spent the next three days writing a detailed report on what had happened; I was pleased to learn that General Holman had received letters from the officer commanding the Don Plastun Brigade, and from the Divisional Commander, saying that at Kardail the situation had been saved by the action of the right flank and by the success of the Lewis guns. The General added that he had recommended me for the award of a bar to my Military Cross; on Colonel Efanov's recommendation the Russians wanted to award me the Vladimir with Bow and Crossed Swords, the equivalent of a D.S.O.

Colonel Julius told me that when I was at the front, an official document from the Admiralty had arrived for me. It was a free pardon from the King for my desertion from the Navy. The Colonel had proposed to keep it for my return, but a senior Russian officer who was dining at the Mission H.Q. said he was going north to the Plastun Brigade and offered to deliver it to me. The Russian was never heard of again.

After three days at the Mission at Taganrog, I went back to Novocherkask and at the arsenal found a lorry all loaded up with spares, plus a young British Ordnance sergeant to refit the Vickers and Lewis guns. We set off with a Kuban Cossack colonel who had been wounded and begged a lift back to the front. The journey north was eventful, the most alarming incident being when the lorry fell through a bridge over a tributary of the Don River. The local farmers teamed up a dozen oxen which managed to extricate us. The alternative would have been to continue the journey by ox-cart; the only car in the Don at this time was the Corps Commander's tourer, in which I once saw him lead a cavalry charge.

We arrived at Corps H.Q. late one evening, to find the General and his staff sitting in the moonlight outside a farmhouse enjoying the company of some pretty nurses who were having a rest from the battle. The fighting was not far away; the rattle of machine guns could be heard over a distant ridge as we had vodka and zakouska, and dined, and performed wild dances with swords flashing and the Kuban colonel shooting off his pistol.

Next morning we pushed on and found the Plastun Brigade. The fighting had been rather desultory since I left them, for the Reds had been consolidating Tzaritzin as a base after they had captured it with much of our kit. The regiments were engaged in night attacks on Red positions; this was good tactics, because the attacks disturbed the enemy with a minimum of casualties to the Whites, and because at night the Reds' strongest weapon, their superb cavalry, was useless.

But these were only pinpricks, and soon the enemy advance continued in earnest. I found myself once again with Colonel Stevanov in an almost identical tight spot, when his regiment was ordered to make a holding attack to permit the brigade to disengage and withdraw. We were to be supported on the left by a battalion from another brigade. In the event, they cleared out, and we were shot up by enemy M.G.s which had worked round to our left rear. It was a very hot corner, in every sense, since it was a scorching morning, and the Colonel and I had to leg it back to where Vasili held the horses under cover. Colonel Stevanov was hit by an explosive bullet which took his left hand off. He was in great pain, but we tied him up and rode on to site the Vickers guns to bring the most effective fire to bear while the battalion withdrew. There were several minutes when I thought it was all up, but the Vickers saved the day, and proved yet again their value shooting from the pony carts as they withdrew.

This was my last action with the Plastunis whom I had come to like and admire so much. When we re-joined the brigade after another long night march, I found orders from General Holman at Taganrog to return. I was loath to do so, and the Brigade Commander asked for my return to be delayed, but the General had made his mind up. I spent a hectic few days with Sergeant Anson doing all we could to refit the guns with the spares I had brought up; and then the time came to say goodbye, and experience a tumultuous send-off from the brigade.

This year had been one long adventure among the sun-baked steppe lands of the Don, and in the seemingly unending miles of swaying river grass along the Volga, and in the beautiful Donetz Basin where birds sang continuously in the water meadows, wild geese called in the pools and cranes passed overhead on their long flight north. The quality of the light was always changing, from a lilac haze over the green-tinted steppe, to the golden light of full day and the violet hues of dusk.

At twenty-four, heat and cold, fatigue and fear, the night marches and the ceaseless riding across the plains were a challenge to youth and strength; a challenge such as moved Conrad to write, 'I remember my youth and the feeling that will never come back any more – the feeling that I could last for ever – outlast the sea, the earth, and all men; the deceitful feeling that lures us on to joys, to perils, to love, to vain effort, and to death; the triumphant conviction of strength, the heat of life in a handful of dust, and glow in the heart.'

I was posted back to the training schools at Novocherkask. All the billets were occupied, so I shared a room in a hotel with a very young officer who had just turned up from the Rhine, Charles Arden-Clarke. We became fast friends and remained so until his death in 1963, five years after he had relinquished his post as first Governor General of Ghana.

Although the coming of the snow put a stop to operations, the outlook was sombre. The defeat of the Don Army had enabled the Reds to cut Denikin's one railway link with his base by the capture of Tzaritzin, and the only way of supplying his main forces to the north was by ox-carts over hundreds of miles of steppe. But in Novocherkask the old retired officers celebrated any festival with huge parties; vodka and caviare were followed by dinner and quantities of Caucasian wine, and by toast after toast with every glass being thrown through the windows into the street below.

In the middle of December, I was given a fortnight's leave in England. I left Novocherkask with Vasili, my orderly, in a Black Sea tramp steamer for Constantinople, and thence on a British freighter to England. A problem arose at Plymouth when the immigration officer taxed me with having a Cossack on board, and asked for his passport. I produced Vasili's paper of appointment, a very impressive document in Cyrillic script and stamped by the Ataman of the Don. I translated all this as a passport, and no more was said.

It was New Year's Day 1920 when we landed and went to my parents' home. It was a memorable reunion, and Vasili was quickly enlisted as a sort of gardener-butler in the household; he has lived in England ever since. My leave was up all too soon, but before I could set off again for the Black Sea I was called to the War Office. The news was most disturbing. The Reds had closed in on Rostov, and crucified and burnt a British transport officer there. The W.O. was about to recall the Mission and was not prepared to send any officers back to Russia.

I was tempted to resign my commission and go out as a volunteer to the White Russians, but my parents dissuaded me. It was as well they did, for Denikin had fallen ill, and Baron Wrangel took over; the armies in South Russia were about to withdraw to the Crimea, from where they were later evacuated by the French. During the coming months the White Armies collapsed on all fronts, and the Bolshevik rule was firmly established in spite of all the efforts to stop it.

E

Chapter Six

UNDERGRADUATE AND SUBALTERN

I DECIDED at this time to stay in the army, and I was recommended for a regular commission. This would take some time to come through, and in the meantime, as a captain in the South African Scottish, I was at rather a loose end. My old friend Hugh Seymour had been at Oxford for a year before the war, and was about to go up again to complete his degree course before joining the Indian Civil Service. He had no difficulty in persuading me to come and see the Provost of Worcester, his college.

My interview went off all right, although I had been brought up in anything but an academic atmosphere, and it seemed curious to meet an elderly gentleman with no contact whatsoever with the world as I knew it. I had to sit an exam of sorts, and was then accepted as an undergraduate. I decided to read Russian, since my colloquial knowledge had been good enough to take me all round the Don; but there was no strenuous striving in post-war Oxford. Life in college was comfortable, and friendships were easily formed.

My life for a year alternated between Oxford and boxing. I had joined the Belsize club in London, and was persuaded to go in for the Amateur Championship. My father was all in favour of this, and helped the captain of the club to arrange for a professional boxer from the National Sporting Club to train me at home, in the vac. We sparred, and then walked and ran over half Surrey; after this, and a walking tour in the spring of 1920 with Hugh Seymour when we walked from Montreux to Zermatt, I felt I could take on anyone.

Unfortunately in the Championship I met in my first bout the eventual winner, but at least I was able to go the full four rounds with him. This encouraged me to enter the Army Championships at Aldershot, where I won the Lightweight after knocking my opponent through the ropes. After the fight, when I was sitting in the dressing-room getting my breath back, the Director of Physical Training, who ran the championship, came in. He was Colonel R. B. Campbell, who later became famous as the head of Physical Education at Edinburgh University.

'What are you going to do, young fellow?' he asked me. I explained that I was waiting for a regular commission: 'What regiment?' I said I had no idea, but that my brother had been in the

Dublin Fusiliers, which was about to be disbanded. He laughed and said, 'I'll tell you what regiment – my own, the Gordon Highlanders. I'll arrange it.' Then he told me that I was remarkably fit, and that I ought to put my name down for the Modern Pentathlon trials at Aldershot in June. I had never heard of this performance, but when he explained that it consisted of riding, running, shooting, fencing and swimming, and that the Olympic Games in Antwerp was the objective, I was full of enthusiasm.

A splendid term ended with a memorable evening at the Commem. Ball at Trinity which Hugh Seymour and I had promised to attend in a party with some enchanting young Danish girls. As luck would have it, I was called for by the President of the Imperial Boxing Association to fight, that same night, at the Holborn Stadium in the lightweight competition against a French services team. The stadium was packed, but my father and some friends managed to get seats. My fight was put on early, about eight o'clock, as I had told the President I had to get back to Oxford; and I found that the British competitors were honoured by having Jimmy Wilde and Jim Driscoll as seconds.

My Frenchman was a good deal heavier (I was fighting at about 9 stone 2 lbs then) but rather fat, and I was able to knock him out in the third round, to an enthusiastic response. I hared off to Paddington to catch the nine o'clock, and changed in the train into white tie and tail coat. I hadn't been marked in the bout, and Hugh and my friends in the party would hardly believe me when I told them I'd been boxing in London. We danced till the sun was up, had bacon and eggs for breakfast and then went down to the Cherwell for a bathe.

A few days later I went to Aldershot for the Pentathlon trials. All my life I had taken an active part in the sports concerned, without being eminent in any one of them; I was selected, and within three weeks was asked to captain the team. We practised hard, ending up with a few days at Aldeburgh, where we attracted some attention fencing with the épee on the front, the only suitable place I could find. In August we travelled to Antwerp for the Games, but were beaten in all the Pentathlon events by the Swedes, who had been training for it since the previous Olympics in 1912. This was disappointing, but we had a magnificent view from special seats of the stadium events, and could see at close quarters Abrahams, Rudd and all the other early Olympic greats.

At last my posting came through, to the 1st Battalion who were then in Constantinople; and on 21st March 1921 Hugh Seymour and I left England in different ships, he for Burma and I for Turkey.

*

Constantinople was very different from the city I had passed through two years earlier on my way to the Black Sea. The Bosphorus was filled with the allied fleets, the largest of course being the Royal Navy. Cutters, whalers and steam launches sped to and fro all day long between the warships and the European and Asiatic shores; sailing boats from Moda and the Anatolian coast brightened the blue Marmara waters with gaily coloured sails, and Greek and Turkish caiques came shooting down the Bosphorus under full sail with the six knot current. The lower city, Galata, was still a pictur-esque jumble of wooden houses, perpetually catching fire; a familiar sight was the fire brigade – primitive pumps carried on the shoulders of six or eight stout Turkish porters – pounding up and down the streets. The Turks in those pre-Ataturk days still wore the fez and baggy trousers. The whole scene was one of movement, life and colour.

The 1st Gordons were in the Haidar Pasha barracks in Scutari, the same barracks which had been Florence Nightingale's hospital during the Crimean War. The army's job was to hold the ring between the Greeks and the Turks, which entailed sending observa-tion patrols to various points where Allied and Turkish territory met. When we were not out on patrol, life in Constantinople was gay, particularly for me with so many friends in the Fleet. My com-panions at Dartmouth were now Lieutenants, and I found myself a constant guest on board. At weekends, we went shooting guinea fowl, pheasants and wild boar in the Alen Dagh forest, or followed the Anatolian hounds in the flower-covered hills of Kaish Dagh and Chamlija on horses lent to us by the Third Hussars. I liked the Gordons, and they made me very welcome as a newly-joined officer.

After some six months, I was given leave and went climbing in the Austrian Alps with our M.O. and Dennis Pasmore, my old friend from *Hyacinth* days, now in Constantinople in the *Iron Duke*. It was my first experience of real Alpine climbing; I had never abandoned my ambition to join an Everest expedition, and I looked on this experience as a proving ground.

In November 1921 we were relieved by the Essex regiment and went to Malta. Here we concentrated on drill, discipline and field training, but found time as well for polo, racing, rugby football and sailing. Another old naval friend turned up in the shape of Claude Butlin, now in the *King George V*; we shared a half-decked sailing boat, and spent many beautiful summer afternoons off the islands, with some anxious moments in the sudden squalls. In the spring, Claude and I spent two months traversing the whole range of Austrian Alps on skis. We camped in the glacier huts, and climbed all the major peaks. When we came down from the Dolomites to Venice on our way back to Malta, we had great difficulty in persuading the porter of an hotel on the Lido to let us in. We were burnt black by the sun, and he thought we were tramps.

A month later the situation in Anatolia blew up and the regiment was ordered back, this time to Chanak in the Dardanelles, a dusty plain on the eastern edge of the Narrows opposite Kilid Bahr on the Gallipoli coast. It was surrounded and dominated by a circle of hills, and was quite untenable. The reason for the flap was the activities of Kemal Ataturk, who had raised a force to drive the Greeks out of Anatolia, and had succeeded in driving them down to the coast in disorder. His forces faced ours at Chanak, and he was said to be planning an attack. I was in command of the Mortar Platoon; since our ammunition was dated 1917, and as often as not burst short, it was as well the threatened attack never happened.

Ataturk's stand was successful in recovering Eastern Thrace for Turkey, and the Greeks were made to withdraw. The Gordons were sent up to Rodosto where we were split up into company areas, to make sure that neither side committed atrocities while the Greek forces withdrew. For my company this meant a march across Thrace, in a blaze of autumn light and colour, to the Gulf of Saros, where we spent weeks visiting the villages and sorting out complaints. In one village I was met by a Greek who claimed to have been headman; his head was wrapped up in bandages and he said that his ears had been cut off. When I said I would get a doctor at once, he told me they were better, and he wanted compensation, not a doctor. So I had the bandages removed, with difficulty, and we found two perfectly intact ears.

Many of the Turkish villagers had served at Gallipoli. It was very interesting to talk to them, and hear their stories of the British attack. They spoke warmly of their enemies, just as everyone I knew who fought in the Dardanelles spoke highly of the Turks.

It was December when Eastern Thrace was declared settled and we were withdrawn to Rodosto. Blizzards had been blowing for a fortnight, and there was seven feet of snow, and a wind straight from the Russian steppes. Constantinople was no warmer, and the battalion spent a miserable Christmas. Our next job was to man a chain of posts across the Chamlija hills, to prevent undercover Kemalists, possibly disguised as policemen, from infiltrating Constantinople. All police had to be checked at the posts, where registers were kept showing how many policemen crossed the line from east to west and vice versa. One day Jock Stewart was inspecting the posts and their registers, and noticed at one of them that seventeen policemen had gone one way and seventeen the other.

He said to the young lance corporal 'It's strange that there should be exactly the same number each way.' The lad replied very seriously, 'Aye, sir, but it wass the same man, sir.' Jock found that this policeman had his house on one side of the line and his farm on the other.

The Council of Lausanne was meeting to determine the question of Turkey, and it became increasingly clear that Ataturk was going to get his way. Chanak was abandoned, the army concentrated at Constantinople and we busied ourselves with sport when we were not training. I coached both the battalion and brigade boxing teams, which were very successful, and went in myself for the officers' lightweight and welterweight championships, winning one and being beaten in the finals of the other. At the same time I was riding to hounds and playing rugger against the Fleet; some days I would play a rugger match in the afternoon, and in the evening, as part of training my boxing teams, would take on six or seven competitors of all weights. Looking back, I cannot think how I produced the physical energy.

In July 1923 I was back in England, and after a short P.T. course at Aldershot, and home leave, I rejoined the battalion. The Gordons had returned to Malta, but with a new commanding officer, Colonel Pelham-Burn. He was an outstanding C.O. in every way. During the war he had commanded the Highland Brigade and for a short period the Highland Division. He had an overpowering and commanding personality, a very practical approach to any problem and was the finest trainer of officers and men that I have come across. He was a bachelor and lived in the mess; since he was a very serious man, this rather cramped the normally lighthearted atmosphere among the subalterns and captains, practically all of whom at this time were unmarried. He was a great shikari, had shot ibex in the Himalayas and tigers in the jungle of Bengal. When warmed up after dinner he would re-shoot the tigers in front of the fire, to the veiled amusement of the subalterns.

He lived for the regiment and during his command in Malta brought the whole standard of training, sport and games to a peak. I have never ceased to be grateful for what I learnt from him of the art of training troops. When two years later I came to command a company of the Camel Corps in the Sudan, and later the Camel Corps itself, I remained very grateful to Pelham-Burn for opening the door to one of the most fascinating aspects of Army life, the capacity to train troops skilfully and realistically for war.

Two nights a week we were paraded for Highland Dancing classes under the Pipe Major, so that we should show up to the best at the Regimental Highland Ball and in foursome and eightsome reels on guest nights. Six weeks before the ball the lady partners were invited to attend the regimental dancing classes on pain of being thrown out of their foursome reel if they missed an evening. There was enormous competition among the female population in Malta to be in on the Highland Ball. When it finally came off with 600 guests and champagne flowing, it was a model of barbaric splendour like everything that Pelham-Burn launched, and was talked about for long afterwards. Anything that brought the regiment to the fore was his delight.

In April 1924 I had a letter from Colonel Campbell telling me that he had asked for my appointment as the officer in charge of physical training and education at Sandhurst, to take over in the spring of 1925. This was a key appointment and really the only one in the physical training world that I would have been keen to accept. Campbell added, 'You will be in a position to train again for the 1924 Olympic Games in Paris.' He had also written to Pelham-Burn, who had agreed that I should go on a preliminary course at Aldershot, provided that I came back to the regiment for the winter training.

While attending the course I lived in Aldershot with the Leicestershire Regiment and used a motor bike to take me to and from the central gymnasium. In late May we started collecting competitors for the Modern Pentathlon team and began training for the Olympic trials. I remember Brian Horrocks turned up; we had much in common, both of us having been in Russia at the same period, and I saw a lot of him. He was fighting with Kolchak in Siberia in 1919 whilst I was with Denikin.

I was on the crest of the wave; immediately ahead of me was an appointment to Sandhurst which any young officer might envy, and the exciting prospect of competing in the Olympic Games. Then one afternoon the fates overtook me and in a moment of time my whole future was changed. I was riding my motor bike back for lunch when a lorry turned in across the road in front of me and the tailboard which was loose fell down and hit my arm. I landed in the ditch on the same arm with the bones protruding through the skin, in such pain as I have never experienced. The driver picked me up and took me to the Cambridge Hospital. I remained there all summer, at one time in grave danger of losing my arm, and in terrific pain, which in those days the doctors would not relieve lest you should become a morphia addict.

Fortunately through the skill of the doctors my arm was as strong as ever again by the autumn and I was passed fit for service by a medical board. But the accident had put paid to all my hopes: the Olympic Games were over, and I had not been able to complete the P.T. course required for the Sandhurst job because Pelham-Burn had wired for my immediate return to the battalion. Colonel Campbell tried to mediate, but 'The Dragon' was adamant. Back to Malta I went.

Pelham-Burn put me once more in charge of the sports and re-fused to discuss the Sandhurst appointment. I felt very sore, and avoided him as far as I could. The battalion was due to go to India that winter, which meant more barrack life: and so I decided to put in for the Egyptian Army.

The adjutant said, 'The C.O. wants to know if you have done this because you are fed up about Sandhurst.' I replied, 'No, not really; but I want more responsibility and a less formal life. And the Egyptian Army is looked on as a crack show.' There was no good keeping up this gloom with 'The Dragon', and gradually our old relationship was restored. When I came to leave in November 1924, he gave me a glowing confidential report; better still, his teaching had given me the confidence to train and command whatever unit came my way.

Chapter Seven

SOLDIERING IN THE SUDAN

And you will list the bugle
That blows in lands of morn . . .
A. E. HOUSMAN

IN November 1924 I received my orders to report to the headquarters of the Egyptian Army in Cairo, and arrived at a critical
moment in the history of Egypt. On the 19th of that month, Sir
Lee Stack, who was both Governor General of the Sudan and
Sirdar (commander in chief) of the Egyptian Army, was assassinated
in Cairo. There had been mutinies amongst Egyptian troops in the
Sudan in August, and trouble had broken out there again. The
High Commissioner, Lord Allenby, presented the Egyptian Government with an ultimatum demanding, amongst other things, the
immediate withdrawal from the Sudan of all the Egyptian officers
of the Sudanese forces, and of all purely Egyptian units.

I reported to the Deputy Adjutant General, Colonel Hammersley.
I was wearing the uniform of a subaltern of the Gordon Highlanders.
In the most pleasant way imaginable he said, 'For God's sake don't
come into this headquarters in uniform at this stage. We are trying
to get officers for a new Sudan Defence Force in the guise of civilians
for the Sudan Government. It will give the whole show away if you
turn up in your distinguished-looking kilt.'

We arranged for my early departure by train to Shellal, the rail-
head for the Nile journey into the Sudan below Halfa. After travelling all night and half the next day in a dusty Egyptian train it was
a delight to board the Sudan Government Railways steamer, a
spotless boat with excellent service, and a clean, cheerful, welcoming
Sudanese staff. There were of course few of the luxuries of today,
but that journey up the Nile in late November was a prelude to
many such unforgettable journeys in the future.

The chugging steamer moved at a little more than walking pace,
leaving a column of black smoke trailing in the still air. Tamarisk
and palms slipped past in a wilderness of sandhills to the west, while
the east bank was as rugged as the rocks of Aden. The desert looked
watery and unreal in the mid-day heat, with the swaying, shifting
mirage of pools merging into ponds and shrinking back to pools
again. Where the sky met the land it threw back a dazzling light
reflected from the burning dunes.

It was as if there was 'no rain left in all the world'. An oncoming steamer, with a barge like our own secured alongside, thrust before it a continuous, glinting wave. Feluccas with their billowing sails half melted in the haze of a distant promontory; their mast and rigging loomed and dissolved unexpectedly, hardening into reality only at our passing. Aboard the barge a Sudanese soldier, silently scraping a perch, its glistening form all silver green, peered into the brown waters of the Nile. In the bow of the barge a white-bearded Arab stood at prayer on his rush mat. It was the hour of the *Assr* prayer.

It was an illusory calm. Egypt and the Sudan were in turmoil after the Great War. In Egypt itself the situation had deteriorated ever since an ugly incident at Denshawi in 1906, where an officer of a British cavalry regiment had been murdered. Of the fifty-two villagers arrested, four were hanged, several were flogged and others imprisoned, a punishment bitterly resented by the Egyptians. Further rioting and murders occurred in 1919, directed against British troops and officials; it was in fact a nationalist rising, and was suppressed by the British army.

All this made the position in the Sudan impossible. This vast territory – about one million square miles, or a quarter the size of Europe – had been more or less thoroughly annexed by Egypt in bits and pieces from 1820 to 1874. Bad administration, heavy taxation and an attempt to end the slave trade led to the successful rising of the Mahdi who defeated every expeditionary force sent against him and, with the capture of Khartoum and the death of Gordon, ruled undisturbed. His successor, the Khalifa, misgoverned the Sudan abominably and when British and Egyptian forces under Kitchener reconquered it in 1896–99, they found an impoverished and depopulated land.

To govern the country, the Anglo-Egyptian Condominium was set up which – while formally recognizing Egyptian claims – effectively left control of the administration in British hands, under the Governor General. Since martial law was in force with the reconquest, the administration at first was naturally very largely composed of British and Egyptian officers of the Egyptian Army, although British civilians were increasingly employed. The armed forces in the Sudan consisted partly of Sudanese battalions with Egyptian officers and partly of Egyptian units, with very few British troops. Thus the effect on the Sudan of the Egyptian mutinies, and the result of Lord Allenby's ultimatum, was critical.

The railway journey from Wadi Halfa to Khartoum was filled with alarms, including a report that two mutinying Egyptian battalions were on their way north. When we arrived in Khartoum

I was met at the station by a member of the Sudan Educational Department called 'Bunny' Field. He said straight away, 'We have had a serious mutiny of the 10th Sudanese Battalion instigated by Egyptian officers,' and went on to tell me that a very ugly situation had been saved by resolute action by the acting Sirdar, General Huddleston. The mutineers had seized the military hospital, where they now lay dead, their officers having escaped by swimming the Nile; the Argyll and Sutherland Highlanders were occupying strategic points in the city; and all British civilians were in the Palace. 'I've got to take you to General Huddleston at H.Q.'

It was already dusk when I reached Force H.Q., a large brick building, with a statue of Lord Kitchener on a horse between it and the Nile River. The General was surrounded by his staff in the midst of a serious discussion. Unwilling to interrupt, I stood in the verandah where they could see me when the conference broke up. Some time elapsed before I heard a voice behind me saying, 'Is that Boustead? I am terribly sorry to have kept you, I thought you were the Argyll's orderly officer until I saw your Gordon kilt.' This was my first meeting with General Huddleston, who was to be both the Commander of the new Sudan Defence Force and the arbiter of my personal future during the coming years.

During my whole service no single officer I have ever met has impressed me more. He had a tall, commanding presence, a quiet and reserved manner, and common sense beyond belief which was indeed his infallible guide and answer to every problem and crisis that confronted him. He was thoughtful and considerate to all he knew, one of the most humble men I have met and apparently quite unconscious of the extraordinary influence that he had on all who were associated with him.

I was sent over in the H.Q. launch to Omdurman, where the Colonel of the 9th Sudanese, Lieutenant-Colonel Bostock, met me. He installed me in a bare room in a three-roomed house which was presently shared with another recruit to the S.D.F., Major Inglis Jones of the Grenadier Guards. We lived in this small bungalow together until April 1925, when I left on appointment to the Camel Corps and Inglis Jones to Equatoria.

The battalion rapidly became a sort of depot for newly joined officers who were going out to join their corps in the Sudan provinces and soon became known as 'Bostock's School of Languages.' We were told that the first and most essential equipment of our new careers was a working knowledge of colloquial Arabic. General Huddleston was so aware of this that he had recently sent for an officer of some months' service, Major Pease, who was then commanding the Police in Medani, and told him to write an easy book for new Bimbashis with the basic illustrations of Arabic rules and grammar in their simplest form. The humble Pease, startled and anxious, had said to General Huddleston, 'But, sir, I am the last person you should ask to do this, as my knowledge is very limited.' The General replied, 'I want a bloody fool to write a book for bloody fools.' So the meeting dissolved in laughter and Pease produced a most practical although by no means highbrow grammar-cum-vocabulary in alliterated Arabic.

I remember on my second meeting with the General, he said to me, 'Keep a notebook and write down every word you can pick up and get the meaning later. Confine your vocabulary to the words you hear and you will soon have a working knowledge of the language.' How grateful I was later when climbing with Sherpas in the Himalayas to be able to learn the essentials of their language in a few weeks by using this method.

The few months from November 1924 till the end of March 1925 were taken up in learning Arabic for many hours a day, mainly listening in Bostock's orderly room or at parades and drills, and working personally with a young Dinka officer, lately from the Gordon College. It was hard work, but I found time to enjoy shooting sand grouse and sailing on the river in the evenings when Nile geese and wild duck were outlined against the glowing sunset during some of the loveliest moments of the Sudan winter.

At the end of March I passed my colloquial Arabic exam after four months' intensive study, and was able to take a fortnight's leave, which I spent in trekking on camel back in the Red Sea Hills, with George Wood of the Dorset Regiment. It was my first introduction to the Hadendoa, a magnificently upstanding Hamitic people with huge heads of hair built up with mutton fat, which gives them a peculiar smell. They are the descendants of Kipling's 'Fuzzy-Wuzzies', who broke the British square when fighting under Osman Digna against Kitchener's forces in the nineties. I was glad to see more of them on the Eritrean border when I commanded the Border Force during the war.

On this trip, the Hadendoa were our guides and ghillies, although they disapproved of our stalking ibex instead of lying up and waiting for them to be driven in by beaters. However, we succeeded in getting a sizeable head each, and in keeping our camp escort happy with gazelle meat and guinea fowl.

It was in May 1925 at the beginning of the hottest season of the year that I arrived in El Obeid, the H.Q. of the Camel Corps, and was met by the Corps Commander, Major Reynolds, local colonel with the Sudan rank of Miralai. We dined under the stars with the heat of the day heavy upon us. I left next evening for Bara, forty miles north, in a sand sea which could not in those days be crossed by car. We motored out some twenty miles to roadhead, where I was met by a camel escort as darkness fell, and we rode through acacia forests over sandy dune country for three and a half hours. I was greeted by Arthur Chater, a Major in the Royal Marines who had distinguished himself at Zeebrugge under Admiral Keyes. I spent a flaming hot summer after Chater had gone on leave, commanding his company which was soon to become mine on his promotion to command of the corps.

The only other European occupant of the station was the District Commissioner, Kennedy-Cooke of the Sudan Political Service, who curiously enough had been in the next rooms to Hugh Seymour and me at Worcester. He had had a distinguished war record, and was both artistic and amusing.

The withdrawal of Egyptian units from the Sudan after Sir Lee Stack's murder, and the gradual disbandment of the old Sudanese battalions of the Egyptian army, led to the creation in 1924 of the new Sudan Defence Force. Sir Hubert Huddleston formed it on the basis of the five irregular corps which were already in existence: i.e. the Eastern and Western Arab Corps which were responsible for internal security in Kassala and Darfur provinces respectively; the Camel Corps in Kordofan province; and the Equatorial Corps in the black south. The fifth corps consisted of three squadrons of mounted infantry companies which formed the central reserve in the Northern Province at Shendi, 125 miles north of Khartoum.

With the exception of the Eastern Arab Corps, whose main role was along the thickly forested foothills of the Abyssinian border, and the Nuba Mountain companies of the Camel Corps, the troops in the Northern provinces were organized on a basis of independent, irregular companies mounted on country-bred horses, mules and camels. The vast corps areas, each about the size of France, called for a high measure of mobility as the first essential in the troops controlling them. The primitive state of the country still neccessitated long treks showing the flag, and occasional operations against warring tribes in the Nuba Mountains or in the black south.

The Kaid, as the commander of the S.D.F. was called, laid down a policy which proved to be one of the most significant factors in the success of the Sudanese forces employed in the campaign in Abyssinia in 1940 and 1941.

With his wide experience of Africa and African troops, Sir Hubert knew their capacity for endurance in their own country, their hardihood and their ability to do without. On trek and in training he stressed these qualities which are born in them and are a part of their lives; they were neither drained out of them by excessive drilling on the parade ground, nor pampered out of them by giving them unneeded clothing and equipment.

Their mode of living as soldiers held one inestimable advantage of first importance to the African soldier: it caused the minimum of disturbance to the rhythm of his life, and enhanced his personal happiness and enjoyment in soldiering.

The men of these irregular corps lived with their families or, if young bachelors, with a brother or cousin in the soldiers' village of grass-built houses under conditions identical with those of the pastoral life of their homes. The men at all times when in station fed in their family groups. They owned their own cultivations in their home villages, looked after by their fathers or younger brothers whom they visited in the rainy season when on leave.

New recruits were the pick of a large number of men outside the company office door clamouring to be enlisted. The companies were such a family affair that in my own company I once had serving together seven brothers, the Abu Kindi, from a nearby hamlet. Soldiering was an honourable profession, and the carrying of arms for *sharaf*, or standing, was the ambition of tribesmen.

Discipline was a simple matter. The greatest calamity and disgrace that could befall a man was to be discharged from the force for a disciplinary offence. During the ten years that I served with the Camel Corps, a court martial was unknown among the six companies of 1,100 irregular soldiers that comprised the corps. The young British company commander had considerable powers; he recruited, enlisted, trained, promoted, punished and discharged his men. In such circumstances it is vital for the commander to be experienced, and not to be changed too often. When I was commanding the Camel Corps, of six British company commanders only one had less than four years' service with his company.

The family atmosphere of the company, the manliness and intense sense of fun of the Sudanese soldier and his complete reliance on his officer produced a feeling of affection between the British company commander and his men which formed one of the main charms of African service with an irregular corps.

My life was full, since I was working hard for the Staff College in addition to running the company. We spent the autumn and winter on trek or training, ranging over wide areas of the northern sage brush steppelands of Kordofan or through the forest and mountain country of the south and west, meeting in the late winter at some well-field for combined manoeuvres. The cycle of field training in ideal training grounds, followed by five or six hundred mile marches showing the flag, was a part of the annual winter routine with a camel or mounted infantry company, unless some tribal operation was called for. In training or on patrols, the endearing quality of the Sudanese soldier was his unfailing zest for it all.

For the British officer to whom the wild unpeopled places of the earth appeal, the life held a fascination of its own. How vivid the pictures of those days remain – the rolling uplands of sage brush in the central belt stretching over the far horizon under the immense dome of the African sky and, in the northern steppes, a horizon pierced with jagged mountains, black at noon and violet in the evening light. Bustard would rise startled from the grasslands as the company approached, and herds of ril and gazelle stare and trot and wag their stumpy tails uneasily or fly bounding in sudden panic across the dunes. 'Hence through the strong unhampered days the tinkling silence fills.'

Vivid too is the memory of the morning arrival at a great well-field, the Arab encampments around the rustling palms, where large camel herds belonging to different sections of the tribe patiently await their turn while the nomad herdsmen fill the mud *hods* for their watering; and of the evening, with the sun setting cloudlessly below the dunes of the Kheiran, as the long file of camel-mounted soldiers follow their lengthening shadows into the still night. How I remember the soft padding shuffle of the camels under the strewn universe of stars, their pace quickening as the cold night breeze rose over the plain. Long lines of white camels couched in squares at the night halt while the men unload them in silence, followed by a loud thumping in unison on the animals' backs to restore the blood; the steady crunching of the grain feed by two hundred camels gurgling and groaning in anticipation, pleasure or disapproval. By now a line of small fires are twinkling in the star-light, warming the fresh night air, and the men are circled in their section messes for their evening meal, 'the cheerful song, the cup at the common fire', talking and joking as the African will, long into the night.

These men were mainly of the Gawama tribes from the central plains of Kordofan. They had that mixture of brown and black blood which seems to combine the intelligence and humour of the Arab, and the vitality and simple cheerfulness of the black. At Omdurman they formed the flower of the Khalifa's infantry. In Abyssinia in 1941 a company of them, acting independently, were to repel Colonel Torelli's battalion of Italians and a thousand Banda in a pitched daylight battle, and having harried his retreating columns from Dangila to Bahar Dar to hold them tied for long months, with their back to the waters of Lake Tana.

Soon after my arrival in Bara I came on a stretch of country

twelve miles to the west which it was clear would form an excep-
tional training area. The red dunes were interspersed with savannah
grass, and haraz trees in the hollows offered excellent shade for the
men and a promise of water near the surface. It was known as the
Kheiran and stretched for many miles north and south. Here we
spent many weeks of the autumn and winter in annual training
camps. The men lived under the trees and the camels were bar-
racked at night in the hollows, protected from the cold winds. I had
a tent which I would pitch on a high dune above the men's camp
with a view of the Kheiran spread out in front of me. The nomad
inhabitants were the Beni Gerar tribe, a friendly and pleasant
people whose grazing grounds stretched across the Kheiran sands.
All round our camps we would come across their *feriks*, temporary
settlements inhabited only during the seasonal grazing of the
camels.

I was preparing the company one Saturday morning in the early
autumn of 1925 for the coming week in the Kheiran. The Sergeant
Major reported that half the company camels had been watered
during the past hour and a half; Bashawish Abdelaal, a Dongolawi,
was about six foot four inches in height, a slim man with a long face
of great dignity in repose and considerable charm when he smiled.

I walked down to the wells with him to see the shape of the
company. The second half were already drinking, half an hour for
each camel over the *hods*. These were then led back to stand and
absorb the water before being taken down for a second drink. This
had to last them till we returned to Bara next Thursday, a period
of five days and nights. To be kept in form they must drink well,
it takes two or three hours to water a couple of hundred camels.
While this was going on some of the men were laying out rows of
camel saddles, ammunition bags, water carriers for the soldiers and
camel blankets in front of the Guard Room.

We were due to leave at four o'clock for Beshiri, a village twelve
miles off in the dunes of the Kheiran. After watering, the camels
were turned out to graze off the trees and grass near the soldiers'
village. A grazing guard of some fourteen men moved out riding
bare-back and under the direction of a sergeant to prevent the
camels from wandering.

We all went off to lunch and by 3.15 p.m. the camels were back
being loaded outside the Guard Room. Every man had brought
his own rations from his tukl (grass hut) in the soldiers' lines, collected his rifle and ammunition from the Guard Room, and
Abdelaal blew a whistle to start loading. I had six pony scouts to
accompany the camel company on trek. The scouts themselves
rode camels and led the ponies, only changing mounts when re-

quired for special reconnaisance. Two of my own ponies accompanied me, led by the *sais*, Mohammed Fadl, a tiny black man with a face like a squashed tomato, who was the butt of the company, extremely stupid but excellent with horses.

We rode out of station two abreast with big yellow and white flags carried at the head of each platoon. The soldiers' wives kept up a long luluing from the lines as we passed, a column over half a mile long, striding out over the dunes. I myself was riding a camel specially chosen by Abdelaal for his paces and on which I used to gallop up from the rear of the company after checking them as they rode past.

On this particular afternoon about half a mile out of station my best polo pony dug in his heels and checked. His reins were attached to the *sais's* belt with a rope. Fadl was already fast asleep and was pulled back, falling from a height of seven feet straight on to his head. His companions were all greatly amused and pulled his leg. It appeared incredible that Fadl had neither broken his neck nor had concussion. It was an unlucky afternoon. Within half an hour I heard a shout from the back, 'A camel is sick.' I went back to find an animal in great distress, shaking and shivering with its fore and hind legs stiffened as in a fit. Presently it fell foaming at the mouth. Abdelaal exclaimed, 'It's been poisoned.' Within half an hour two more were taken the same way and we left them lying dead in their tracks. This was Chater's company which I was caring for whilst he was on leave and as a new Bimbashi I was greatly disturbed. As we continued our ride Abdelaal showed me the poison bush which is normally avoided by the camel guard. The grazing sergeant was up in Orderly Room next day.

It was late evening when we arrived in the dunes. The camels were couched in lines and a picqueting rope was stretched out in front of each platoon to which the head ropes were tied. In the meanwhile grain feeds were issued in a canvas cloth carried by each man, two or three pounds of grain per animal. These were laid out in front of the camels, and when the feeds were finished, the animals were turned over to a camel guard responsible that none of them slipped their line at night or started biting the backs of their neighbours, a common habit among rutting camels. In Arabia only *nagas* (she camels) are used for riding, but in the Sudan the Camel Corps bought short-haired male camels from the Red Sea Hills. Their normal pace on level ground was a trot of about four or five miles an hour with their full load of about 400 pounds, including the man and his kit. Camels which became tiresome when rutting would be castrated; later it became the practice to castrate most of them.

F

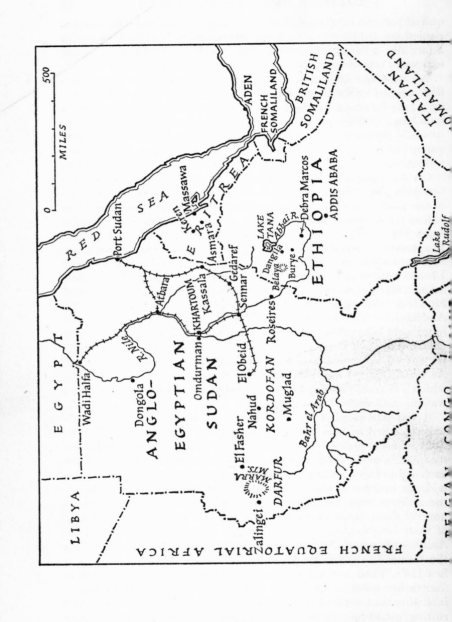

The sections lit groups of small fires under the trees and cooked their evening meal with an immense amount of chat which went on long into the night. The men slept in their blankets on a canvas sheet to keep out the thorny grasses. The main pest in the sands was scorpions, and sometimes two or three men were bitten in a night. Up on the dune, behind the men's camp, my servants had a drink ready, on an Abyssinian table placed with camp chairs and a camp bed outside the tent. Candles with glass globes lit the table and in a short time the cook had a three-course dinner cooked over the fire.

In training camp, the men were woken at five to drink tea and to turn the camels out with a grazing guard who took them over from the night guard, counting them carefully to see 'all present'. On this particular morning Sergeant Major Abdelaal came up to me with a slightly amused look and said, 'I have put Sir El Khatim under arrest.' He went on to explain that the night guard discovered a camel missing from the lines, and had found an unoccupied blanket under the trees. Shortly before dawn while it was still dark the camel stole into the lines ridden by a young Shaigieh lad, lately joined. He tied up the camel quietly but was held up by the guard before he reached his blankets. Sir El Khatim was brought up before me. He looked about sixteen years old and as if butter wouldn't melt in his mouth. Abdelaal of course had the answer to it. Sir El Khatim had a liaison with one of the soldiers' wives and had ridden back to have a night with her. He covered twenty-four miles between our arrival in camp and first light and became known as 'The Night Rider'. He did not deny his visit to Bara but told a nice story of visiting his sister who was sick.

It was not long before Sir El Khatim became an N.C.O. and was a platoon sergeant before I left the Camel Corps. The N.C.O.'s were the key to all our field training and were as enthusiastic and responsive as if we were on operations. If an N.C.O. forgot some essential detail during training I devised various schemes for making him remember it. Kerer Magufa, when in attack with his section, was always forgetting to give them the number of rounds in his fire orders. I sent him out onto a high dune above the camp where he repeated every ten minutes, 'I must not forget the rounds.' It became known as Kerer Magufa's *goz* and a roar of laughter from the company greeted his repetition.

In the winter of 1926 the District Commissioner of Northern Kordofan asked that a camel company should visit the Nazir of the Northern Hills in Jebel Haraz. This entailed a lengthy trek through the northern Kheiran and then over the wide steppes north of Kagmar, where the Kababish tribe under Sheikh Ali Tom had their grazing grounds. The country was full of ril and gazelle, and when I told Abdelaal and the sergeants 'We will do some mounted exercises, using the gazelle as our enemy,' their eyes shone with excitement. We settled the rules: 'The leading scouts, riding in pairs, when sighting gazelle on their front from their camels, will be responsible for stalking them and may only shoot when within a hundred yards. Anyone shooting over this distance will be fined ten piastres.' More laughter and excited chat.

Riding in the centre of the advance guard, I spent a number of fascinating mornings watching the skill of these soldiers as we advanced on a wide front in cavalry formation. There was great competition to be a scout and we swapped them over in turns. We collected some eight gazelle during that march and about eighty piastres in fines. The whole company enjoyed it immensely. Nearing Jebel Haraz we adopted our normal formation on the march and rode into the Nazir's camp with flags flying and our full column in file stretching back for half a mile or more.

The District Commissioner had forgotten to warn him and the Nazir was very worried that we had come to arrest him. He pulled himself together pretty quickly, and came to meet us, a distinguished grey-bearded man mounted on a grey horse. In no time he had five bulls herded as a guest present for us; two of them quickly escaped, and the pony scouts had the perilous job of trying to round them up. We feasted for two or three days up there and the enjoyment was only broken when Ibrahim Ahmed, a young soldier who had been given charge of a rutting camel, bent down inadvertently to prepare its evening feed. To my horror I saw the camel dart its head down, seize Ibrahim by the neck, lift him up and shake him like a rat while grinding his neck to pieces. He was buried in the Northern Hills.

Another year we were called out suddenly to deal with a tribe in the Nuba Mountains who had murdered their *Mek* (chief), disobeyed Government orders and refused to pay their taxes. The Camel Companies were ordered out at short notice and I, then commanding No. 2 Company, made a forced march down to the jebels of the Nuba Mountains. The camels, accustomed to the sandy plains of Kordofan, suffered severely from sore hoof pads and many were lamed by the time we reached Dilling, the district H.Q.

We made a base in the Gulud Hills to the south and spent the next three months endeavouring to subdue a most primitive people who refused all overtures of peace and shot at us from caves. We blockaded them in groups and eventually obtained their submission with few casualties. One of my memories of this campaign, high up in the mountains, is of a violent storm which flooded the wadi where temporary grass shelters formed the base camp. The Camel Corps Commander lost his false teeth which caused a major furore, and most of the H.Q. personnel spent the next day in the floods searching for them. I remember another rainy night when I had come down to the main base camp for discussions. I was asleep in my tent, shared with a brother Bimbashi, when I woke with a feeling that there was a snake in my shoes under the camp bed. In the early morning when I got up and was about to put my foot into my shoes I was suddenly aware that there *was* a snake and a krait at that – one of the most poisonous. My companion jumped up on his bed and the krait disappeared under the tent flap.

No sooner had we finished with this patrol than another tribe at Tuleshi, west of the Nuba Mountains, was reported in trouble and we were asked to deal with them immediately. We organized a night operation in the mountains at the District Commissioner's request and surrounded the mountain villages. Unfortunately a few of the ring leaders had got away into some caves. The D.C., George Bredin, now Bursar of Pembroke College, Oxford, said he thought they were frightened and rashly went into a cave after them. I was unwilling to see him go down alone so I followed him with the patrol doctor, Dr Cruikshank, and an orderly. The cave opened into another with a narrow opening, completely dark. As George Bredin put his head up to peer into the opening, there was the blinding flash of a Remington rifle discharged in his face, and the bullets ricocheted around the cave. All hell was let loose when Bredin's policeman, who had slipped in behind us, fired two more rounds into the cave. We three rushed back to the main entrance and got jammed in the mouth, but managed to wriggle out one by one, in fits of laughter. By good fortune George Bredin had escaped with a face blackened and pitted by powder but otherwise intact. When the recalcitrant Nubas were eventually rounded up Tuleshi settled down to a period of quiet prosperity.

After short home leave in 1926 I returned to my Camel Company in Bara and found myself compelled to weigh up the pros and cons of soldiering in the Sudan. During the course of a number of brief meetings at home with a girl whom I had known some years previously, we became formally engaged, with the proviso that it should not be announced officially and that the date of our proposed marriage be left open. At this period and for many years later the Sudan with its harsh background was not considered suitable for married officers; so marriage would mean my resignation. I was forced to come to terms with the future; here was a life in which I was entirely absorbed and one which I knew that I would be most unhappy to leave. During the following months it became completely clear to me that to embark on a marriage which would take me away from this background would lead to unhappiness for both parties. I adopted the coward's course of cooling off in my letters which became more and more infrequent, and the engagement was broken off. Each succeeding year found me more absorbed in the life of the Camel Corps and more convinced that the decision had been right.

That winter General Huddleston himself conducted manœuvres for the whole Corps and was delighted by the standard of the Camel Companies. He knew that I was very keen to visit the Meidob Hills in Darfur, a vast waterless upland 700 miles north-west of El Obeid, the home of barbary sheep, a comparatively rare animal only found in the wildest dry mountain and desert areas. The General gave authority for the motor machine gun battery in El Fasher, the Province H.Q., to take me and Major McDougall and our servants up to Meidob on a patrol in their cars. There we had arranged for camels to carry our kit into the hill country which is wild and almost waterless for thousands of square miles; the hills are savannah ranges, intersected by dry gorges. The Meidobis are an attractive pastoral negroid race herding sheep and camels, and continually in dispute with the neighbouring nomad tribes over camel thefts.

Fortune favoured me on this expedition. McDougall and I each choose our own hill and set out with full water bottles to spend the afternoon and night on our mountains and return to camp the following evening where we had all the reserve water in tanks. I was accompanied by my escort corporal Ombashi, Guma Mohammed Ali, a most intelligent and courageous young Dongolawi. At an early stage on the first afternoon I came on a Meidobi herdboy who had just sighted six or seven barbary sheep with one splendid male lording it over the females. We slept that night on the mountain leaving them quietly grazing and followed them in the early morning. My particular quarry was the ram which had a magnificent head. After an hour he detached himself from the females. I stalked him relentlessly for a further five hours before I could get a shot. It was now 11 a.m. and he was standing majestically on a hill slope when I floored him at about 150 yards range.

McDougall, who had seen no game, joined me that evening on the hillside when I sent him down the news. The Meidobis shared the meat and McDougall, who was a keen student of hunting form, immediately said, 'By God, I think you have got a world record here'; when he measured the head with his tape it proved to be so. I agreed to leave the hill to him and make my way back to camp over another group of hills.

I rashly left the herd-boy with him and early the following day went off with Guma Mohammed Ali, in whom I had the greatest confidence. He assured me that he could find the way through the hills to our camp, the only water supply for hundreds of miles around. Noon came and found us both parched with thirst, the water-bottles more than half finished and a tin of sardines for food. I was hungry and shared the sardines with Guma. This was a rash act and increased our thirst. We wandered on over the hills looking uneasily at each other, for I now knew he had over-estimated his capacity to find our way back to camp by this different route. Guma presently admitted that each valley looked like the next and only God would lead us to the camp. By now the sun was falling low over the hills and Guma had finished his own water-bottle; his lips were white with foam, but he would not touch mine. I began to feel that I had had it, and an hour or so before sunset, exhausted, I drank my last drop.

Dusk was already setting in when we saw smoke rising from a fold in the hills. We caught hold of each other and ran towards it, terrified of being overtaken by darkness before we could reach water. When we arrived, it was already dark, and I felt how stupid I had been to have left my Meidobi guide with McDougall, who returned twenty-four hours later empty-handed from the chase.

After four years commanding the Camel Company I was called in by the Kaid to act as G2 on his staff in Khartoum. This was in the Spring of 1929. The Camel Company had been like a family, and leaving them for an impersonal job on the staff was an unhappy break with a life and people to whom I had become intensely attached.

After two months I went to General Huddleston and said I really could not stand this any longer and must get back to command troops outside. He was typically understanding and said, 'Don't you want to go on in the Army to higher command? If so, you must learn to express yourself on paper and learn the normal staff organization.' He added, in tones of great sympathy, 'I know exactly what you are feeling,' and said, 'This is only a period and you should see it through.' Coming from him this was unanswerable. About a month later I regained complete happiness in the thought of the future and the work of the present when Charles Adair, the

Adjutant General, told me confidentially that the Kaid had ear-
marked me to command the Camel Corps when my time in Khartoum had closed.

I spent most of my time away from H.Q., visiting the various
corps, attending manœuvres and operations, or framing and revising
defence schemes. This involved a lot of flying. The planes were
Gordon Faireys, with open cockpits and water-cooled engines. The
water jackets often leaked, which entailed a crisis with over-heating
and as often as not a forced landing. I remember ten perilous days
spent trying to find suitable landing strips and sea-plane bases on
the Red Sea Coast, north and south of Port Sudan. We landed in
the most impossible places and sometimes took off from strips sand-
wiched between dunes which would be cleared only by a few inches.
On the return journey to Khartoum we had no less than three
forced landings, the last just before sunset. Fortune was with us;
had any of these taken place among the jagged peaks of the Red
Sea massif we might well still be there today, with the remains of
the burnt-out plane.

During that period the Dinka and the Nuer tribes had been continually skirmishing, which entailed flights down to the Upper Nile
Province to help over the Nuer Settlement, which consisted of
arranging agreed tribal boundaries. In September 1929 General
Huddleston himself decided on a trip to the South in the *Metemma*,
an old Nile steamer with a barge alongside. He was accompanied
by his wife who was an ardent naturalist and a crack shot. We
visited most of the southern stations and I was introduced at first
hand to the Equatorial Sudan, the home of the southern pagan
warrior. It was a fascinating tour which took us down the Zeraf
River winding through the game reserves where herds of elephants
and wild game of all sorts roamed freely along the banks of the Nile.
We met D.C.s and soldiers and covered the country from the
Ethiopian border in the east to the Bahr al-Ghazal border with the
Congo in the west.

Huddleston was a prodigious reader. I remember he came on
board with among other books three volumes of Lord Ronaldshay's
life of Lord Curzon, heavy volumes with close print. I was anxious
to read Curzon's life and asked him to lend me them in turn as he
finished them. To my surprise, he presented me with the first volume
after two days; then I remembered an incident in his office when
I had given him a file with a thirty-page report on the Nuer Settlement. He turned the pages over as if he were counting them and
then looked up and began to comment on each page in turn without
reading it. He had an astonishing photographic memory and quite
evidently had taken in the whole report while turning over the

leaves. Within five days he had finished all of Ronaldshay which lasted me the remainder of our trip.

It was a sad day when he handed over his command later in the same year. He had first come out as a Bimbashi in 1910 and had acquired a great name among the Sudanese after the capture of Darfur, when Sultan Ali Dinar, the Ruler of Darfur, was defeated at Berengia and fled to the Marra Mountains. Huddleston boldly followed him with a small mounted patrol, and by hard riding and good information came up with him in the early dawn, and killed him in Western Darfur. 'Huddle' was known to the Sudanese as the *Morfain Abuhigl* (the hyena with white feet), on account of his famous night marches and his habit of wearing white spats to protect his ankles from thorns.

General Sammy Butler, who replaced Huddleston, had had a very similar background but was a completely different personality. I found him most engaging and friendly and spent the succeeding months of 1929 as his staff officer. During this active year on the staff I took the opportunity of working successfully for an Arabic interpretership with a Syrian teacher from the Gordon College. At the same time I seized the chance to pass my promotion exam for Major.

I spent a few months in the winter of 1929–30 as second in command of the Camel Corps, and in the spring of 1930 was sent home for a six months' refresher course in Aldershot. I enjoyed this, and also the opportunity it offered of a short leave in Switzerland, where I climbed the Matterhorn and other peaks with my old friends Claude Butlin and Dennis Pasmore. This was my first experience of Alpine climbing in high summer rather than in the dangerous spring.

In October, returning in the *Shropshire*, I was delighted to find myself sharing a table with Douglas Newbold, then Commissioner for the Red Sea Hills, where the Fuzzy Wuzzies live. Newbold was shortly to become Governor of the Kordofan province and my opposite number on the political side when I was commander of the Camel Corps. His wit and charm and ready laughter, and real intelligence combined with wide erudition, made him a greatly sought-after companion. After four years of outstanding work as Governor of Kordofan he was knighted and appointed Civil Secretary to the Sudan Government, Head of the Political Service.

He had come to the Sudan four years before me, in 1920, while I was still at Oxford, and he resigned twice but had been persuaded by some wise Governor to withdraw his resignation. He was tremendously attached to the Sudanese though fully aware of their shortcomings. He infused into his group of D.C.s, agricultural, forest, and irrigation officers, an astonishing spirit which emanated from himself; it combined an immense wealth of technical learning, sheer common sense, enthusiasm and humanity. The Sudanese, and particularly the younger generation, thought the world of him and when he died in 1945, really as the result of overwork engendered by the war, large crowds flocked to his funeral.

In the spring of 1932 Major (now Brigadier) Bagnold, who won such fame with his Long Range Desert Group, had asked Newbold, an ardent archaeologist, to accompany him on the longest of his journeys. It was planned as a geological and archaeological expedition and survey of the Libyan Desert, Jebel Owenat and the outskirts of the Tebesti and Enneddi Mountains, thence south-east to the Wadi Hawa and on to El Fasher in the Sudan. Newbold was unable to take part in this expedition, though he had done two previous explorations in the Libyan Desert with Shaw, the author of *The Long Range Desert Group* and later curator of the Jerusalem Museum. He asked me if I would take his place if Bagnold was agreeable, and recommended me to Bagnold as a member. This offered a singular opportunity of seeing this vast tract of country in company with interesting and cheerful companions. I jumped at it.

After some correspondence we met in Cairo in early September, a group of eight, all British Army officers except Shaw who had been in the Forestry Department in the Sudan Service, and Dr Sandford who was the geological authority on the Nile Valley at Oxford. Guy Prendergast and Rupert Harding Newman of the Tank Corps were the two technicians of the party and very expert they were; Guy himself later took over the Long Range Desert Group from Bagnold during World War Two in the Western Desert. The know-how and the ability of the Desert Group were largely founded on the knowledge gained in the sand seas and Libyan Desert exploration carried out by Bagnold, using a sun compass and studying all the techniques of sand travel. We actually used Model T Fords with ordinary thin tyres. Balloon tyres at this stage were unknown and we were forced alternately to pump and deflate the tyres every time we crossed from soft dunes to stony going. Water was one of our main problems and we kept a permanent reserve of thirty-six four-gallon tins on the running boards of the cars. We confined ourselves to one water bottle a day each and a pint mug of tea for breakfast, a pint mug of lime juice for lunch, a pint mug of water for the evening drink. The September weather was fiercely hot and we lived in a state of permanent thirst. The worst days were when we had a good deal of pushing and shoving on the cars when they were stuck, and repumping tyres which had been deflated.

Craig, who was a sapper, was largely responsible with Shaw for the dual map-survey, and Dr Sandford would constantly want to stop to examine stones and rocks. For the rest of us the most fascinating finds were the archaeological sites in the blinding desert, hundreds of miles from water, where we would find pottery shards, grindstones and sometimes coins. The most fantastic were the rock pictures of giraffe, lion, buffalo, gazelle and antelope, beautifully drawn and wonderfully preserved in a dead land where now only hawks could survive on the blood of migrant birds. All this indicated a country where water and grass must have been abundant and where herds of game had roamed. It was Shaw's and, I think, Newbold's theory that this was about the time Ptolemy I was ruling in Egypt.

The migrant birds were numerous and the ornithological societies were anxious to have a line on the passage of migrants through Libya. I was responsible for the fauna and collected sixty-seven specimens of migrants shot with a dust-gun and injected with formalin and then wrapped in cotton-wool. These were sent to the British Museum at the end of the expedition, with the latitude and longitude and the details of the locations in which they were found.

In the Wadi Hawa, north of Kuttum, where we had reached the grass country of the northern Sudan steppes, we came on a hundred ostrich eggs with the male birds keeping them warm. This enormous collection was due to collective laying, and their safety to the male birds which protect the eggs. We tried blowing out two of them and they made a sizeable omelette for the party.

Before turning west to the foothills of the Tibesti Mountains we climbed Jebel Owenat, a 6,000 foot massif at the junction of the Tripolitanian, Egyptian and Sudanese frontiers. My most vivid recollections of that climb, which was in no way difficult as a mountaineering feat, was the intense, unquenchable thirst which rendered the whole operation one of the most tedious and tiresome I have ever experienced.

On returning to the Farah spring which was our base under Jebel Owenat, we found a group of cars led by an Italian officer from Kufra, Colonel Rolle, a squat, broad, grey-faced, serious-looking man. At this time the Italians were disputing the area known as the Sarra triangle which lies in the Sudan and the centre of which is the Sarra well, dug by order of the Grand Senussi long ago. According to the Moslem tradition, he, like Abraham, had a vision that water lay beneath this featureless desert plain. Under his holy orders men dug and dug; water was there, and was used for centuries by passing caravans on the route from Tibesti to Kufra.

We moved on to Sarra the next day and found another Italian

convoy camped at the well in charge of a very dashing looking officer with a large beard and a most ebullient manner. Colonel Lorenzini introduced himself to us and we soon learned all about him over a most excellent dinner which he kindly cooked for us and presented on white tablecloths, with china, glass, silver, and an abundance of Spumante and Chianti. He was an excellent host, deprecated the idea that anybody who had lived in these parts should be stupid enough to want to acquire the territory, and told us that after fifteen years of service in the Libyan Desert he was known throughout the Italian Army as the Lion of the Sahara. It was about this time that Mussolini declared that he was not a collector of deserts and was no longer interested in the Sarra triangle, and was turning greedy eyes on Ethiopia. The next time I heard Colonel Rolle's name was in the winter of 1940, eight years later, when at the head of a raiding column he crossed the frontier into the Sudan. As for Lorenzini, he was a brilliant commander, and when he was killed on the heights of the Keren battlefield ten years later he was deeply mourned by the whole of the Eritrean army.

It was late in October when we reached El Fasher and I left the expedition and flew down to El Obeid in a R.A.F. plane to rejoin the Camel Corps.

Chapter Eight

HIMALAYAN INTERLUDES

I'll walk where my own nature would be leading—
It vexes me to choose another guide —
Where the grey flocks in ferny glens are feeding,
Where the wild wind blows on the mountain-side.

EMILY BRONTË

ONE of the most relaxing and delightful features of service in both the Sudan Defence Force and Sudan Political Service was the very generous leave, three months a year and travelling time, which enabled officers to give of their best in the harshest of climates and conditions with none of the comforts which modern science has now brought to life in the tropics. It was indeed a wise government which realized that it would benefit by the generous leave rules. I gratefully seized the opportunity which they offered to enjoy, on my way home to see family and friends, visits to Palestine and Turkey, spells in the Adriatic, ski touring in the Oberland or Austria, climbing in the Alps or the Himalayas.

Paradoxically, these long leaves were made more enjoyable by the fact there was no air travel. We would return primed for nine months of intensive hard work with no amusements other than the odd game of polo or tennis, but happily absorbed in the life of our company or district. This is the very important point; by virtue of these prolonged breaks, with their mental rest and change, the officer could retain real vitality of approach to his task, and enjoy life thoroughly with these delightful and simple people without irritation at their peculiarities.

I had always been fascinated by climbing, and had tried to spend part of every leave in the mountains. In 1924, when home on leave, I visited Brigadier Norton who had recently returned from the Everest expedition of that year, when he and Somervell had achieved the highest point then reached. I told him that my ambition was to climb Everest.

He asked me to tell him about my Alpine experience – which by then was considerable – and said 'If you can pull off an expedition to clear the Zemu Gap on the north-east shoulder of Kangchenjunga, I will personally back you for the next Everest expedition.' Apparently two parties had been turned back by snow conditions and avalanches. Norton very helpfully offered to ask for assistance for me, if I could get out to the Himalayas, from Shebbeare, the chief forest officer in Bengal who had been transport officer to the two previous expeditions, and from that great Everest climber Somervell who was now working in southern India as a medical missionary.

In the winter of 1925–26, after the Nuba Mountain expedition was over, I decided to give up working for the Staff College which would only have taken me away from my beloved Camel Corps. This meant that I could plan to spend my next leave climbing, and I decided to take April and May in the Himalayas when the snow could be fairly good, and before the monsoon broke.

I found Shebbeare had lined up six Sherpa porters, fully equipped for the snows and with Everest experience. The youngest, Ang Penba, a lad of about seventeen and extremely tough, he had detailed as my personal bearer; he had been Somervell's bearer on the Everest expedition. He had also produced a most excellent Chinese cook called Takbu who was completely undismayed by any weather or conditions and would produce a marvellous meal in a Whymper tent in a howling gale on a glacier at 18,000 feet. The sirdar, Nur Sung, who had watched Mallory and Irvine on their last climb up above Camp Six, was in charge of the porters. He was an intelligent Nepalese, and using the technique I had acquired in the Camel Corps for learning Arabic I quickly picked up with his help enough colloquial knowledge of Nepalese to get on terms with the Sherpa porters before we reached the snows.

The route that Shebbeare recommended took us along the Phallut Ridge, which is about 12,000 feet high and forms the border between Sikkim and Nepal. It presents the most splendid mountain scenery that I have ever seen anywhere. As we moved daily on moderate marches from dak bungalow to dak bungalow, the whole of the Kangchenjunga massif was spread out to the north-east, with Makalu and Mount Everest to the north-west.

Shebbeare's advice was admirable. This interlude enabled me and the party to become acclimatized gradually to the heights. Where the ridge ends we dropped down into the Sikkim forests where I was able to get a sight of both the black bear and thar. We emerged from the dark jungles into a thick forest of rhododendrons of every shade and colour which covered whole mountain sides. Here we had already reached the snow line. We camped at Chematang at 17,000 feet, below the Gyocha La and the splendid mountain of Pandim, 21,000 feet, which had towered above us all the way up this final valley before crossing into the glacier region. Sirdar Nur Sung and one porter stayed to look after the surplus kit that we could not carry on the glaciers.

The Zemu Gap that we hoped to reach lies at the south-west end of the Zemu glacier and is a pass connecting the Zemu and the Tongshyong glaciers. To get there we had to cross the Gyocha La pass, drop down to the Talung glacier and strike across it to the mouth of its tributary, the Tongshyong glacier: then up the length of the Tongshyong to its head and, I hoped, the Zemu Gap.

It was a nightmare journey, with heavy snow and a thick mist blotting out our landmarks. I had to rely on compass bearings, which slowed up our rate of march, already slow enough through thigh-deep snow, with our heavy loads. The echoing roar of avalanches of soft new snow filled the valley. We left Chematang on 5th May, plodding over the Gyocha La and camping above the Talung glacier. On the 6th we got well out on the glacier bed, and camped where I hoped we would be safe from avalanches (before our return journey, a hanging icefall from the mouth of a glacier had crashed into the valley across the slope we had traversed). We were soaked through, and the men were very cold. Sixty pounds of stores, when you are wading thigh deep through soft snow on a mountain side, is a heavy load; and they were weary. In addition, two of them had been in the earlier Everest disaster when seven porters had been killed by an avalanche, so they were, very sensibly, frightened.

Morning showed a new world. On either side above us towered the mountains, in a mantle of freshly fallen snow. It was 4 a.m. and the sun was just touching the topmost peaks. I left the men to make tea at once, and went down the valley to where I thought I could see the Tongshyong glacier stream pouring into our moraine. It was there ahead, there was no mistaking it. But again the amazing deceptiveness of these distances struck me. At six o'clock I was back in camp to find no tea, as the Primus had jibbed. This was exasperating, as the danger of avalanches was great with the new snow and a glowing sun rising over the mountains. We eventually got away at 7.15.

It was an hour's march to the foot of the Tongshyong glacier stream. Below we left a three days' dump of rations, and then on this brilliant sunlit morning started for the pass. I had misgivings about the entrance to that glacier stream when sighting it alone in the first light of dawn, but it looked as if we might hope for better things inside. The overhanging cliffs near the entrance were dropping stones as we went up, few but dangerous. Higher, things got worse. Loose cliffs on both sides looked as if they might fall in at any moment, and barrages of stones were rolling into the chu (the glacier stream). For the sake of morale, I kept the party together, though it would have been better to be killed singly than all together. And then a thick mist rolled up the valley and obscured everything. All around was the roaring sound of falling snow and stones. I set the men down under the largest boulder we stumbled on, and went slowly up through the mist.

The right bank of the Tongshyong glacier gradually loomed up, a steep wall of rock. Above it there appeared to be no cascading snow and stones, as was happening across the moraine. Once under the shoulder of this wall, with the tents up and making tea, the party could smile once more. We had had four rather nerve-shaking hours, though we must have come up that chu in record time. It was now 1 p.m.

I had a sketch of the Zemu Gap with me, made by a previous expedition. It showed the ice pinnacles of the Zemu glacier hanging down over a dark rock cliff, the head of the Tongshyong valley; and on the east of the Zemu pinnacle there rises the towering shape of Simvu. There is a couloir running up to an ice slope below Simvu and thence on to the Zemu glacier. The mist cleared later, and it was all there. But down this couloir, our route to the pass, an avalanche of snow was pouring into the Tongshyong valley. I left the porters and went to look at the west side of the pass hidden behind our rock shoulder. The last rays were falling on Simvu peak. A couloir on the west side looked steep, but safer from avalanches.

It was 3 a.m. on 8th May when Ang Penba came with me up the couloir that runs up to the west of the Zemu Gap. We had slept the night under the rock shoulder, and left the other porters sleeping. The couloir was steep, and we were hurrying and rather breathless, fearing the coming of the sun. Above we could see a snow ridge running up to the pass above the Zemu glacier. It was 4 a.m. as we reached the ridge, and the rocky peaks above the Zemu on our side of the pass were glowing in the first rays. On the far horizon over the centre of the Zemu gap some peak was alight. We turned towards the south; Pandim was now lit up by the sun, a mass of white and blue, hanging in ice-ribs, with its splendid dome of snow and ice over all. And so we moved breathless to the crest of the pass (19,300 feet) and there opened before our eyes the fluted blue ice pinnacles of Siniolchum in long serried ridges against the perfect blue of the morning sky. She is written of as the Jungfrau of the Himalaya, the queen of mountain beauty. She towered in morning splendour over the level ice mass of the Zemu glacier.

We descended to the glacier across the pass, and then reluctantly returned, for the morning sun was already softening the snow. Where we had trodden during the ascent to the pass on a surface as hard as ice, it was now knee-deep. As we reached the tents clouds were rolling up the valley from the south-east, and presently at

5. A young Hadendoa

At the lake above Gautsa

In the Chumbi Valley:
Ruttledge, Shebbeare, Greene, the author

9 a.m. the hills were echoing once more with the sound of falling stones. Snow fell that day and late into the night. On the morrow we were faced with the descent through the Tongshyong valley; there must be no delay, and orders were given to start at 3 a.m.

In our wildest fears during the ascent we had hardly anticipated the scene of destruction and debris which we were to cross. Our tracks of two days previously were covered in many cases by whole hillsides which had crashed into the valley and filled up the racing chu. There was not fifty yards of our going uncrossed by some enormous landslip. We looked fearfully through the half-light at the hanging walls above us, bound at the moment by the night frost.

In a short time the first warm rays would loosen them, and then perhaps some trickle of water from a mountain stream might send us to destruction beneath those walls. We raced down the chu. In forty minutes we had reached the foot of the valley, and arrived breathless and thankful in the Talung glacier. And no stones fell during our passage.

The entrance to the Tongshyong glacier may be less dangerous at other times of the year, but should always be made in the very early hours, as it is a three hours' climb before one is free of the danger of avalanches and falling rocks. Another party, knowing that the Zemu Gap can be traversed on the west side of the ice-fall, could cross over on to the Zemu glacier, returning by Lachen. In clear weather a day's march could take one from Chematang to the junction of the Talung and Tongshyong glaciers, and another day's march over the Zemu Gap.

This was my first experience of snow and ice in the Himalayas, and made me fully realize the importance of moving early. The snow was soft by 9 a.m. nearly every day and the mountains obscured in mist by 10 a.m., so that the day's journey had to be made between 3.30 a.m. and 9.30 a.m.

On our way back I had a shot at climbing Pandim from the Talung. I got as far as 20,000 feet with Ang Penba up a very steep couloir, but a precipitous ice fall turned us back. The monsoon broke, and cloud and heavy snowstorms surrounded us, turning to continuous rain as we dropped down to Darjeeling by forced double marches. We arrived on 18th May, and I said goodbye to the cheerful and courageous Sherpas and the imperturbable Chinese cook.

I have a note still of the expense. The cost of food, porterage, pay and equipment for the party (including some extra coolies from Darjeeling to the snow line) amounted to 1,200 rupees, or about £90, for thirty-two days.

I returned to England to complete my leave after the monsoon

G

broke and gave Norton my story of the expedition. He was delighted and said, 'I never thought you would make it, and I will
give you all my backing for the next Everest show. Your knowledge
of Sherpas and snow conditions, and the actual height you have
attained, should prove invaluable to you in the future.' Six years
were to elapse before Hugh Ruttledge in 1933 was allowed by the
Tibetan authorities to take an expedition to the North Col of
Everest.

I actually heard the news that I had been selected to go on the
Everest expedition while I was exploring the Western Desert with
Bagnold in the autumn of 1932; our second day out of Cairo an
R.A.F. plane landed beside us with mail and a welcome case of
iced beer. There was a telegram for me from the President of the
Royal Geographical Society, who was also President of the Everest
Committee, asking me to join Hugh Ruttledge's expedition which
would gather in Darjeeling in March 1933. The pilot of the plane
took back my answering wire, 'Both keen and delighted.'

The manoeuvres that winter were much more strenuous than any
I experienced before or since. The exercise set by the Kaid pitted
the Camel Corps against the Western Arab Corps and covered a
large part of two provinces, Kordofan and Darfur. The Western
Arab Corps, operating with aircraft and motor-car patrols, had to
try to intercept the camel- and horse-mounted units of the Camel
Corps, who were moving from Southern Kordofan through the
dense bush country of Southern Darfur to occupy the Rajaj Wells,
200 miles away, without being discovered. The exercise entailed
moving through dense bush at night and lying camouflaged while
grazing the animals during daylight. The camel, mule and horse
companies covered forty miles a night by forced marches, and the
men were extremely short of sleep. The animals had to be grazed
for at least six hours daily, and grain fed during the night, in order
to keep their strength.

It was a tired-eyed crowd of British and native officers and
Sudanese soldiers who eventually arrived at Rajaj Wells undis-
covered. It was an exciting journey since both planes and car
patrols had been extremely close to the companies without spotting
them. After a conference at the Wells conducted by the Chief Staff
Officer, and a long rest, one of my companies went off on a 1,000
mile march to Northern Darfur where there had been trouble on
the French border, while the remainder set off on the return march
to their station in Kordofan, 500 miles away.

It was now early March, and I was due in Kalimpong, east of
Darjeeling, in a fortnight's time to join the Everest party in the
Chumbi Valley. I set off from Rajaj Wells with a lorry and a Ford

V8 with big tyres. We drove all night and stopped to make tea at first light on the sand track which runs through thick dried bush near the Kordofan border. I was cramped and tired, and while the cook was making tea I wandered up a thin green belt of bush reflecting on the past manœuvres and on the Everest expedition ahead. Musing in this way I had not realized how far I had walked from the sandy track which served for a road, when it suddenly dawned on me that the green belt had petered out and I had no idea where the road was. For hundreds of miles in this area there is nothing but bush, dried up except in the rains, on a sandy floor. I was wearing only a shirt and shorts and the sun was already up and hot. The only sound was the rasping note of a singularly exasperating grey bird. Taking my direction from the sun, I started to walk south, since on my map the road had been shown running east and west. After some twenty minutes' walking there was no sign of the track, and I began to wonder whether I could have crossed it without realizing it, in that sort of fevered panic which is apt to overtake one when lost in the bush.

I sat for a bit and then thought, 'Perhaps the road turns south east and the map is wrong, so I must walk south west.' This was actually so, and after an hour I came on the track and then judged that I must turn right to get back to the cars. I had only gone some 300 yards when I came upon the shawish (sergeant) of my escort, Agib Atitullah, with a soldier and my head boy, Adam Sabil, all looking dreadfully anxious and worried. They greeted me with enormous relief and gave me a very severe dressing-down. 'What should we have done if you were lost? How could we go back to our people? We are responsible for you and our faces would have been blackened for all time. May God give you more wisdom.'

At El Obeid I found that the Kaid had kindly arranged for 'Maori' Coningham to lay on an R.A.F. plane to fly me down to Port Sudan to pick up the boat to Aden, whence I went on by P. & O. to Bombay. I crossed India by rail and joined the Everest expedition east of Darjeeling.

I was warmly greeted by Shebbeare who had helped me so much seven years before, and who was again acting as transport officer on this, his third expedition. He said, 'I've got a young chap who insists on coming with you as he was your bearer on the Kangchenjunga party.' I was delighted to see Ang Penba again, looking only very slightly older. Nur Sung, my sirdar on the Kangchenjunga expedition, was also there awaiting me, full of smiles.

The journey up the Chumbi Valley and across the great plateau of Tibet, some 200 miles to the base camp, was made on horseback. We rode and walked in groups, getting to know one another. We used to breakfast in the open shortly after daybreak, the air freezing but very still. It was impossible to cook or eat a mid-day meal in the open, since a high wind always rose about noon and blew in impetuous gusts until late afternoon; and so the mess and kitchen tents were always sent forward at dawn. At night, dinner was served in the mess tent, and there were long discussions on every aspect of the climb ahead of us, on the best methods of acclimatisation, the debilitating effect of too prolonged a period of acclimatization, whether or not we should use the oxygen we had with us.

With such a mixed party, I found the whole company enormously interesting. Apart from Ruttledge himself, Eric Shipton and Frank Smythe were redoubtable climbers, the latter very quiet and very impressive. The party included Raymond Greene, a great raconteur who was often asked to give us a story, Jack Longland, Wyn-Harris, Wager and Bill Birnie. Wood-Johnson was our Stores Officer; when Shebbeare at base camp sorted out the high and medium camp stores – all distinguished by different colours – we found Wood-Johnson was colour blind. Fortunately the discovery was made before all the good work of the Army and Navy Stores in marking the packages was nullified.

The expedition must have looked like the retreat from Kabul to Kandahar in the First Afghan War. Our pack transport consisted of yaks, mules and donkeys, all moving at a different pace and forming a column a mile or more in length straggling over the vast Tibetan plateaux. The Himalayan peaks lay to the south, dwarfed by distance and the height of the plateau. We rode across iced-up rivers which had ceased to flow with the approach of winter and would not run till May or June. My most vivid memories are of monasteries perched on the flank of great hills rising out of the plain, of the monks and their butter-tea, a taste not easy to acquire.

We were not allowed to fish or shoot, or kill anything, in deference to the Buddhist law. The Sherpas, whose religion is very lax, cared little for these rules; and at Tzinki Dzong they broke the river ice and produced some fish for their supper. That day a mule died, and the Tibetan coolies considered this act of God was a punishment for the offence against taking life, and they went on strike.

Along our route it was discovered that the high-climbing boots and other articles of equipment were missing, believed stolen by some of the coolies. This was a serious blow to the expedition. The matter was reported to the Tibetan District Commissioner of the monastery town where we were camped that day. He had been presented by Hugh Ruttledge with a beautiful homburg hat, the usual form of headdress of Tibetan high officials, with which he was delighted. He held a court, convicted two of the coolies and ordered a hundred lashes for each of them. The punishment was administered by two men, one on either side of the victim whose trousers were stripped; after every ten or fifteen lashes there was a pause and the accused's hair and ears were pulled while he was told to produce the missing articles. Eventually they were produced and the thieves must have regretted their daring.

I only had leave till early July. Hugh Ruttledge agreed that I should take part in the early establishing of the high camps because if we were delayed I should have to go back. It was generally agreed that we should not use oxygen which was somehow at that period looked on as off-side. Our acclimatization was probably better than that of any previous expedition and we established our camps with this object. I found like others that a new camp entailed one or two bad nights, the second less trying than the first, with heavy asthmatic breathing, headaches and lassitude.

The first hazard was the North Col where Camp 4 was eventually established on a ledge of snow and ice about 1,000 feet above the ice glacier plateau. Hugh Ruttledge found it necessary to set up an intermediate camp near the foot of the North Col in order that the parties might get to work early each day clearing the route. This intermediate Camp 3A was subject to violent winds which eventually cracked the strong arctic tent which was our only real source of comfort and shelter. We all hated 3A, the most unpleasant camp below Camp 5.

From 8th May to 15th May Frank Smythe, Eric Shipton, Raymond Greene, Longland, Wyn-Harris, Wager and myself set out with the rising sun, cutting steps and fixing ropes to make a safe route for the porters up to the Col. Later in the day a gale would force us back to the arctic tent whilst the snow filled every step we had made.

On May 12th we were faced with the ice wall which formed the most difficult and dangerous obstacle to be overcome in establishing the North Col camps. Frank Smythe, Eric Shipton and Jack Longland, working just above us, continued with the skill based on their Alpine and Himalayan experience to cut foot and hand holds and drive in pitons which enabled Frank Smythe, backed up by Shipton supporting one of his feet with an ice axe, to clear the ice wall. At its lowest point the ice wall was about forty feet high, of which some fifteen feet were vertical and possibly even overhanging; to right and left it rose abruptly forming impossible ice cliffs over one hundred feet high. Since the 1922 and 1924 expeditions the face of the North Col had altered with the rapid downward movement of the ice masses. A projecting rope end, a relic of one of these expeditions, was hanging from the ice wall.

In *Camp Six* Frank Smythe wrote a superb description of his attack on it. His skill with the ice axe, cutting steps in the vertical wall, enabled us to get up it. We lowered a rope ladder down the ice wall to let the porters climb it with full loads. The porters were eventually tied together on one long rope, not more than two being on the ladder at the same time.

It was a relief to reach the new sheltered position below the North Col ridge where we set up Camp 4. On the 15th we were joined by Birnie. The next five days a tremendous storm virtually stopped all work, although on the 18th a slight improvement in the weather in the afternoon enabled us to complete the route to the crest of the North Col. We had become acclimatized to the new height and unlike previous parties felt an urgent call for more solid rations, those provided for the higher camps, as a result of the experiences of the 1922 and 1924 expeditions. So we asked brazenly for full glacier rations.

On the morning of the 20th I left with Wyn-Harris and Bill Birnie and a party of ten porters with the object of establishing Camp 5. We were hoping to reach 25,500 feet and return the same evening. We moved on up to the North Col and thence up the ridge above it. On reaching the rocks at about 24,500 feet there was a dispute as to the exact direction that we should now take. Bill Birnie, who was in charge of the porters, considered they had about had it. Wyn-Harris, who was in tremendous fettle himself, was all for pushing on. After some discussion we left the loads on the rock face and returned to Camp 4. On the following day Frank Smythe and Eric Shipton moved up with red bunting to ensure that the route was marked clearly. They encountered a fierce gale and were forced back from 24,200 feet. Next day the wind had lessened and I left with Wyn-Harris, Bill Birnie and Raymond Greene to establish Camp 5 at 25,500 feet, and on the day following to take up Camp 6, leaving Wyn-Harris and Greene at 6 whilst we escorted the porters down to Camp 5. In the meantime Eric Shipton and Frank Smythe were to come up in support and occupy the empty tent at Camp 5. Alas, Raymond Greene was not sufficiently acclimatized and was forced back to Camp 4 with a bad heart. However, Wager came up and took his place.

The next three nights were hellish. The wind blew continuously, rising to 100 miles an hour at intervals across the North East Shoulder where we were camped. It was impossible to move forward and upward on these slopes in these conditions. We waited patiently at Camp 5 in desperate discomfort, gradually eating our food away to keep warm. With my slight knowledge of Sherpa, I was helping Bill with the porters. He and I were mostly cooking for them in turn.

They were disheartened by the delay and the cold and during the subsequent three days all suffered from frostbite.

To make the early morning cocoa entailed first chopping ice and melting it in a tommy cooker balanced on your knees. At this height when the water was boiling you could comfortably put your finger in it. We carried the brew through to the porters who certainly looked as if they had no great desire to move on in these fierce winds.

Smythe and Eric Shipton came up to relieve Wyn-Harris and Wager in case the weather turned, and brought up some more stores. The howling wind continued, always rising at that time of the morning when we hoped to make a break. Frank Smyth would step out of his tent and shake his head and say, 'Impossible.' We used to prepare early at 5 a.m., but the wind would rise with the sun.

Outside the tent at Camp 5 we gazed over a scene which looked like the top of the world. The great mass of Makalu and all the wilderness of Himalayan peaks were ranged around us, seen through mist and driving snow. A white sheet of snow flew like a pennant from the top of Everest, in effect a snow curtain blown by the wind. The summit looked so near across the great yellow slabs of the last gully which led up to it.

After three days the food in camp had given out and the porters were in poor condition. News had come that the monsoon was upon us and Hugh Ruttledge sent a message up telling us to come down. My own time had run out and I had to set off without delay for Darjeeling. The descent to the base camp was painful to a degree. I had not realized till then that I was suffering from frostbite, not severe but extremely painful and increasingly so as I went further down. Each time I put my foot on the ground it was like treading on red-hot bricks.

This was the end of the attempt for me. The expedition had two more tries at the summit, after re-establishing Camp 6, but were defeated by the dreadful winds and blizzards and by Eric Shipton's sudden illness when climbing above Camp 6. The monsoon had broken early, and the whole party had to withdraw from the North Col to avoid the danger of avalanches which had overcome the 1922 expedition. The whole story is described in Hugh Ruttledge's official *Everest 1933*, by Frank Smythe in *Camp Six*, and by Eric Shipton in *Upon that Mountain*.

At base a horse transport convoy was arranged with the local Tibetans because I could go no further on foot. Since leaving the Chumbi Valley, like everyone else, I had grown a very thick beard which I found most ticklish and uncomfortable under the chin. I shaved it off in base camp where at the same time I bought a sheep.

We had been living entirely on tinned food at the forward camps and the craving for fresh food was acute; we ate this sheep all the way across Tibet. The journey was one of the most memorable and enchanting of its kind that I can remember, despite the fact that I had to be lifted onto a Tibetan pony at eight o'clock in the morning and lifted off at noon for lunch; lifted on again at one o'clock, until we made camp at five.

Rivers that had been iced up when we crossed were running streams with teal and mallard swimming and diving in their waters. The great white plains of the plateau were now green with new grass and violet with flowers. Mountains two or three days' journey away looked as if you could hit them with a stone. Wild asses, gazelle and Ovis Ammon roamed over the countryside and to the south the snow peaks of the Himalayas were spread in a jagged chain of ice pinnacles. For the past two months the only sounds we had heard were the roaring of the winds, the gurgling of a glacier or the fall of ice and rock. We saw no sign of life other than the occasional chough up on the high rocks. We had breathed with increasing difficulty as the height increased, but here, although the altitude was 15,000 feet, every breath of air seemed to fill me with so much life that I felt I could never be tired again. Ang Penba, my Sherpa bearer, accompanied me on a horse with a trotting baggage column of five animals carrying my tent and bedding and their riders. We rode solidly for eight hours a day, crossing these vast and beautiful plains. I felt I could have done another four or five hours daily without fatigue. My pony had been taught to tripple, the easiest pace for long trekking.

It was not until we came across the Natu La down into the forests of the Himalayas, already rain-swept by the first monsoon showers, that the pain of the frostbite began to disappear in the damp of the warmer atmosphere. The mountain sides were perilous and terrifying, whole tracks had been swept away by the force of the first monsoon torrents, and I rode down feeling that the horse and I might disappear at any moment into the torrent two or three thousand feet below. When eventually I reached Calcutta my feet were totally recovered.

I arrived back in the Camel Corps in July. It was not until the following year that I saw General Norton again. He was now in the War Office. We talked for a long time and he asked me what I thought was the most enjoyable part of the expedition. I told him of the return journey across Tibet alone, with all the immense contrasts that it held compared to the weeks of striving among the snows. I found that my senses had been so keyed up by the weeks of high altitude that I was able to appreciate all the beauties of the

Tibetan spring in a way I couldn't describe. Norton entirely agreed, and said, 'I found exactly the same. The whole expedition was worth the return journey across those enchanting plains in spring.'

In the summer of 1933 fighting was reported on the Bahr el Arab river between the Dinka and Baggara tribes in Southern Kordofan. Douglas Newbold, then Governor of Kordofan, asked me if I would send a force to deal with it.

I sent off Bimbashi Hussey de Burgh, a most able and amusing Irishman, with his mounted infantry company of mules and horses to deal with this problem, and myself followed some days later in a Ford V8 and lorry, my animal transport having left with Hussey. We arranged to meet in the bush country on the north bank of the Bahr el Arab, which forms a border between the Homr, a Baggara cattle-owning tribe of Southern Kordofan, and the Aliab Dinka, south of the river. Alec Findlayson, who was my Staff Officer, accompanied me. This southern country of Kordofan, in contrast to the dunelands of the north, is covered with thick scrub bush and was in those days teeming with game. Lion were abundant throughout the area and caused considerable anxiety to Hussey who on three occasions had his mules stampeded at night by lions roaring round the camp. The mounted infantry were excellent for this job as they could slip through the bush with their loads; if the rains came they were still mobile where camels would split in half, slipping in the mud, and motor transport would bog down.

It was late morning when I stopped at Muglad to see the Sheikh of the Homr on my way south. Nazir Baboi was then quite a young chap, slim and handsome with a thin brown face and a ready smile. We spoke about the troubles with the Dinka, mainly the outcome of cattle-stealing by raiders from the opposing tribes. Nazir Baboi said to me, 'Well, of course, the Dinkas dislike us from the old days on account of our slave dealings with Dinka babies. They now outnumber us and cross the river at night to steal our cattle. Our young men resent this enormously from a people we looked on as slaves in the old days.'

We drank tea together in his ferik and then I went off with Alec Findlayson to have lunch under a tree, asking Baboi if one of his chaps would give me any news of lion. He said, 'I'll send somebody out now and I've no doubt he will show you a lion this afternoon.' After lunch I lay down under the trees on my camp bed and had a siesta. After about half an hour I heard the soft voice of a Baggara Arab say to my servant Adam, 'Is that the Government?' Adam replied, 'Yes, that is the Government.' 'Is the Government asleep?'

'Yes, the Government's asleep.' 'But there is a lion lying up quite nearby.' 'All right, I'll wake the Government up.'

By this time I was already sitting up and stretching out for my rifle. The visitor from the Nazir was a Homr herd boy, a young lad of about sixteen wearing *sirwal* (short cloth trousers, loose and knee high, and tied with string) and a tobe of *damur* (woven cloth) over his shoulders. He carried a broad-bladed spear which is used by all the Baggara cattle-owning tribes for protection against lion or for fighting against each other or with the Dinka. Like most of the Baggara of the Homr this boy was very black with a thin face like the Nazir and bright-eyed and cheerful. We shook hands and he pointed excitedly up the green wadi bed where we were camped to a thicket of acacia bushes some half-mile upstream. He said, 'There's a lion lying up there now, waiting for my cattle. Please come and shoot him.'

It was a perfectly still afternoon, so we chose the most concealed route regardless of scent. When we came up with the lion the boy, who could see it long before I could, kept clutching my shoulder and pointing excitedly. It was lying in the long grass on the side of an ant-hill and yawning, having, I think, just woken up from a mid-day sleep. As I was now within fifty yards of it I rolled it over with one shot and the Government was able to continue its journey south leaving the Baggara tribesmen very pleased with the afternoon performance. I took the skin with me.

It was two days later that I met Hussey de Burgh at our rendez-vous on the banks of the Bahr el Arab. We spent the next ten days trekking and camping in this fascinating piece of country. The river itself was full of hippos and crocodiles, and almost every tree overlooking it was tenanted by a fish-eagle, occasionally taking off to soar over the water, plummet down and emerge with a fish in its claws. Hussey was tired from lack of sleep; his men had to keep big log fires burning all night to keep the lions away, and he had a horror of losing half his mules in a night. His men were in great form, well supplied with meat thanks to his skill as a shot. Lack of sleep troubled them little, as they were inclined to talk half the night anyway.

We spent our time talking with the quarrelling tribes. Our party now included the District Commissioner of the Homr and the D.C. of the Dinka across the river, who in private were almost at war with each other in support of their respective tribes. Hussey and Alec Findlayson and I teased them by taking sides. Eventually, both tribes, who were anxious to stand well with the Government, settled their differences fairly amicably in a series of almost interminable discussions, and the soldiers could withdraw.

I was now into my last winter as Commander of the Camel Corps. During it, Sir Stewart Symes, Governor General of the Sudan, came down to the province H.Q. at El Obeid on an official visit. The Camel Corps staged a final full-dress parade for him, the last that was ever held by a mounted corps on animals. The whole of El Obeid's population, 100,000 odd, turned out for the parade which was held on the Maidan. The soldiers were dressed in their white zouave jackets with white baggy trousers, dark blue puttees and a wide belt of green cloth round the waist. This dress, worn with white rolled turban and black ostrich feather, was most striking. The mounted columns marched past first in platoons in line and then in fours at the trot and finally closed up *en masse* and rode past the Governor General at the gallop – camels, mules and horses in a massed charge with the riders waving their whips and cheering. It was a tremendous spectacle and the population of El Obeid were overcome with delight. Sir Stewart said afterwards that it was one of the most impressive sights he had ever seen. Alas, with the arrival of balloon tyres all this pageantry of the Camel Corps would be lost in a cloud of dust, grinding gears, and blowing horns.

In August 1934 I said goodbye to everyone. A guard of honour was mounted in the station at El Obeid and then the whole station rode out with me on horseback to wave farewell at the waiting plane on the air strip two miles out. I felt much the same as I had felt in Bara, five years before, when I said goodbye to my Company to go to Khartoum. But the pang was even keener as the intervening years had brought a closer link with the Political Service officers, so many of whom were my friends and whose work under the guidance of Sir Douglas Newbold I had come to realise was providing the country with its greatest chance for the future.

I had invitations from my Sudanese officers of the Camel Corps to stay with their relations in Dongola on my way north to Egypt. I journeyed slowly round the bend of the Nile from Abu Hamid, where the Nile turns west through Dongola Province, up to the Battn el Hajer, staying with chiefs in Argo and Delgo. It is a fascinating quiet backwater of the River Nile inhabited by the intelligent and charming Shaigieh and Dongola tribes who were perfect hosts. All this was done by boat from Merowe, thence by car through the Valley of Stones to Halfa.

From there I contrived to hire a sailing boat – which I had long wanted to have the leisure to do – to sail down the Nile at high river to Aswan. The felluka was manned by two young lads and I was accompanied by my cook and bearer, Adam Sabil, and a camp bed and primus. We sailed by moonlight as well as day, stopping off at Toski where Lord Grenfell defeated Wad Negumi, one of the bravest and most intelligent of all the Mahdi's generals who was beaten very largely by thirst.

On the return journey the two lads manning the felluka battled for two and a half months to get the boat back up stream to Wadi Halfa.

During my slow journey back to England and after my arrival I kept receiving letters from the Sudanese officers of the Camel Corps thanking me for my assistance and asking me to return if possible. Ten years in the Sudan had indeed attached me to the people. They have the humour and quick intelligence of the Arab and underlying this the basic balance, practical ability, and boyish humour of the African. The combination is a marvellous mixture.

As a result of my years in the Camel Corps, I had obtained a considerable insight into the life of the District Commissioners in Kordofan, and had become increasingly impressed by the practical and human value of the work the D.C.s were doing for the people under Newbold's administration. It seemed to be intensely constructive, and I realized that here was a life integrated into the life of the country and directed entirely to the betterment of the people's wellbeing.

Here, I could in the future use the experience of the past. I had acquired a very adequate working knowledge of Arabic, enormously enjoyed trekking, working with and talking to the peasants and nomads and all whom I came across, and felt an instinctive sympathy for them and all they stood for. It was borne in on me increasingly that my ten years in the Sudan would help to fit me to become a part of the Sudan Political Service.

When my leave was up, I returned to my regiment, the Gordon Highlanders, in Edinburgh. One miserable, cold grey day in February 1935, I was commanding a company of seventy men on guard duty in Edinburgh Castle, and thinking back to sunlit days on the steppes of Kordofan, with a whole country to secure and some 1,200 troops under command. Out of the blue came a telegram. It read:

'For Major Boustead, Gordon Highlanders, from Civil Secretary, Sudan Government. I am authorized to offer you an appointment in the Sudan Political Service, the rank of District Commissioner, and the appointment of Resident of Zalingei Emirate in Darfur, provided that you will resign from the Army.'

It seemed that all my hopes had materialized and I sat down and wrote a reply immediately saying, 'Have resigned and gratefully accept the appointment you offer.' Then I went in to see the Colonel.

He looked at these two telegrams and laughed and said, 'We realize you are sold to the Sudan, and did not think we would be able to hold you.'

Within a week I was on my way by sea from Southampton to Port Said.

Chapter Nine

DISTRICT COMMISSIONER

Up lad, 'tis late for lying,
Hear the drums of morning play.
Hark! the empty highway's crying
Who'll be to the hills away?

A. E. HOUSMAN

IN Khartoum I lunched with the Governor General, Sir Stewart Symes, who gave me some wise advice. He said, 'You have served always in a service where the gravest mistake is to defer decision when action is called for. Here in the Political Service it is far more necessary to wait and defer your decision until you are sure it is sound. In the army no decision is a bad decision. Here no decision may be far the best, since so many political crises work themselves out without our interference.' He added, 'You are going up to a very backward district where the chiefs in the past have had absolute control and there has been a good deal of oppression. Some of it is healthy oppression, and do not forget this. You cannot alter the chief's rule suddenly without undermining the discipline of the whole people and the status of the rulers.'

I left the next day for El Obeid, my old Camel Corps H.Q., where I stayed for three or four days as the guest of Douglas Newbold, still Governor of Kordofan Province. Then I set off up the Fasher road, over four hundred miles of rolling, grass-covered dunes to El Fasher, to report to Charles Depuis, who was then completing his twenty-seventh year of service with the Sudan Government and who had been for some seven years Governor in Darfur. He had applied for me personally and was very welcoming.

Darfur – the Land of the Fur – was a very unusual province, as well as a backward one. In the Sudan, the provinces were roughly grouped as the Northern, and the Equatorial or Southern; the people of the former were Muslim, much affected by Arab blood and Arab traditions, while the peoples of the Southern Sudan, bordering on the Congo and central Africa, are black and pagan. Throughout most of the nineteenth century the black south had been the hunting ground for slavers from the Arabic provinces of the North.

Darfur is one of the Northern provinces, and is predominantly Muslim like the others. But it forms the western edge of the Sudan, with what used to be French Equatorial Africa as its neighbour, and its people are very different from those of Kordofan. The Fur are negroid and wholly non-Arab, and although they adopted the religion of the Arabized races round them, they successfully maintained their independence for centuries, despite Darfur's nominal annexation by Egypt in 1874, and the subsequent rule of the Mahdi. After the fall of the Khalifa and the reconquest of the rest of the Sudan by Kitchener's forces, Darfur was left alone under Sultan Ali Dinar until 1916. Wingate, then Governor General, was nervous of trouble on the west of the Sudan at a time when the Turks in Palestine and Arabia were threatening Egypt from the east; and when the Sultan made some equivocal moves, Darfur was invaded, and the Sultan was driven from his capital, El Fasher, and killed.

Darfur had thus been administered as a province of the Sudan for less than twenty years when I went there. It was still subdivided into the Emirates which had existed under the Sultan, and local control under the emirs was largely exercised through *shartais* or hereditary chiefs. It was a large area for Charles Depuis to govern – about the size of Italy – ranging from high desert and steppes in the north through a downland belt of grass to thick thorn bush in the south, cut by sandy wadi beds which form broad rivers in the rains. In this well-watered land south of El Fasher live the Baggara tribes, cattle-owning peoples, part Arab, part indigenous black Africans; they ride their bulls between their villages and their feriks.

On the west lie the Marra Mountains, 10,000 feet high, running approximately north and south into Northern Darfur District. This great range contains two huge extinct volcanoes and from them flow the mountain rivers through a countryside shining with leaf and blossom, giant acacias and gambeel trees in the forests that fringe the river beds winding in ribbons of white sand out to the west. These forests, filled with the song and vivid flight of birds, are the haunt of lion, leopard and cheetah, antelope, and of herds of small elephant in the more secluded ranges. The blue line of the massive Marra Mountains is never far distant, and the foothills are glimpsed continuously through the forest glades. Grass, water, and shade are plentiful and the soil is rich, its fertility not yet exploited by its increasing population. The country forms Western Darfur district which was to be the scene of my administrative activities for some ten years.

Here in the rains, the high mountains are enveloped in cloud and the lower ranges in transparent mist, thickening and fading in the showers. Torrents plunge down the mountain gorges to swell the flood of turgid waters which sweep out to the west. Islands break off from the main banks and large trees are swept down in the floods.

A carpet of lush grass is spread below the forest trees. From noon onward, behind the mountains the clouds are piled in high white pillars, and sharp bursts of sunshine alternate with the torrential rains. In spring in the forests and valleys and on the hills, flocks of wild geese and duck, white egrets, and ibis, cross the evening and morning sky in flight between their nests and feeding grounds by the river beds, where the grey-blue herons lurk in the marshes.

The rains finish in October, leaving a flowering countryside sparkling beneath a sky still flecked with white clouds. The warm shimmering mornings of light and colour and the lovely solitudes of these green valleys below the Western hills remain for me a vivid and enchanting memory.

I spent two days at El Fasher with Charles Depuis, discussing all the essential problems of my new district, some two hundred miles away to the south west. I learnt that the previous D.C., Edmund Battye, had died of blackwater fever that summer whilst on trek in the district. The Emir, Abdel Hamid, a direct descendant of the Sultans of Darfur, who had been installed as ruler of the Zalingei Emirate a year previously, had died of a heart attack within a few weeks of Edmund Battye. His son, Mohammed Fadl, who had inherited his father's position, was already 34, of an unstable character, and quite careless of his people's welfare. Charles Depuis was much disturbed about the future, and had asked that I might be sent for to pull the Emir together, and to make something of him as a ruler.

I set out in a lorry with servants and police down the road which runs out to the western border of Wadai in French Equatorial Africa. We passed over the Marra Mountains and then turned south into the Western District. It consists largely of tumbled stony hills, covered in thick bush and intersected by great valleys cut by the rivers, and adorned by the beauty of the haraz forests. These huge and graceful trees have a great spread of branches with a blue-green leaf; their peculiar property is that the leaves dry up when the rains come, allowing sunlight to penetrate so that crops can be grown within the forests without the interference of forest shade. They flower when the rains are over, shedding a yellow leaf which is regarded by both Arabs and Fur as a valuable food for cattle and goats.

It was late afternoon when I crossed the bed of the Wadi Azum or Great River which runs from the Marra range west to the French border. At that time of the year it consists merely of a great sandy bed three or four hundred yards across, with sand so heavy that a grass and mud bridge had to be laid for cars to cross. After May the heavy rains came and the river became a fast-flowing flood which

On tour in the Marra Mountains

7. Darfur

A *shartai* and his retinue

Camels in the Shankalla Wilderness

8. Ethiopia 1941

Patriots at Debra Tabor

sometimes for days on end could not be crossed on horseback or by car.

We drove on some four miles through a splendid haraz forest, across the bed of a smaller river, the Aribo, and up to a low range of hills with a commanding view of the whole country to the north east. Here was a brick three-roomed house with a thatched roof, the D.C.'s headquarters. Below the house to the north-west was a square brick fort, castellated and built in Beau Geste style round an inner courtyard. It had been put up in an emergency shortly after the occupation of Darfur and served as offices for the administration and as a prison; a wireless set was installed to keep us in contact with El Fasher, two hundred miles away.

Zalingei village itself was a comparatively small community. The Emir lived on the Aribo River well away from the fort, so that in the future his administration should be quite independent of the D.C.'s headquarters; our hope was that the D.C., now known as the Resident, should act largely as an adviser. This clearly could not happen immediately as Mohammed Fadl, although educated, required both training and experience. The whole Emirate, about the size of England, was split up into regions known as dars under hereditary feudal chiefs who had considerable powers. In recent years the chiefs' powers had become increasingly oppressive in certain dars, although their hereditary position was respected by the people who were accustomed to rough and tough justice.

My task, in a nutshell, was to encourage the Emir to govern his own people well; to curb the oppressive chiefs without upsetting the whole structure of the Emirate; to introduce a proper system of justice dispensed by courts and not by chiefs; and to encourage in every way I could the building of schools. But first I had to meet the people.

It was the custom in Darfur for tribal gatherings to be held at the district centre once a year in the winter. The tribes would ride in on horses and camels from all over the district, each with its own band of tribal drums, and, sometimes, reed pipes. They were a merry party and much marissa (native beer) was drunk. These gatherings gave an unequalled opportunity to find out all that was going on, and for the Fur to meet on friendly terms and discuss one another's difficulties and problems.

The first of these gatherings was due to take place within a fortnight of my arrival and the Emir was already preparing for it. Knowing little of the form, I left it in his hands. It struck me as being very formal and without the fun and games which are an inherent part of the Sudanese character and life. I think that this was due to the Emir, pompous and inexperienced, endeavouring to

H

assert his position. In the coming years all this was altered and the tribal gatherings took on the colour and laughter and horseplay which are natural to the people.

When the tribal gatherings were over and when I had surveyed the administration at H.Q., my most immediate concern was to get round the whole district and meet the chiefs on their own ground. I had to hurry, for the rains were due in two months' time.

When I arrived money was only used to pay taxes to the chiefs. Cash was raised by the sale of cotton cloth, chillies, or wheat, or onions, but it had no other value than to pay the taxes. All trade was carried on by barter, and it took some years before the Fur markets used money as a means of purchase.

In a district so primitive as Zalingei was then, there was no end to the activities of the District Commissioner, and it would be quite easy for any keen, energetic young man to wear himself to a shadow in a very short time. It became clear to me at an early stage that the first essential was to sort out the priorities and to concentrate on them according to their importance. The District Commissioner who nibbled here and there at everything accomplished nothing; one had to maintain a steady front against being distracted from the essentials. Education and hygiene had to take second place on the list to suppressing the oppression of some of the Shartais, which in turn meant setting up courts. The first task here was to find out who were the most influential men among the *agawid* (the elders) in each chief's domain, and persuade the chief to make them into a court of elders.

The rains were early this year and the rivers were already running, so that trekking by car was out of the question. I set out, with mule pack transport and two of my polo ponies, accompanied by the Emir, his young brother Abbas, a boy of twenty-one, and certain of the elders of his court.

Trekking in the rains was a most arduous task and nothing could have been more unpleasant than the nights in a hot tent with the rain pouring down at intervals and hordes of mosquitoes buzzing round. The clouds gathered in the early afternoon in great banks of cumulus which burst at any time from four o'clock onwards, so we spent the mornings riding and moving camp with pack mules. The Emir obviously loathed every minute of it and after a few days returned to Zalingei, sick.

In mid-July I was down at Garsilla in the southern part of the district where the grain at full height towered above a man on horseback. The harvest was still young but very thick. It was early morning when I rode out with Shartai Ali Bakheit to look at the crops. We were on horseback watching a party of young Fur 'hishing' (clearing) the weeds between the crops in line, when I heard a scream and looked up to see a leopard bounding away through the young grain with the young men chasing him with spears. But one of them was lying moaning in the crops. We rode up to find a Fur lad with both his eyes torn out and the whole of his face torn open with lips and nose missing. He had startled the leopard while he was 'hishing' and it had made straight for him. During the coming summer no less than five similar cases appeared in the Zalingei health centre. They all survived but were blinded and their faces mutilated.

The road to Fasher was closed and it was four and a half months before I spoke English or saw another white man. I had by this time covered most of the district, and when September came round I rode into Fasher, some hundred and eighty miles through the Marra Mountains, for a break to stay with Tony Arkell, the acting Governor. The first words I said to him after settling into his comfortable house were, 'I must make it quite clear that only one person can talk for the next four days and that will be me, as I have not spoken a word of English since March.'

I was trying desperately to learn the Fur language since Arabic was still very little used by the common Fur, although the chiefs and some of the elders spoke it. I was set on gaining their confidence by talking to them in village groups during my tour. It was not a written language, which made learning it doubly difficult. By November I had got so far and then stuck, and was finding it increasingly difficult to get at the grammar and construct sentences properly.

The process of learning up to this time was ridiculous, infuriating and humorous. I had at my disposal a Fur orderly who talked Arabic, but his idea of helping me when I was trying to turn sentences from Arabic into Fur would be to put the first person into reverse. For example, I would say to him in Arabic, 'Tell me in Fur how you say, "I will go to Fasher tomorrow." ' He would reply, 'You will go to Fasher tomorrow.' I would say, 'But I said, "I will go to Fasher tomorrow." ' To which would come the rejoinder, 'But I *said* you will go to Fasher tomorrow.'

At this juncture A. C. Beaton arrived to become my Assistant D.C. He was a brilliant linguist with a first in Greats. He quickly set to work to compile a Fur grammar and vocabulary, and eventually, entirely thanks to him, we both passed a Fur interpretership.

By the time the winter came I had a fairly clear idea in my own mind as to where the main courts should be set up and which of the chiefs should be given courts to restrain their present unfettered powers of sentencing. The setting up of the courts and the regulation of the Shartais' powers in so feudal a state had to be tackled with a certain amount of delicacy, for too sudden a switch-over might have endangered the authority of the chiefs, without which the administration could not possibly be run; furthermore people such as the Fur would become immediately most unruly.

I had my first experience of this with Shartai Yussef Abdullahi, one of the barons of the Jebel Marra. In spite of being a most oppressive old man, he was a likeable character. His disregard for Islam was notorious. He had about fourteen wives and eighty or ninety children. Whenever I visited him he used to put the children on parade and I walked down and inspected them, asking their names. It was as good as a play to watch Yussef trying to remember the names of the children. He started, Yussef, Ahmed, Ibrahim, Mohammed, Ali, Ismail and then a sudden blank look came on his face and he said, 'And you, you little bastard, what's your name?' The main purpose of the wives is, as in the pagan south, to assist the Shartais in their cultivations. Yussef Abdullahi was a short, thick-set man, with a well-bearded dark brown face, always laughing – the result of great quantities of native beer which used normally to leave him speechless from late lunchtime until evening. He was the most attentive host, kind and thoughtful to his guests in proportion to his beer.

Like all the other shartais, Yussef Abdullahi had a team of Felagna or Chief's orderlies. These toughs, some armed with rifles and a number mounted on horses, were a sort of tribal police and responsible for bringing in delinquents. This practice was general throughout all the Dars. Yussef's Felagna were notoriously brutal at times.

Fornication was looked on as a criminal offence and was dealt with by fines or restrictions. It was very common among the young Jebel Fur and Shartai Yussef took full advantage of it to keep the offenders – girls and boys – in his jurisdiction working for him on the cultivation for long periods. His redeeming feature was generosity which saw that everybody was well fed.

When it came to regularizing court powers it gradually dawned on him that the young Jebel Fur of Dar Lewing, his fiefdom, were becoming increasingly disobedient to his sentences. A mass of them came to him insisting that past punishments had exceeded the powers laid down in the new courts, and that Shartai Yussef should pay up most of the past excessive fines. Poor old Yussef was terribly frightened that his mountain kingship would be upset and he would come toppling down. Eventually I had to be pretty tough myself in order to ensure that his dignity and position should not be affected. I learnt a great deal from this incident. When I left the district, Yussef was suffering from arthritis and rheumatism, and no doubt from the effects of the massive quantities of marissa which had accumulated in his system. A number of his sons came on well and one was running the whole administration for his father on my departure.

Setting up the courts required endless travelling, talking, persuading, explaining. There was no intention of the District Commissioner taking charge of the courts personally – this would have got us nowhere. Instead, we had to regularize the chiefs' powers by a code of offences and penalties, and for this we had to have court clerks to keep record books. At that time the Fur were so backward that clerks had to be recruited from other provinces: indeed, the need for court clerks was one of my main propaganda points in the drive for more schools. Within the next five years, before the war held things up, we had covered the district with a web of courts, and had put an end to oppression, which could easily be detected in the court books during personal visits of inspection.

One of the early problems was the impossibility of preventing the plaintiff and the defendant and half a dozen witnesses all talking at once. I therefore devised a plan by which a large stone was held in each court, called the Talking Stone. The only person allowed to speak during a case was the person holding this stone; anyone else interrupting was immediately fined five piastres (one shilling) by the court clerk. It produced much laughter and amusement and discomfiture among the Fur, but it worked. The obtaining of witnesses was another difficulty. They could not read or write, so we made small metal plates with a number on them. The defendant would go out and present this plate to the witness required who seeing it came from the court, would come in; without this they were too occupied with their own affairs to bother to turn up. These badges of the court authority worked like magic.

It had always been a problem for the shartais to ensure that prisoners who were under arrest did not get away. They used to put ordinary offenders in the stocks. Those accused of murder were treated more harshly. The trunk of a tree would be split at the top into a fork which would be fitted over the neck with an iron bar to close it behind. This would then be carried by another man, who had to be careful when putting it down not to break the neck of his prisoner. Sleeping in a fork of this sort was extremely uncomfortable. As conditions became more up-to-date we were able to replace these ancient methods with leg-irons and handcuffs.

The commonest cases before the courts involved insult, assault, and – following the local customs – fornication. The Fur are extremely sensitive to insult, and it was interesting to see how many cases came up. They are a very superstitious people, and one of their strongest beliefs is in 'were-hyenas' – in other words, that certain people can turn themselves into hyenas at night. To call a Fur a hyena is a deadly insult. The sentences were heavy, anything from 50 to 100 piastres (10s to 20s); an insult was regarded as anti-social. Despite the laws of Islam, the Fur were heavy drinkers, and for a large part of the year, for a large part of the day, most of them were half-seas over. When the harvest was over, vast quantities of marissa beer were made, and the drinking and dancing went on all night, with the boys and girls stepping off intermittently into the fields. Large numbers of illegitimate babies always appeared as a result of the summer dancing, and by custom the young fellow responsible and the girl were heavily fined. Since the Fur all carried spears and short stabbing knives, the fights that broke out after too much marissa had been drunk often led to serious injuries.

To set up the courts meant almost continuous living in the field, visiting villages, learning the language and establishing confidence by getting to know the people. The most trying hazards in so forested a country were the flies and mosquitoes and the damp heat; two of my staff died of blackwater fever, as my predecessor had done.

For over a year I strove to get the Emir to work for his people, but it was like ploughing in sand. He was entirely wrapped up in his own idea of enjoyment, marrying and divorcing freely. He scandalized the royal family of Darfur, some hundred and twenty of whose sons and daughters were alive, by bastinadoing one of the princesses whom he had married. This punishment was normally reserved for slaves and roused great resentment in the royal family. His final act of folly was to help himself through his accountant, a brother-in-law, to the treasury funds and then to burn down the office while I was on trek, with the object of destroying all traces of the accounts. He botched this so badly that eventually we were able to ascertain from the remains of the books the exact amount of money missing. He was then dismissed from his post to the general satisfaction of the Chiefs.

It was decided to revert to the ancient custom of having the Dimingawi, the local chief of the pastoral area of Kas District, as head of the Fur in Zalingei. So the Dimingawi took over the leadership of the central court in Zalingei and the running of the local government headquarters. He was a weak character, but much liked by everyone and extremely well mannered. Unfortunately, he had a tremendous thirst for marissa, and would pass out for two or three days at times. This of course, as his responsibilities increased, distinctly interfered with his administration, but he fortunately

improved. From now on he presided at every annual tribal conference attended by the Province Governor.

The annual gathering became of cardinal importance to plans
for development. The Fur were a curious mixture of religious
delinquency and fervour. Few of them could afford to have more
than the specified number of wives, which by the Koran is four, but
several of the shartais would run their wives up to twenty or thirty.
The Koran preaches cleanliness and habits of cleanliness, but the
Fur were allergic to washing, and it took some twelve years of
schooling and propaganda to bring about a marked change. On
the other hand, they were very zealous in their praying and the
young boys from eight to about seventeen were taken in hand by
local Fikkis from whom they learned the Koran by rote, and would
inscribe the 'suras' in ink on boards which they carried everywhere.

With two mounted infantry companies in the province, polo was
one of the most welcome pastimes, and in order to play in Zalingei
I started playing with the Emir's brother, Abbas, the local Health
Assistant, and my head boy. With the help of Lord Mountbatten's
book, *Polo by Marco*, some clay dummy horses and a small wooden
demonstration polo ground, these people with a natural eye for the
game became so good that for two Christmas seasons we defeated
every team in the province.

The next priority after setting up the courts was to try and get the
chiefs' sons educated. During these first five years before the war
I put the young sons of school age through Zalingei school and
then sent them on to intermediate schools at province headquarters
or in El Obeid. We were to reap the benefit of this during my second
spell as District Commissioner after the war when these boys
returned, educated and trained, to become the executive officers
of their fathers' lands.

I can remember now Shartai Omar Ahmed Zurug, a fierce old
Fur with a very genial eye, saying to me, 'Well now, if I educate
my sons as you suggest they will be better than me and I will get
no respect and no obedience from them. I would much rather
keep them like myself and respectful and under my control until
I die.' I would say, 'If you take this line you will merely have people
from the east coming in over you to give you orders and to take on
all the administration of your Dar. You will die and your sons will
be the donkeys and the eastern Arabs will ride on them and they
will curse you as being their stupid father, and they will curse me.'
And so the talk would go on until eventually the Shartai gave way.

The problems of education were almost unbelievable. The fathers,
from chiefs to peasants, refused flatly to send their children to school,
and it required endless persuasion and illustration to make any

headway. The most valuable analogy I was able to give them was that of a distinguished officer in my regiment who was for many years Governor of Dongola Province. Sir Herbert Jackson was a man of tremendous personality and greatly loved by the people. In the early part of the century he denied them education since he considered that their agricultural background made it unnecessary. In the years that followed, education went ahead in all the neighbouring provinces and by the time he died young Arabs from outside were already beginning to hold comparatively highly paid positions in Dongola province. Sir Herbert Jackson died in Dongola and he was mourned throughout the Sudan; thousands attended his funeral, but a few years after his death the sons of the fathers who were his friends were cursing his memory for having denied them the chance to hold positions of authority and prominence in their own country.

By the time I left the district there were eleven sub-grade schools in which hygiene, sadly lacking among the Fur, and physical health played as great a part as intellectual education; and the chiefs' sons were conducting all the administrative duties in their fathers' fiefdoms.

Hygiene was a vital subject in the schools and in all my village meetings. The otherwise delightful Fur had an astonishing inhibition about washing themselves or their clothes, despite plentiful supplies of water. One of my first aims in a newly established school was to drum in the need of clean clothes and the use of soap and water. Fifteen years of propaganda in the schools and under the haraz trees meant that washing twice a day became quite the thing, and I was able to see the young Fur showing off their clean clothes and shining black skins in the markets on a Friday.

I was on a tour of the district in March 1937, when I found huge areas of forest and grass lands on fire. I came on a whole line of young Fur from the village of Kurgula, near the Azum Valley, with throwing sticks and knives, chasing mice, rats and lizards escaping from the forest fires. Away beyond them was another line of young Fur setting fire to the grass. This was in some of the finest forest areas of the Azum Valley where the haraz trees cover the whole countryside. Fortunately the shartai of the Dar was riding with me, with some of his tribal police; they were out after these youngsters as fast as they could go and in the ensuing days most of them were before the chief's court.

As we went on we saw some of the bigger haraz trees burning, where the trunks had been set on fire to smoke out the bees and to collect the honey. In a year or two these magnificent forests would have disappeared unless drastic steps had been taken. Shartai Ibrahim immediately got hold of the nearest villagers and told them that either the delinquents would be produced or the whole village would be fined. Within twenty-four hours four young lads were in the district prison. The young Fur were adept with the throwing stick and would knock over partridges, guinea fowl and hares, as well as rats and lizards. It was a normal custom for hunting parties to go out every Friday and this continued, but the grass burning gradually abated as the shartais took action. In this way some of the most magnificent timber in the Northern Sudan was saved.

The Fur had problems with their neighbours on either side. To the west lived the Masalit tribes in an independent Dar under their own Sultan, the border running along the Wadi Azum. Unfortunately the arable land on either side of the river bed was partly in Fur and partly Masalit ownership, and some savage tribal fights were the consequence. I remember one in particular when a quarrel led to a melee between men of the two tribes; spears and stabbing knives are dangerous weapons, and three Fur were dead and some twenty-five Fur and Masali seriously wounded by the time mounted police from Zalingei had stopped the riot by opening fire. The doctor from Dar Masalit took two days to patch up the wounded.

It was essential that an example be made of those responsible, and John Owen, who had succeeded Beaton as my Assistant, and I spent long days living in the damp wadi bed holding a major court. At the time we were still short of handcuffs and leg irons, so the principal offenders sat or lay uncomfortably in 'shaibas' or forked tree trunks, until tried. Sultan Audoka of Dar Masalit himself came down and was highly displeased to see some of his pet tribesmen in this ignominious captivity; but it was essential that they did not escape before trial. Eventually several men were sentenced to seven to ten years imprisonment at Fasher, and the border was heavily policed next year.

Across on the eastern side of the district the trouble lay with cattle-owning Arabs letting their herds break into the Fur cultivations and eating the grain. The Arabs would pretend that the animals were out of control, having deliberately urged them on. Here again we had some heavy tribal fights; the Arabs were armed with huge broad-bladed spears, which inflicted very ugly wounds. Again this entailed long days under trees adjudicating on the guilt of accused.

During this year, 1937, I was confronted with the same problems of heart and mind which had worried me in 1927. Again on a leave in England after a period of climbing in the Alps, I became engaged to a girl whom I had known for some years. On returning to the district where I was completely absorbed in the life of the people, and on trek some three weeks a month, I became increasingly certain that she could not physically take this life, and that it would lead in consequence to much unhappiness later. However, I took it more slowly this time and it was not until the time of Munich, nearly two years later, that the engagement was broken off. War followed shortly afterwards and I did not return to England for five years.

It is hard for anyone nowadays to realize how much a girl had to put up with in those years as a wife of a D.C. in one of the wilder districts of the Sudan. Modern comforts which are taken for granted, such as electricity, fans, refrigerators, were non-existent. On trek the D.C. would be fully occupied interviewing tribesmen and villagers, inspecting courts, schools and health centres, dealing with agricultural and irrigation problems and the building of roads, and so on; whilst his wife would be sitting in a tent or in a grass tukl, worried by flies, bitten by mosquitoes, flayed by dust storms and fierce heat, and with no female company at all.

Although I was wholly taken up in my work as a D.C., and in Zalingei was about as cut off from world events as one could be, the Italian conquest of Ethiopia concerned me deeply. The then commander of the Sudan Defence Force, General Franklin, was convinced that trouble would come from this quarter and was planning ahead. He had visited me in my district, and arranged for me to receive copies of his Intelligence reports. 'This appeasement will get us nowhere,' he told me; 'there are the Italians with 150,000 troops, and here we are with 4,000-odd Sudanese in the S.D.F. When the storm breaks, we will have to hold them until reinforcements come, and we can go on the offensive. What I want you to do is come back to the Army when the time comes, and command a mobile independent column operating inside Abyssinia.'

I jumped at this proposal, which tied up with my experiences in Russia after the First War, and was correspondingly depressed when Franklin left the Sudan in 1938. But I soon had a signal from S.D.F. that his successor, General Platt, would like to visit me in Zalingei.

An R.A.F. plane arrived in the afternoon and General Platt jumped out, lean and brown with quick restless eyes and rather ferrety nose. He greeted me cheerfully with, 'I've heard all about you from Franklin, but for God's sake where can I relieve myself? These open planes are hell.' We talked over tea on my verandah overlooking the Koygnia hills, and he said, 'I understand you are getting all the Intelligence reports on Italian East Africa from my Headquarters.' I said, 'Yes, I am, and I'm planning a trip into

Ethiopia during my next leave.' The General said some kind words about my work with the Camel Corps, and left me cheered up at the prospect of having something useful to do if war came. In the meanwhile I was utterly and completely absorbed in the task of getting to know the chiefs and people, the basis of all progress for a D.C.

Fortunately in Western District major homicide crimes were rare in comparison with the neighbouring cattle-owning district of Southern Darfur. With the Fur during my first five years as D.C. I convicted in possibly some twenty-five cases, an average of five a year, of homicide amounting to murder; in the neighbouring Baggara Arab District of Nyala this figure could be multiplied by four. It was during the latter half of my final year before leaving for the war that an elderly Fur peasant said to me one day, 'What happened to old Ahmed whom you tried some five years ago in Kas for murdering his wife?' I replied, 'He was sentenced to be hanged by me and the court who sat with me.' The old boy said, 'But he's working in Port Sudan gardens.' I asked him, 'What makes you think that?' He said, 'Oh, everybody knows that.' I replied, 'This may be, but it isn't true. He was hanged in Fasher.' The old man then said, 'But tell me how many people have you hanged since you came?' I replied, 'About five a year, altogether about twenty-five.' 'But what is the point of this?' he asked. 'Twenty-five people murdered and twenty-five people more killed for murdering them, that makes fifty. You are forty-eight down on Grant Bey.' I said, 'What do you mean?' 'Well, he came to Zalingei in 1920 just as a murder had taken place and he hanged the murderer in the market-place on a market day on a tree.' 'And what then?' 'And then there were no more murders for five years.' This gave me much to think about, for it was clear that with a primitive people the visual effects of a public hanging acted as a very strong deterrent.

An amusing incident happened during one summer leave while I was at home and the rains were heavy over the whole countryside in Western Darfur. The rivers were flooded and lion and leopard were encroaching on the station. One night a lion got into the bathroom of one of the resthouses and was discovered by the rest-house keeper in the morning as he opened the wooden latch of the window. The resthouse keeper was terrified to hear a roar from inside and found himself faced with a huge snarling male lion. He withdrew quickly and reported it to the very junior Sudanese Administrative official who was holding the fort during the quiet summer period. The junior official, a nervous little man, was so agitated that he immediately sent off a wireless message to the Province Governor reporting the lion in the bathroom and asking for instructions. The Governor wired back: 'Re lion in the bathroom. Bathe lion. Do not get soap in lion's eyes. Or else shoot lion. Best wishes.'

During this period John Owen and I worked together intensively training the chiefs' sons when they were on leave from school. We dressed them simply in white damur (local cotton) gibba and shorts, with a green turban as a distinguishing mark for a chief's son. They were nicknamed either Green Hats, or the *Abu arbain* (Fathers of Forty), because they received forty piastres, about eight shillings, a month. When I went on trek, they sat on top of the lorry; and at each chief's centre they had to prune the forest trees around the area in the early morning and check over all the books of schools, courts and health centres. They poured tea for the elders and their fathers, and attended all conferences. On the return journey from tour they were dropped off the lorry to find their own way home on foot, forty or fifty miles across country, within a time limit. There would be bets on the way home as to who would be dropped off, and every time the lorry stopped I would see Ahmed or Ibrahim or Yussef nudging each other with a laugh to indicate it was the other's turn. This somewhat Spartan training paid a hundred-fold; in later years many of these lads became a driving force in the development of the district. I looked on this training as vital for the future; the reward came after the war when, after a further final period of training with me, they were fit to join their fathers as administrative executives to their regions.

In 1938 Marjory Perham, a great friend of mine, visited the Sudan on an official tour. As Darfur was within her terms of reference I had the pleasure of having her as my guest for some days. We rode through the Marra Mountains together, where she was reminded of early visits to Basutoland. She was on one of her numerous official tours to the territories of Africa, connected with her work on the administration of underdeveloped territories.

Later that year on my return from leave as I rode into Kas village in the late rains, I saw a tumult of young Fur crowding around one of the tukls on the outskirts. There was a hullabaloo with women weeping. Full of curiosity I rode up to the crowd where I saw a Fur lying on a string bed, covered in blood and with a foot severed at the ankle. His wife was weeping beside him. It had been a hot night and he had slept outside with his feet hanging over the end of the bed. It appeared that a hyena had come along and seeing this enticing joint had bitten it off and made away with it. Ahmed had lost a great deal of blood; fortunately the Health Assistant, who had been out on trek, turned up whilst I was still there and we were able to save his life. Attacks by hyenas were not uncommon, but the greatest danger in the district was the leopards during the cultivating season.

I had two months at home in 1939. In late August London seemed to be filled with utter gloom as it became increasingly clear that war was inevitable and that the country was by no means ready to meet the Nazi threat. The 'In and Out' was full of my old regiment, the Gordon Highlanders. Chamberlain's Government appeared hopeless to most of us; and when the news of war being declared came through on the club radio, the atmosphere was very different from what it must have been in August 1914, when actually I was on the high seas off Madagascar. There was none of the bursting enthusiasm of 1914, the spirit with which Julian Grenfell wrote *Into Battle*. In no time the regiment was off, and I longed to go with them; but was ordered with all Sudan Government officials to report to the S.S. *Montcalm* which was lying in the Firth of Clyde.

When I returned from that leave I stayed with General Platt on my way through to Zalingei. He said, 'We shall not want you yet, but I will call you down in good time when we know what the Italians are going to do. It can only be a matter of time before they are in the War. In the meantime you remain in your district.'

Very many District Commissioners and Assistant D.C.s of fighting age demanded freedom to enlist, but the Sudan Government resisted this and in general only those with some special background were allowed to go. I remained in Zalingei that winter while the phoney war continued. John Owen, who was about twenty-eight but had no chance of being spared, manfully suppressed his gloom.

At the end of March 1940, General Platt wrote officially to the Civil Secretary, Sir Douglas Newbold, saying, 'I should like to have Boustead before any officer and I want you to send him home now for some refresher training in England.' Newbold then communicated with the Province Governor, Phil Ingleson, who wrote to me urgently, saying, 'I have had good news for you from Douglas. The General is now wanting you back immediately to serve with the Sudan Defence Force, and I gather that you are to go home first in order to pick up the latest training. You are not a civil servant any more; you are returning to be a soldier and you'd better get back into your kilt again.'

Chapter Ten

THE FRONTIER BATTALION

MY refresher course never happened. I reached London on the night of the 10th May, and woke up next morning to the news that the Germans had broken into Holland and Belgium; the phoney war was over, and I was ordered back to the Middle East. A small party of us flew from Hendon, after reports of German fighters over the Channel had delayed our departure. At Bordeaux the French Air Staff told us, 'Le Roi des Belges s'est rendu'; and as we flew on into the bright June sunshine of the Mediterranean I wondered how quickly Italy would come in.

Cairo was expectant and excited. For nine months the Middle East Command had been waiting on the side lines; everyone knew that the balloon was now going up. I reported to General Sir Arthur Smith, Wavell's Chief of Staff, whom I had met before. He was friendly and forthcoming, and arranged for me to attend some training exercises in the desert, as well as settling down to do some homework at the Special Operations Branch at H.Q.

After ten days of this Sir Arthur Smith sent for me and said, 'I would like you to meet General Wavell.' I was taken into the C. in C.'s room, where Wavell was sitting at his desk, his craggy face quite unreadable. He was about to speak to me when the telephone rang, and he picked up the receiver. He listened impassively, and in silence, and then put it back quietly. Turning to Smith, he said, 'That is to say that the Italians have come in'; he appeared unmoved at the news which committed his forces to action on two fronts against vastly superior numbers. Then he carried on with his interview with me. He asked me a number of questions about the Sudan, and went on, 'I understand that Platt wants you to raise and command the Frontier Battalion to cross the Abyssinian border. Have you met Sandford who is going into Ethiopia with a mission to raise the patriots?' I replied that I had had two or three talks with him in the past week, and expected to see more of him in the Sudan. 'Well, Boustead, you'd better get on a flying-boat tomorrow morning and go down and raise your Frontier Battalion. Good luck to you. We shall hear more of you later.'

In Khartoum I reported to the Kaid, General Platt, who had already set the wheels spinning. 'I've instructed every Corps of the Northern Sudan Defence Force to detail N.C.O.s and trained men,' he told me. 'They will form the nucleus of an extra company in every Corps. These companies will remain in their Corps station for administration until they are fully trained, by you. I want them brought up to the highest possible standard of platoon training. You must have them ready for me by November.'

General Platt had now, in June 1940, been commanding the Sudan Defence Force for two and a half years. From the time of his arrival the Kaid had been drawn to the Sudanese people, conceived a strong liking for the Sudanese soldier and an equal understanding and regard for his qualities. These warm-hearted and responsive men, like most African troops, were conscious of their commander's reactions, and they responded warmly in their respect for him. He had promptly adopted the Sudanese soldier as a son, a relationship which the young Sudanese fighting man both understood and appreciated in his commander. The effect of a few words in his own tongue on the African soldier from a higher Commander on exercises or inspections is electric, and the results repay the toil of study which is a wearisome burden to the ordinary man over forty.

The Kaid had sensed this. In spite of long and arduous journeys by air and over bad roads in a climate which would have tried men ten years younger, he had persisted in his study of Arabic, and established that essential human contact which command of a language strengthens enormously. The soldiers' affection, regard and loyalty were his reward, and his prestige was high in the Force when the testing time came. There is a saying in the Sudan: 'If you show him kindness, you may pull the whiskers from a lion.'

On his inspections his approach to the men was friendly, his eyes laughed and a perpetual smile hovered around his lips. They sensed his humanity, his humour and sympathy. The added word of Arabic, and the slow tempo and infinite pains of these inspections, where every man received a personal penetrating and cheerful scrutiny, made a lasting impact. I remember his coming when the Frontier Battalion was trained and ready, and the march across the frontier was only a few days ahead of us. The men were aware in some measure of the hazards that lay before them, the uncertainty of supply into the mountains of Abyssinia, the Italian and native armies which, if concentrated *en masse*, would swamp our small columns. The General, more fully alive to the ardours and endurances, risks and chances that would confront the Force, went round punctiliously shaking hands with all the Sudanese officers and senior non-commissioned officers, and patting a man here and there on the shoulder with an infectious smile. Unhurried, he inspected each company appraising the men. The line of brown and black faces were lit with gleaming white teeth, the answering grins of a whole battalion whose hearts responded to the inspecting General's anxiety to show each man his personal importance to his Commander. He won their hearts, and for days afterwards the men talked of his visit.

I remember a farewell speech he made at the Native Officers' Club when he was leaving the country, in which he said that, on his arrival, Sir Stewart Symes gave him three invaluable pieces of advice. 'Meet the Sudanese with a smile, and when in doubt what to do next, shake hands.' The third, he admitted, he had found more difficult – to learn Arabic.

Raising the new Frontier Battalion was no problem – young men of fine physique clamoured for enlistment in the new Patrol Companies. The name was fortunate; the Arabic word *doria* or patrol was used in the Sudan for all military expeditions, and added to the appeal of the battalion. We had the pick of the volunteers. Training them was less simple, despite the N.C.O.'s and trained men seconded from the Corps. For a start, the Nuba Company – 270 six-footers – had to be taught Arabic. These jet black hillmen from the Nuba Mountains have a long tradition of soldiering, and late into the night they could be heard drilling each other, like Ghurka recruits. Their fitness could be taken for granted, for their physique is superb. Wrestling is a traditional pastime, and in the southern hills they box with a metal gauntlet, like the Roman cestus, which will split open a man's skull with a blow.

The companies were scattered over the Sudan, the eastern on the Abyssinian border, the western a thousand miles away in Darfur, the others in Kordofan and the Blue Nile Province. To supervise and coordinate their training meant immense journeys followed by long hot days in the sun, on foot or on horseback, watching the training of the troops and setting and demonstrating exercises to the officers. The Sudanese officers were irregulars, like the men; the British were either regulars, or seconded from the Political Service, or planters from the Gezira Cotton Company. The Kaid had picked them all personally – as he told me, 'I have chosen your officers for their toughness, adaptability and leadership.'

It was clear that operating in the Abyssinian mountains would mean limited supplies, brought in on animal transport, and no reinforcements. We had to learn to meet the enemy again and again at close quarters while avoiding casualties ourselves, and to control our expenditure of ammunition by the strictest fire discipline. We trained intensively at section and platoon level. Mobility and endurance could be taken for granted; we concentrated on the

9a. Hugh Boustead, mounted, talking to the Ethiopian Mortar team on the summit of the Chokey Mountain pass, 14,000 feet, *en route* to Mota

9b. The halt to adjust loads on the Gojjam plateau

A tribal march past

10. Zalingei

Umpiring a Fur wrestling match: John Owen on the right

development of bold leadership, use of ground, fire and movement, fire discipline, a great deal of patrolling, and a large number of field firing practices, often with ball ammunition. The tirelessness and zest of the officers and men were heartening, and speeded up the whole process.

While I was out in the field, the central administration of the battalion was in the hands of Jock Maxwell who had been appointed second-in-command. He had commanded a company of the Eastern Arab Corps at Gedaref for five years after secondment from his regiment, the Royal Scots Fusiliers, and had been to the Haifa Staff College.

Wilfred Blunt describes in his diaries a young Vice-consul in Bizerta: 'He has the rare virtue in an Englishman of being never bored or in a hurry or out of temper, or too busy to speak to the poorest man that calls on him.'

This is a pattern of behaviour increasingly difficult for an administrative or political officer to attain in the growing web of administrative tangles around him. Yet many come very near the mark and their reward may be seen in the high regard in which they are held. For the young officer commanding native troops, it is possible in the life of the station, but in the field where time is an ever pressing factor, where a hot African sun blinds the sight, a myriad insects irritate the senses and fatigue and thirst cloud the temper, it is an almost superhuman ideal never to appear out of temper or in a hurry. Of all the British officers with whom I have served in command of native troops, I believe that Jock Maxwell came nearer to it than any other, and he was correspondingly loved by all ranks.

With his knowledge of the country and the Sudanese soldier, combined with his staff and regimental ability, Jock was invaluable to me, and remained so for the two years we were together. Later he was to command his regiment at Anzio and on the Rhine, where his leadership, skill and courage won for him a fine D.S.O.

As adjutant for the new battalion I was lucky to have Colin MacDonald, who had joined the Sudan Political Service only a year or two earlier from Edinburgh University. He was astonished at his luck at being released to join the army, and his vitality and high spirits were as irrepressible as his eager welcome of the adventure ahead of us. I have seldom seen such positive and conscious enjoyment of life as he displayed in the nine months left to him.

Doomed to know not winter, only spring, a being
Trod this flowery April, blithely for a while,
Took his full of music, joy of thought and seeing,
Came and stayed and went, nor ever ceased to smile.

I

There had remained the problem of a Native Staff Officer, who in a Sudanese battalion is largely the father of the young native officers and an adviser to the Commanding Officer on matters concerning the men. There was no one available of the right seniority in the Sudan Defence Force at that time, and the Political Service offered Adbel Razak, a seconded officer with twenty years' service with the political. A massive man with a perpetual twinkle and a laugh that made his whole fat frame shake like a jelly-fish, Abdel Razak filled the post admirably. His strong personality impressed the young Sudanese officers, and his sense of humour kept him at all times unruffled. He could talk only a few words of English, but had a quick ear. His prowess on the polo field in pre-war days was interlarded with English exhortations to his horse whom he had endearingly named 'Come-on-bloody-fool'.

Training went on so well that by September 1940 it was possible to move our H.Q. from Khartoum to Sennar, on the Blue Nile, in readiness for the concentration of the Frontier Battalion on the Abyssinian frontier, ready for action.

The position that autumn was very threatening. In Egypt General Wavell was confronted by the ponderous invasion of the Western Desert by Graziani's enormous and then untested army, while Syria and Iraq were both danger spots. In August the Italians, encouraged by the surrender of the pro-Vichy forces in French Somaliland, had over-run the defences of British Somaliland, and their obvious next move was an invasion of the Sudan. They had already occupied the border towns of Kassala and Gallabat in July, and the way seemed open to Khartoum and the Nile, or up the Red Sea littoral to Port Sudan.

On paper, the enemy forces in East Africa had overwhelming superiority, with an army of nearly 300,000 men, both highly trained and determined Italian units and native Eritrean regiments; over 400 guns, 250 aircraft, and 60 somewhat inferior tanks; against a total of some 7,500 men in the Sudan and about 10,000 in Kenya. The Italians had some able commanders, including officers capable of inspiring their men to great achievements, like Lorenzini and Rolle. They were well supplied with ammunition and petrol, although clearly they were not equipped for a long war, cut off as they were from their homeland; on the other hand, no one was equipped for a long war. Everything should have led the Italian to strike at once, and vigorously, across the 1,200 miles of frontier into the Sudan, defended by three British battalions and 4,500 men of the S.D.F.

One of the inhibiting factors was their new Abyssinian empire. Unlike Eritrea, the oldest Italian colony and a safe offensive base, Abyssinia was still 'occupied territory' and could not be denuded of troops. Bandits (or patriots) still operated in the highlands, and large forces were tied down by the need to protect settlers and colonists from the disaffected inhabitants, bitterly resentful of Italian oppression. The position had been eased by the appointment in 1937 of the Duke of Aosta as Viceroy; a humane and cultured man, and a good soldier, he had moderated his predecessor's ruthless policy and gone far to reconciling many Ethiopians to Italian rule. He was also a shrewd politician, and exploited the divisions between the barons who were the hereditary rulers of vast areas and who in some cases had no love for the exiled Emperor. In the Gojjam, for instance, he reinstated as ruler Ras Hailu, who had been imprisoned by the Emperor before the conquest; the Viceroy thus secured the help, in an untamed province, of some 6,000 irregulars, foot and horse, of the Ras's feudal following.

Even so, the 'banda' were not very reliable allies, and 14,000 white and Eritrean troops were tied down in the Gojjam in a series of protective forts from which they occasionally emerged in strength to sweep the linking roads; and the position was very similar in all Abyssinia. To make the most of Italian anxiety was a key point in the British plan.

The strategy was simple and effective: to invade Eritrea and there bring to battle and destroy the main Italian armies; simultaneously to invade Italian Somaliland and southern Abyssinia from Kenya; and to deny the enemy any reinforcements from his central position by raising and arming patriot forces to pin down and destroy his garrisons in Abyssinia. The first task was accomplished by the 4th and 5th Indian Divisions after bitter fighting, above all at the prolonged battle of Keren, and the second by General Cunningham's force of South African and East and West African troops. In the centre, the backbone of the fighting force which penetrated Abyssinia was to be the Frontier Battalion of the S.D.F.

In the meantime, before this three-pronged offensive could be mounted, the Italians had to be held in check by the handful of S.D.F. troops scattered along the frontier. Relentless and vigorous patrolling made the enemy overrate our strength, and kept him largely on the defensive. In September the 5th Indian Division arrived, and the immediate threat to the Sudan was eased; in January 1941 the 4th Indian Division arrived from the Western Desert, and the Eritrean campaign began; and in the same month the Emperor crossed the frontier back into his homeland.

His return, and the entire Ethiopian venture, were made possible

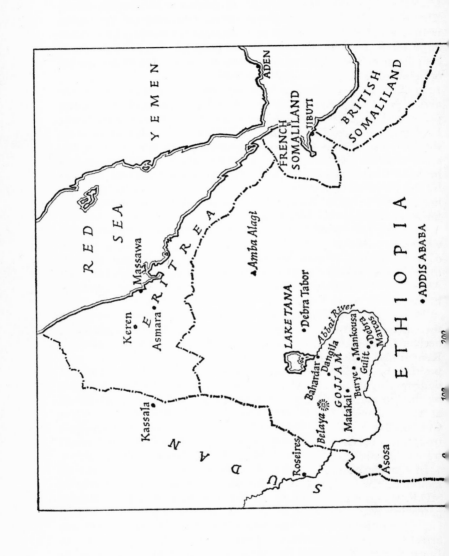

by Colonel Sandford's mission. He was a remarkable man, already 58, who had lived for many years in Abyssinia before the Italian conquest. A close friend of the Emperor and many of the chiefs, and with a sympathetic understanding of the peasantry, he was the ideal leader of the enterprise; his astonishingly sanguine temperament – he had the faith of a Gordon in the success of any of his undertakings – gave him great strength.

After our discussions in Cairo, my next meeting with him was at Gedaref, where I had gone to watch the training of the Eastern Arab Corps company. It was a very good company of Beni Amer, hillmen whose light-boned, almost delicate, appearance belies their strength and endurance, and officered by two Britons from the Sudan Cotton Syndicate. Henry Johnson's grave, quiet manner and firm command inspired me with confidence from the first. He was an international footballer, and his toughness and leadership were proved in the forthcoming campaign in which he was awarded two D.S.O.s. Peter Hayes, his number two, was a tall, fair intellectual and a master of languages. He trained the best Bren-gunners in the battalion.

Of the native officers, Yuzbashi Ishag Effendi Musa had been my staff officer in the Camel Corps for three years, and was an old and tried friend. An outstanding figure in the company was the Bash-shawish (sergeant-major) Musa Mohammed, a short, wiry, square-built man from the Red Sea Hills; intelligent, full of laughter and fun yet a good disciplinarian, he was Johnson's right-hand man in a number of precarious situations. He is now a Yuzbashi, with the D.C.M.

'Dan' Sandford turned up at Gedaref on his way to meet the Abyssinian chiefs of the Ermaccio hills at Gallabat on the frontier; he asked me to come with him to spread the news that the Emperor had arrived in the Sudan, and to hand over the first supply of arms. The other members of his mission were with him – Donald Nott in charge of admin., Ronnie Critchley, their doctor, Drew, and Lance Corporal (now Lieutenant-Colonel) Grey, their signaller. We were periodically bombed by a Savoia at Gedaref; I felt that Clifford Drew was a poor companion in a slit trench, since his cheerful, red face uplifted to the sky looked to me like a flaming beacon to the Italian pilot.

Sandford and I had a long day to reach Gallabat; this was just before the Italians occupied it, nearly 2,000 of them taking a day to push out one platoon of the S.D.F. Sandford seemed inexhaustible and at midnight called a conference to plan the morning's meeting. In the daylight, we walked down through the forest to the river bed to meet the chiefs – thin-faced, grave men who had been putting up a sporadic resistance to the Italians. The meeting seemed to me inconclusive; it went on until noon, but the chiefs were not very impressed by the arms Sandford had brought. They wanted magazine-loading weapons: but so did we, and so did the still largely unarmed Home Guard in Britain.

We set off at dusk for Khartoum, and drove all night for 180 miles over the trackless Butana Desert. Sandford was still smiling and fresh, and went straight off to see the Kaid. In a few weeks' time, he slipped across the frontier with his little party, and established himself at Sakalla in the Gojjam Highlands, in an area held by the patriots. It was the first step in the offensive.

My object was to have the new Frontier Battalion ready to force a way into Abyssinia, to let the Emperor return to his people and, we hoped, raise them against their Italian rulers. The plan was given an unpleasant jolt in October by a brave and resolute Italian commander.

I had been ordered in July to take over the defence of the so-called Fung frontier – the area of the pre-Mahdi Fung Kingdom, more or less where the Blue Nile leaves Abyssinia and runs for about a hundred miles over cataracts until it breaks into deep, navigable water at Roseires, the district headquarters and market centre. I was uneasy at taking on this additional responsibility when I had to spend so much time travelling round the Sudan to visit my newly formed companies: I hoped that the Fung Frontier Police, then only 110 rifles, could keep tabs on the Italians, who had 800 native troops at Gubba, just across the frontier, and 4,000 men with guns and planes at Asosa, not very far away. The position was made more difficult by the veiled hostility of the Wat-a-Wit, a border tribe who resented Sudanese suppression of gun-running and the slave trade; intelligence was hard to come by.

The Sudanese of the Frontier Police, under Bill Davies, later Governor of the Upper Nile Province, did wonders, patrolling intensively and keeping the enemy on the hop; for three months, in soaking rain, this handful of men kept the enemy in a mist of ignorance.

The blow fell while I was inspecting No. 5 Company – the Nubas – and watching them sweating at their section training in the bright sun, below Jebel Dilling. Telegrams started to arrive, all marked urgent, so we adjourned to Guy Campbell's company H.Q. to decipher them. The uneasiness that always oppressed me when I was away from the frontier crystallized as the word FUNG emerged. An Italian force was already well into Sudanese territory. The truck was loaded up while the next wire was decoded. 'The enemy are moving down the Blue Nile burning and looting.'

It was 120 miles to El Obeid over a road made heavy and some-times impassable by the rains, and a further 300 miles on to Roseires. At El Obeid I was lucky enough to find General Platt. A serious discussion was brightened by an urgent wire from Fasher in Darfur; it read 'Please re-direct the spate of urgent ciphered telegrams for El Miralai Boustead Bey to his proper address, or send me a team of cipherines.'

I flew on to Khartoum in the Kaid's plane, and then on to battalion H.Q. at Sennar where I learned that the enemy force was within forty miles of Roseires. It was under the command of Colonel Rolle – a name that took me straight back to Bagnold's trip eight years earlier, when we had met Rolle at Jebel Owenat in the Western Desert. I learned later that he was confident that his column could live off the country, and capture Roseires, so threatening the vital communications at Suki and Sennar; his success was to be exploited by a mobilized column from Asosa.

He very nearly did it, but lack of local knowledge wrecked the plan. The crops were not ready for harvesting, and the villages along the Blue Nile had practically no stocks of grain. His hill-bred Ethiopians were not used to the heat of the Sudan low country, and above all did not know that the water they desperately wanted was theirs for the taking, only a few feet below the surface. They died in large numbers of hunger and thirst.

I found Jock Maxwell at Roseires, his usual calm self, with all dispositions made. This crisis had one good consequence: it led to the immediate concentration of the entire Frontier Battalion, and the companies were already on the move from Fasher, from north Kordofan, from the Nuba Mountains and from Singa, down the Blue Nile. I immediately sent out a column from Roseires, but the Banda had had enough, and Rolle withdrew without contact. It was the last Italian offensive.

I now had my battalion under my hand; the next problem was transport for the march into Abyssinia. The chosen site for an advanced strong point, and the Emperor's base, was the Belaya Mountain; and the route from Roseires led through Umm Iddla on the Dinder River across the Shankalla wilderness – a waste of stony ridges covered with thick scrub, waterless, and quite impass-able to motor transport without months of preparation and an army of labourers. From Belaya Mountain the way led steadily upward to the great Abyssinian Escarpment, some 4,000–5,000 feet high and standing 2,000 feet above the hot wilderness below. It was hoped that Sandford's mission would be able to organize large mule convoys on the actual plateau, but it was clear that any expedition must rely on camels for the main carry up to the Escarpment. In the event, the patriots could muster no mules, and camels bore the burden all the way.

So the immediate need was camels, not only for the supplies for the expedition, but to carry in all the weapons and ammunition to arm the patriots: a lot of camels. The Governors of Kordofan, Ewen Campbell, Blue Nile, James Robertson, and Kassala provinces, Kennedy Cooke, set about providing the prodigious herds that were required, and soon an immense throng of 18,000 camels was winding in steady procession up the west bank of the Blue Nile, over the glowing parklands of the Fung province on the long road to Roseires, itself 100 miles from the frontier. The tall trees that line the river provided them with grazing and complete cover from the wandering Savoia bombers.

I had no difficulty in finding men for the camel transport of the battalion; old friends of Camel Corps days, who had served before mechanisation started, flocked to re-join. On their efficiency and care of their animals we depended for our capacity to keep the field, and their long service in the mounted Camel Corps bore fruit in the campaign.

They crowded round me at El Obeid, these veterans out of a past phase of my life. Some had been in my own company, some in other companies when I commanded the Corps. Lately retired, they were longing to return to the companionable life of the service. As the news went round of the huge herds of camels that were to be driven across the enemy frontier, their enthusiasm intensified.

Guma Mohammed Ali in particular stands out. A Dongolawi Arab but born in Kordofan and educated in the El Obeid school, his quick intelligence, attractive manners and outstanding capacity as an instructor won him early promotion. Unfortunately his career was chequered by his love of native beer. However, like Browning's hero, 'each time he fell to rise again'. In that autumn of 1940 I found him as a prison warder in El Obeid jail; he, the late Bashshawish instructor of the Camel Corps. He swore on the Holy Book that no drink would pass his lips if he might 'list the bugle' once more. I took the risk and made him Bashshawish to the camel train of the Frontier Battalion. I never regretted this step, though his eventual promotion to Mulazim (Subaltern) two years later was celebrated so universally and successfully by himself and his friends, that from that time on he was never again able to say No to drink. He had been the crack marksman of the Camel Corps for several years, and in the coming campaign he dropped four Ethiopian shifta (brigands) dead in their tracks on the Debra Marcos road one

night when a band attacked his isolated convoy of a few unarmed
camel drivers. Terrified by his swift and deadly shooting the
remainder of the band made off. The campaign was over when I
saw Guma, in his own home at El Obeid among a host of friends,
a full-blown subaltern:

> Dressed to the nines and drinking
> And light in heart and limb
> And each chap thinking
> The fair was held for him.

During these late November days, the river bank at Roseires was
an astonishing sight. The vets of the Sudan Veterinary Service –
John Jack, Ian Gillespie and Percy Durran – sweated the day long
in the scorching sun, serving and sorting the convoys, turning away
immature animals, repairing the gaping wounds that rutting camels
inflict on each other; settling the countless queries of their drivers;
arranging rations and pay. Their combined efforts introduced order
out of the chaotic herds of grunting, gurgling, snuffling and groaning
animals, and sent the convoys out into the unknown efficiently provided for the hard days ahead. The question of saddles was soon
settled. The Frontier Battalion first-line transport and their camel
column used government saddles with stuffed horsehair pads; these
ensured secure loads, but clumsily or inefficiently used meant sore
backs.

The tribesmen loaded their animals with the native *baladi* saddle
which has a large surface of straw pads, and so ensures an even
weight over the maximum area and the continual access of air to the
camel's back. This rough structure of wood and straw had the great
advantage that the materials for its repair were provided by the
country, and their drivers were accustomed to repair them themselves. Wounds on the back were invariably due to the drivers
allowing the wooden structure to bear down on the animals' backs.
Loads rarely exceeded 250 lbs. The light hill-bred camels of the
Camel Corps would cover up to forty miles a day on forced marches,
carrying over 400 lbs including their rider; but this can only be
achieved by grain-feeding. The nature of the campaign ahead
precluded any such ideas, and the whole camel column and camel
train were to rely on the trees and grass of the countryside.

In January 1941 the Shankalla wilderness was burnt black by
giant grass fires spread by the Gumuz honey hunters, who burn
down the trees in their quest for hives. All day columns of grey
smoke circled the wide horizon, rising hundreds of feet into the sky,
and the seared trees and blackened grasses presented a picture of
desolation and distress for the camels and their drivers. Hot stony

ridges cut and burnt the feet of animals accustomed to the soft sand of the Sudan plains.

The years of mechanization in the S.D.F. had inevitably affected the old skills of animal management, and the relative mortality of the separate camel trains reflected the knowledge and care of the convoy leaders. The wise leader would move whenever possible at night, but if need be would press on till he found grazing in some green *khor*, untouched by the blistering grass fires. He would hold his camels six to eight hours on such grazing at all costs, for they are slow and choosy feeders and need bulk for their seven stomachs.

Too often, on poor grazing, exhausted by travelling in the heat of the day and by the appalling terrain, the camels died. Uncomplainingly they fell in mid-stride, unable to breast one more ascent; in minutes, the eyes glazed and with a pitiful gurgle the animal was dead. By the end of the campaign, every 200 yards from the Sudan border to the Ethiopian Escarpment was marked by a group of corpses, and men vomited as they marched from the reeking, cloying smell. Enough camels survived to make the Frontier Battalion's operations possible, but the cold of the high plateau finished them off in time.

On his journey to Belaya Mountain, the Emperor counted fifty-seven dead and dying animals in one day. He came to one isolated corpse and very truly observed, 'He died for Ethiopia.' The expedition owed its very existence to these patient, long-suffering, unlovable creatures which smell horribly and show no response to the care of their Sudanese drivers; whose delicate system is upset by heat and cold and wet, and whose grazing needs as careful attention as a horse's feed. Out of the vast throng of 18,000 camels assembled at Roseires and Umm Iddla for the campaign, some 15,000 perished.

Our first move across the frontier, in November 1940, was made by Peter Acland's company of Western Sudanese from Darfur; their task was to take in a supply of arms and ammunition for the patriots in the Gojjam Highlands, and to blaze a trail for the main force across the Shankalla wilderness to Belaya Mountain, the area chosen on Sandford's advice for the Emperor to rally his countrymen. Wingate was acting at this stage as the Kaid's staff officer for the Gojjam operation, and at the same time organizing the Ethiopian Refugees Battalion and the Operational Centres – groups of Ethiopians, with British and Australian officers in most cases, and British N.C.O.s, whose task was to contact the patriot chiefs and encourage them to move against the Italians. He had been flown over the Belaya Mountain to spend a few hours at Sandford's headquarters;

and Peter Acland and I followed his example. Belaya is a huge mountain massif towering above the plain which lies between the frontier and the precipitous Escarpment of the great Abyssinian plateau. It was an obvious choice for a main base from which we could probe forward to find a route up the Escarpment.

The wrinkled grey cliffs looked very unpromising; and quite clearly it would be a real problem to find a landing ground near the mountain because of the thick bush and bamboo forest of the plain, and the great ribs which radiated from the mountain mass. But it was clear that the least difficult route for camels would be to the south of the mountain.

On the last day in November a long column of 180 men and 30 horses filed out from the cover of the green shelter of Roseires into the open desert. We watched them disappearing into the gathering dusk. An envious crowd of young friends from other companies lined the routes with shouts of *Maak Saleen, Inshallah nashufkum gudam, Shid a heilkumtaib, El hamdallilah wallahi, Dughum samme* – 'Peace be with you; Pray God we may meet ahead. Buck up. Health to you. Praise be to God. By God you must hit them a crack.' Partings and greetings in Arabia and the Sudan are protracted affairs with an infinite number of phrases and good wishes to draw on. Everybody shakes hands with everybody else at least three times, the left breast is touched with the right hand between hand shakes and the calls to God are unceasing. Pray God, in the name of God, praise be to God. Allah is the beginning, the end, the cause and the effect of greetings and partings, health, wealth, happiness, war and peace, misfortune and misery.

Acland's operation order directed him 'to pass through and hand over a convoy of arms, 1,000 rifles; ammunition 250,000 rounds, 70,000 Maria Theresa dollars to the report of Colonel Sandford. To occupy and establish a defensive position on Belaya Mountain plateau in co-operation with the Fitarauri Taffare Zelleke, Chief of Belaya, which would serve as a forward base for the passage of arms to the Escarpment and a centre for patrolling operations against the Italian forces. Thirdly to clear a landing ground 1,000 yards square to the east and north-east of Belaya.' There was at this time not a single spare wireless set in the country to give him, to communicate his information and requirements to headquarters.

Thirty days later Charles de Bunsen, the second in command, rode into Roseires with 160 camels of the returning convoy for further loads. The journey and setting up of the base had both been extremely tough. The rains were only lately finished and the uncut track was overgrown with thick thorn, scrub and high grass, impassable to loaded camels. For seventeen days of arduous toil, with cutting parties working half a day ahead, the Sudanese soldiers tore down the thorn and choking scrub that closed their passage. The African soldier's panga, half chopper, half knife, is admirably suited to this task. The thickness of the going made night marching practically impossible, and the steepness of the rocky gullies entailed hours of banking the approaches to them. Grazing had been good through the 180 miles of their passage. But the days of toil that followed, dragging loads of arms and ammunition to safety in a mountain fortress 5,000 feet above the plain, had been even more exhausting than the journey.

Fitarauri Taffare Zelleke, who met the company on their arrival, had made a great impression on the British officers. The local Gumuz (black tribesmen) gave little or no willing assistance. Acland's report was disturbing; there were no spare supplies in the Belaya villages on which the column were relying to purchase their food, and the men were carrying out these Herculean labours on meals of dead camel meat as practically their sole sustenance. Sandford had failed to obtain mules in any quantity, though Acland had managed to send him some 400 rifles in two small convoys of mules and donkeys. The prospects of finding a landing ground were discouraging. Finally Acland wrote that though the local tribesmen were naturally eager for firearms they showed no enthusiasm nor disposition for fighting. Only the arrival of regular forces would stimulate them to action.

Chapter Eleven

INVASION OF ETHIOPIA

The soldier, the king and the peasant
Are working together as one,
Till our dream shall become their present
And their work in the world be done.

G. K. CHESTERTON

AT Christmas Wingate appeared at Roseires to expound the operational plan. The Ethiopian Refugees Battalion was to escort the Emperor across the frontier, and to operate with the Frontier Battalion in the initial stages, while Operational Centres were to be infiltrated into various territories where the chiefs and people seemed likely to rise if encouraged. The Frontier Battalion was to consolidate Peter Acland's grip on the Belaya massif as a stronghold for the Emperor, and to prepare a landing ground for his arrival by air. Should this not be possible, he would get to Belaya by lorry, following an as yet unreconnoitred and untraversed route to the north of the mountain, which would have to be opened up by a company from the Battalion, accompanied by a camel convoy.

I had another look at the ground on 4th January, from an old Vincent plane. It was impossible to land on the mountain, and we found that an innocuous looking plain of white grass, which some staff officer had reported as eminently suitable for a landing ground, was in fact a huge bamboo forest with deep ravines beneath the canopy of leaves. The proposed northern route for the Emperor in his lorry and my company and its camels led across a tangle of ribs and escarpments running north-west from Belaya.

I flew next day to Khartoum to try to dissuade Wingate from the folly of his proposed route, and to urge him to follow the track that Acland's men had cut. On my previous visit to Khartoum, in December, I had first met the Emperor Haile Selassie. He was seated in a brocaded chair in the verandah of the Pink Palace, and obviously feeling the heat, his small Imperial head hidden by a huge service sun helmet which ill became him. He greeted Wingate and me with a charming smile, but was clearly fretting at the hot months of waiting to return to his own country. I knew the urgent need to restore him to his throne; Anthony Eden, the Foreign Secretary, had visited Khartoum, and Churchill was reported to be taking a personal interest in the shaping of the patriot campaign. All the more need, I felt, to start on the right foot.

I arrived at the Grand Hotel in Khartoum in the early afternoon. Wingate was in his room, and sent down asking me to come up. He was lying in a cold bath reading *Pride and Prejudice*, a suitable title, I felt afterwards, for the conversation that ensued. I had known Wingate at intervals since he was a subaltern and a junior Bimbashi in the Eastern Arab Corps in 1929, and had once attended some large-scale tank manœuvres with him in 1930 on Salisbury Plain, when his car ran out of petrol and we were stranded for some hours on an open down with 'nothing coming our way'. His strategic conception for the type of operation that lay ahead was arresting and brilliant. But his tactics were not at that time practical, taking into account the topography and means of supply. His previous experience of commanding troops was limited to the command of a battery, of a company of the Eastern Arab Corps, and of small groups of Jews in the Jewish–Arab operation in Palestine in the thirties. In these latter operations he had distinguished himself. Our relationship during the coming campaign was rendered more difficult from my own point of view by his acute lack of experience at this stage of his soldiering in dealing with anything but small bodies of men to whom he could give personal commands. This inevitably led to his interfering in the chain and details of command, which I would not stand for, and over which we had various violent altercations, since my own position in command of my battalion would have been insupportable if I had accepted his attitude.

However, it was clear to me that Wingate, who was still staff officer to the Kaid for the coming operations, was going all out to bring the Frontier Battalion into battle, and this conception dominated all else in my mind. I differed fundamentally with him over the route he had chosen for the Emperor and the camel convoys, and told him so. We argued for several hours. A further point of contention was the landing ground at Belaya, which Wingate said in an airy way could be constructed easily and quickly on the north-east of the mountain. I told him frankly that if this was his view, he was signally ignorant of mountain topography.

However, Anonymous, as the Emperor's move was called, was firmly fixed in Wingate's mind and the Affidavit, as the Emperor was referred to in this top secret document, was due to land by air at Umm Iddla a week later with a bevy of war correspondents in attendance. He would not budge, and only his own arrival at Belaya in late January on a jaded horse, without the Emperor, finally convinced him of the folly of his northern route which more than doubled the mortality of the camel convoys.

'The most important of a General's qualities is what the French call "le sens du practicable", and we call common sense, knowledge of what is, and what is not, possible. It must be based on a really sound knowledge of the mechanism of war – topography, movement and supply. These are the real foundations of military knowledge, not strategy and tactics as most people think.' I quote from *Generals and Generalship* by Field Marshal Lord Wavell.

For the men and officers of the Frontier Battalion, the journey to Belaya was a confused blur of camels marching all night through a forest of fantastic shapes. Uncontrollable fits of sleepiness came over them night and morning. In the drowsy darkness the branches of the thick tree scrub looked like camel heads, and boulders looked like camel loads lying beside the track, or like fallen bodies, till the mind started into wakefulness for a moment, when the overpowering drowsiness would again cloud the senses. Continually from the company commander would come the question *Kulle tamam wara?* (Is all well behind?), passed in endless repetition down the column, one and a half miles long. Back would roll the answer, *Wara tamam – wara tamam* (All is well), sounding like the mouthings of ghosts staggering through the stony darkness. More frequently over these steep khors and stony ridges the reply would come back, *Wara mush tamam. Gamel fil khor* (All is not well, a camel has fallen into the gully), and the drowsed company commander would ride back down the column to sort out the trouble. And so through the long dragging hours of darkness or indeterminate moonlight.

At intervals a short halt would be made to allow the tail to close up on the column. The soldiers would sit down in their tracks and rock off into complete oblivion. As the order was given to advance, frequently an unconscious soldier would be left asleep on the stones with half a column behind him, and an accompanying trail of anxiety for the anxious company commander when it was discovered. The early hours of the morning were the most agonizing time of this weary march across the wilderness, but it was during these hours of darkness that the camels went their best, striding through the black night in the moonlit forest with their silent tread, their saddles creaking with each step, with every now and again a complaining roar as some unfortunate animal stubbed his toe on a rock or caught his load in the overhanging branches.

With the dawn, after a short halt to look at the loads, the men would start broad awake and the company commander's *Kaifa-halkum* (How are you?) would meet the usual smiling face, and the laughing reply, *Wallahi shedid, taibin genabak, mafish taab el ham-dallilah* (By God we are fit and strong, your Honour, there is no fatigue. Praise be to God).

The journey took the companies and camel convoys about ten

or fourteen days: setting out after them on horseback, I reached
Belaya in seventy-two hours of day and night riding, stopping only
to bait the animals. My two Darfur ponies were undistressed and
might have come fresh from a normal morning ride. My civilian
Sudanese sais, Ahmed, who had been with me six years, accompanied me throughout the campaign and tended the horses as if
they were his own family. I had bought Strombol, a stocky roan,
and Sheikh, a large chestnut, at a horse fair in Darfur. Both were
useful polo ponies, but Strombol was Ahmed's favourite. If for
any reason he was off his feed, Ahmed would weep and would
spend the night tending him. The ardours of the campaign were too
much for Strombol. The day and night marches and the flies wore
him down, and eventually serat fly bite finished him and he died in
Debra Marcos. It was many days before Ahmed recovered his
spirits. He still speaks tenderly of those good ponies. Sheikh reached
Addis Ababa and was absorbed into the ranks of His Imperial
Majesty's Army as an officer's charger.

Our destination was a great horseshoe valley on the north-east
flank of Belaya. It was some thirty miles from Dangila, on the
plateau, where Colonel Torelli commanded two brigades of Italians,
with some artillery. From the air the valley had looked a suitable
base. The Birgi River flowed across the entrance, bubbling over
rocks and pebbles; the forested ridges on either side ran up to the
broad summit, 5,000 feet above the plain. Within the mountain
wall, the highland scenery was inspiring in the morning sun – green
grasses, streams, shady trees and ferns. Here Peter Acland welcomed
us; all the lads in his company came running up to shake hands
with us in the delightful manner of the Sudanese. *Salaam a leikum,
Keifel hal min el taab, el hamdallilah, wa allah yabarik fik* – Peace be
to you, how are you after the fatigue, praise to God, God bless
you.

The tasks in hand were immediate and pressing, and after lunching
with Peter Acland I rode down to where, after days of reconnaissance, he had chosen a possible site for the landing ground, six miles
away. After seventeen days' trek through the Shankalla, and the
hauling of hundreds of rifles up to this 5,000 foot mountain, the
task of clearing the strip entailed very heavy work, and Jarvis's
men of No. 3 Company took it over. Jarvis had only just arrived
by the northern route which had proved a death trap indeed for his
unfortunate camels, and wearying and tiresome to the soldiers. I
wondered wistfully how Wingate and the Emperor would fare.
Jarvis with a trained company of camel masters from the camel
column in Kordofan had lost forty-seven camels in a single journey,
with broken necks and broken legs where they had fallen over the

Two young 'Green Hats'

11. Zalingei

With Margery Perham in the Marra Mountains

A meeting of chiefs

12. Zalingei

In the Meidob Hills

cliffs and ravines, or dead from sheer exhaustion. The Operational
Centre which accompanied them had fared worse. This Centre was
commanded by Brown, an Australian, with four tough Australian
sergeants; they were to be our constant companions, and their
mortars formed our only artillery.

I had to see for myself what our mountain base consisted of, and
so spent two days reconnoitring Belaya. The plateau on top was
parkland and open country, rich in tumbling streams. At the village
of Gedami we met the Fitarauri Taffare Zelleke. Round faced and
smiling, with a quick intelligence and energetic manner, he was
charming. He had remained hostile to the Italians since the conquest, but his isolated position had saved him from their reprisals.
His brothers had been collaborators for years, and formed part of
the banda at Tumha, on the edge of the great Escarpment, guarding
the approaches to the Italian base at Dangila.

Next day the Fitarauri came with us, as we pushed north at dawn.
About noon I found what I had been looking for – an easily defen-
sible position in case the Italians were to besiege us and the Emperor.
The plateau was split by a deep chasm, bridged by a narrow neck
of land which a couple of machine gun sections could hold against
an army. My satisfaction was interrupted by the zoom of a Caproni
bomber; we slipped away among some broken rocks while it circled
round. A thunderous roar from the direction of Gedami signalled its
departure, and meant, we learnt later, the destruction of the
Fitarauri's grain store. He was stoically calm; he was lucky not
to be in the house, he said, and anyhow the days of the Italians were
numbered.

The activity had been noticed, and Capronis now began to
bomb Belaya regularly. They could see nothing in the horseshoe
valley, owing to the cover, but the smoke of patriot camp fires
attracted them to the landing ground. We promptly built a decoy
camp, with grass huts and camp fires. It proved a sure draw to the
raiders, who never dropped a bomb in the valley, even when it
concealed 3,000 men, hosts of mules and horses and, above all, His
Imperial Majesty. I was very struck by the reaction of the Sudanese
to bombing, which we had often discussed in the past, wondering
whether modern weapons would worry them. Not a bit of it; the
pleasures of being allowed to shoot at the planes (under strict orders)
outweighed anything else. One great day, a large chunk fell off a
Caproni after a burst from a Lewis gun; the bomber made off,
smoking, as the soldiers raced for the fragment. *Wallahi yom tamaan!
Darabna samme, shuft el duchan?* (By God, it was a good day. Hit
it fine, did you see the smoke?) The lucky gunner was the envy of all.

Sandford now arrived in camp, and reported some favourable

K

progress. Some villages of collaborating banda had been attacked
and burnt, and some of the disaffected chiefs, including the Fitarauri's brother, had begun to hedge their bets and declare their
loyalty to the Emperor. Above all, highly exaggerated accounts of
large regular forces at Belaya were unsettling the Italians. On the
last day of January 1941 Wingate rode into the valley, bearded,
dishevelled, filthy and worn, on a drooping horse. The party had
been on the way for a fortnight, and the route had been indescribable; he had left the Emperor ditched in a ravine, sitting dejectedly
among some dead camels beside the overturned remains of the last
lorry.

Wingate, Sandford and I discussed the next move. It would be
a week before the Emperor could reach Belaya on horseback, and
could there start to receive the allegiance of his chiefs. In the
meantime, Torelli's forces, nearly 10,000 men, in the Dangila area
were a threat which had to be countered by vigorous patrolling to
keep him on the defensive. Beyond that step, we had to try and reach
the Escarpment with a fully equipped force, which meant finding
a gap in it which camels could climb. Time pressed, for in Eritrea,
to the north, the invasion by the 4th and 5th Indian Divisions had
begun.

I sent Bill Harris with a patrol to reconnoitre the Tumha lip of
the Escarpment, Johnson sent Omar Effendi, a young Sudanese
officer of his company, to find a southern route, while I set off
with Peter Acland and a platoon to examine the northern route; I
was armed with a letter from Sandford to Ayelu Makonnen, the
local magnate.

We had ridden half the night, and after two hours' sleep pushed
on at sunrise through a maze of forested hills rising up to the escarpment some two miles ahead. Suddenly below the escarpment we
heard a few shots, followed by a regular crackle of musketry and
M.G. fire, not far to the south in the direction of Tumha. Presently
there was the crunch of bursting mortar bombs. We wondered
whether Torelli and Harris had met at Tumha.

The track rose steeply through a thick dark forest, then started
to zig-zag along the slope. As we reached the crest we emerged
suddenly into bright daylight. The ground fell away from our feet
to the east in rolling fields of close grass, cropped by fat cattle. There
were scattered copses of cyprus and eucalyptus, wild flowers grew
in profusion amid gorse, bracken and broad-leaved trees. A grass
banked stream wound into the valley below us. The air sparkled
like wine, and a European light flooded the scene instead of the
harsh light of Africa. Spiked trees, thorns and rank grass, rotten
soil and rock were left in the warm plain below us, and we breathed

the thin air of the rolling uplands in a new, fresh and sparkling world.

The Sudanese soldiers were a study. *Ya salaam, shuft el bahaim, el samin dol* (Good gracious, did you ever see such fat cattle!). Peter's Baggara herdsmen were thunderstruck; cattlemen from the thorn scrub and wadis of Southern Darfur, their hearts went out to such fine beasts and rich pastures.

It was a Wiltshire scene of rolling grassy downs and arable lands. The soldiers were full of questions. We told them it was like England. *Wallahi balad tamam* (By God, what a country), *Fi daiman moya?* (Is there always water?). This to a Sudanese from the western plains is almost unbelievable.

We camped by a stream, and sent word to Ayelu Makonnen at Amsiti Ambo, while we reassessed the route up from the plain. Camels could make it, but it would be a heavy haul and the loads would have to be dragged up by the men.

Fitarauri Ayelu arrived mounted on a fine mule and surrounded by his followers. An impressive figure of a man, solid-looking, less sharp featured than his people, with a grave, steady, composed face, he had been with Sandford when he first came up. Their camp was in the middle of a thick clump of cyprus and eucalyptus trees which concealed the Amsiti church. Throughout northern Abyssinia these hilltop clumps denote the presence of a church, past or present. Amba Maryam, Amba Georgis, the same names are constantly repeated throughout. From one high point in the Debra Marcos region no less than twelve churches were visible.

We rode forward that same morning on a reconnaissance of Dangila. Riding through these straw-coloured downlands of wheat and tef, and stubble, and fine grass, we were surrounded by a throng of Ayelu's braves, all armed with rifles. Homespun jodhpurs and tunic, and a tob (shawl) thrown over the shoulders is the national dress. They go barefoot; plunging through the streams, and running swiftly up the hillsides, these small-boned, thin-faced people, with huge black mops of hair, impressed us with their astounding and tireless lightfooted energy. Their movements were quick, and their bodies were as spare as their features, due no doubt to the thin air of the uplands and their sparse diet and hard life. On either side of the Fitarauri strode two young lads each carrying an Italian machine gun. These captured weapons had long been out of action for want of spares and proper attention but made a brave display. This mediaeval procession seemed out of a past world; so rode Henry to Agincourt with his men-at-arms.

It was already high noon when we looked down from the commanding ridge over the pale fields of stubble on to the Dangila forts, about 6,000 yards away. The scattered rows of huts, tents and horse lines were clearly visible; in the north-east rose tiers of mountains, range on purple range, set in a framework of drifting cloud.

I had been looking doubtfully at our many followers and then at the sky when, as if reading my thoughts, Ayelu said through his interpreter, 'They rarely use air action against us, as they never quite know who are friendlies till afterwards.'

We lunched behind a screen of tobs in Ayelu's headquarters with the chief's own bodyguard standing round and shielding us from view to keep off the evil eye, while his cup bearers filled our glasses with tej or honey wine. The meal, as usual, was of tef cakes with red pepper, and tej to drink.

Ayelu Makonnen was very keen to operate against the garrison at Sankirkana, one of the outlying forts, and optimistic of the results of an attack on the banda brigade stationed there; so we rode north the same afternoon by a track running across the eastern shoulder of Zibisit mountain, where a few months back Sandford had narrowly escaped being captured with his whole mission.

The force of patriots had swelled on our way north. The solid black core of Sudanese troops was set in a horde of running, skipping figures in white homespun. From a high upland on the slopes of Zibisit, we viewed the Sankirkana fort and its approaches, but could see no movement. We were clearly visible and wondered what the Banda Brigade were thinking of this great white army with its black core. We knew that the arrival of the Sudanese troops with British officers would be noised abroad, greatly exaggerated.

I returned with my party to Dir Ambo, where I met Bill Harris. He reported a brisk encounter with hostile banda – the firing we had heard – but a friendly reception from the villagers round Tumha; the only complication was that one patriot chief had been cattle raiding at the expense of another, and the national cause was quite eclipsed by the local feud. It was like trouble between the clans in the Forty Five. It was clear that the Tumha route to the Escarpment was not possible, so I pressed on with work on the northern route.

At this point Wilfred Thesiger turned up from Sandford with important news: Torelli had been so alarmed by the apparent concentration against him that he had started to withdraw part of his forces to the north, into the friendly country of the pro-Italian chief Gizzar. Thesiger played a notable part in the campaign. His father had been Minister to the Emperor, and a great personal friend, and Wilfred had been brought up with the Crown Prince. He had made as a young man an arduous exploration through the dangerous Danakil country, and was enthusiastic in his affection for Ethiopia and its people. He had joined the Sudan Political, and as a D.C. in Darfur had found plenty of scope for his love of the wild, camel trekking with the nomads or lion hunting on horse back, armed with a spear, with the Beni Hussein.

He had come straight from Sandford at Sakalla, after living on the country for two months; he could not understand why people travelled with rations. He took a bathe in the icy water of the stream, and then with enormous appetite demolished the last of Bill Harris's stores while we watched with amusement and sympathy for Bill. It was a memorable meal for Wilfred, and in later years he would be reminded of it by his hosts: 'It's no good offering you anything, is it, Wilfred? You live on the country,' while the marmalade pot would be ostentatiously hidden.

The news was good: Jarvis and his whole company were now up on the Escarpment and in a position to harry the retreating Italians: and I hurried back to Belaya to get the main force moving.

At Belaya I found that Wingate had at last succeeded in bringing up the exhausted Emperor and the Ethiopian battalion, which had lost most of its camels on the disastrous northern route.

All day the Emperor sat under the trees in the horseshoe valley, receiving the patriots who came in ever-growing numbers to pay homage and swear allegiance. Their chiefs led them in parties into his presence. As they approached, they dropped in obeisance on one knee, head bowed to the earth, and then sprang up with a wild cry in the strange and ancient bragging custom. Their voices were normally harsh and grating, but now rose to a metallic scream as they boasted of their skill at arms and the numbers of Italians they had killed in battle. The Birgi River tumbled heedlessly over the rocks as the Emperor listened in still dignity, his pale, serious face lit occasionally by a charming smile. As the lines of tribesmen knelt to him, my mind was filled with visions of Loch Shiel and Glenfinnan in the Forty Five.

At tea in his tent in the evening, the Emperor spoke French, easily and with humour, a quick smile lighting up his face, as he recalled old days in Addis, or his exile in Bath, or the frustrations of waiting in the Pink Palace in Khartoum to return to his own land.

Wingate had borrowed my tent, where he had seized avidly one of my books, *The Nazarene*, a remarkable life of Christ. He was an ardent Zionist, and his experiences as a subaltern commanding bands of Jewish youths in the Palestine troubles had fired him with the qualities and genius of the race. He had learned Hebrew fluently, and in this tongue would chant to us the psalms, in the high-pitched nasal monotone which passes for singing in the East. I swopped *The Nazarene* for a repeating pistol of formidable size, with which I was later tempted more than once to spray Wingate in his really exasperating moods.

Almost immediately after my return to Belaya, young Omar Effendi of Johnson's company turned up with vital news from his patrol in the south. He had been able to take loaded camels up the Escarpment, and had found that the supposedly pro-Italian Matakal district was in fact awaiting a sign from the Emperor to rise. Wingate, Sandford and I immediately re-cast the whole emphasis of the campaign; the harrying of Torelli's force in the north became a secondary operation, since Matakal could be used as a forward supply base on the Escarpment. From it we could attack and isolate the main Italian force under General Nasi in the forts of Burye, Dembecha and Debra Marcos, a force of 20,000 men. Apart from splitting Nasi's and Torelli's forces, the operation would have the enormous advantage of pinning down Italian forces which might otherwise be released for the defence of Eritrea. There, the British offensive had been held up at the immensely strong position of Keren, and it was imperative to prevent reinforcements being sent from Abyssinia.

Jarvis's company was to remain up on the Escarpment to the north (it was two months before I saw him again), and Harris and Johnson, with a month's rations, moved out from Belaya to clear the route up the Escarpment for camels, reconnoitre a base at Matakal and prepare it for defence. The main force was to follow, to thrust forward at Nasi's positions in the Burye–Debra Marcos area. Fortunately Jock Maxwell had settled the whole base organization of the Frontier Battalion's supply base at Roseires, and was now able to start on the arduous task of arranging the forward move to Matakal of the mass of supplies and ammunition which the camel convoys had brought to Belaya. Only his remarkable ability and foresight kept us supplied, until at last he could hand over the burden and join me in the field at Debra Marcos. I was always torn between the desire to have so experienced an officer with me and the fear of failure in our slender line of communication.

Our plan for a bold thrust forward depended on active help from the patriots; and yet as allies they raised as many problems as they solved. In the Gojjam their quality was hardly representative of the best of the patriot forces in other areas, but this was because their spirit was dimmed by four years of fighting against foreign oppression. They were no longer disposed to take any serious risk of death in a cause for which so many of their comrades had already fallen without result. The rivalry of the feudal chieftains meant constant mistrust; the arrogant independence which stiffened them against the Italians made them suspicious of all foreigners, and especially the Sudanese who had been their enemies since the Emperor John had defeated the Mahdi's invasion at Kassala. They would ignore any opportunity to destroy the Italians if there was a chance of loot; the information they brought in was so vague as to be often positively misleading; and it was almost impossible to tell patriots from the pro-Italian banda.

It may be asked, then, what part they could play, and why we equipped them with such quantities of scarce British weapons, which they would either not use at all or only fire at extreme range? First of all, of course, Ethiopia was their country and they had to be given a full share of the task of liberating it and restoring their Emperor. They played an invaluable part in protecting and helping the early missions, and they denied information to the enemy. Their existence and their arms prevented the enemy from patrolling for reconnaissance; indeed, from Dangila Colonel Torelli would promenade the Gojjam with never less than a brigade column, with clouds of irregulars on the flanks. Their presence confirmed the Italians in their siege mentality, and kept immobile in the various garrisons large forces of foot, cavalry and guns. Above all, the threat of being cut off in a completely hostile country made the Italians unduly nervous about their line of retreat. The object of our campaign was to exploit this fear.

The Escarpment rose steeply, but the road had been graded by the leading companies; at the foot Johnson had left a notice board, 'This way to the promised land.' It was already high noon and I had been riding since morning through the thorn bush and stony ridges of the plain. There was a delay while we sorted out the loads; the camels could not take this with full loads, and it meant heavy going for the men. At the top the same sense of exultation filled me as at Amsiti Ambo, when we first caught sight of the rolling downlands, the short cropped grassy turf, a woodland valley lying between the great downs, smelt the fresh mountain air and saw once more the pale northern light.

The companies had off-loaded all spare kit in this, the Matakal valley, which was to form the forward base. The Ethiopian Battalion, leading some hours ahead of the others, had pushed on to a rendezvous south of Engibara.

We had covered fifty miles since the previous evening and the animals were too tired to push on that night.

A cold grey mist was rising in the valley as we moved out at daybreak with a small party on horseback to meet Wingate in the

Achefar area forty miles east. The track led by villages and solitary farms, across downlands, through flowering woods, copses, fields of tef-barley, crossing a number of running streams and two large flooded rivers. A smiling and gracious countryside, this downland of Damot.

Long shadows were already slanting across the downs when we sighted the main Engibara–Burye road crossing a brown valley below us. Suddenly the sound of firing disturbed the wide plain, and we could see herds of cattle streaming south amid columns of dust. We halted in a hollow. Presently the Emperor's guide returned, agitated and talking at great speed. Only yesterday General Nasi had sent a column up from Burye to escort the Engibara garrison of two battalions to the shelter of the Burye forts, thirty miles south; and Mamu's irregular banda cavalry had been herding all the peasants' cattle for miles around to feed the Burye garrison.

Mamu, the son-in-law of the great Ras Hailu of Taklahaimot, now the restored feudal King of Gojjam, shared with his father-in-law the unusual distinction of being treated with respect and as a European by the Italians. He was popular in the Gojjam Province and commanded a big force of irregular cavalry.

At Engibara, next afternoon, the Frontier Battalion joined Boyle's Ethiopian Battalion. All the signs of a hurried evacuation showed in the looted shops and buildings, with their contents strewn about the streets and lanes of the village – macaroni, tins of sardines, giant tins of tunny fish, tinned fruits, books and clothes, films and sugar.

An enemy plane came over in the late evening with red-cross markings, circling the town very low down. Fortunately the camels were well under cover in eucalyptus groves outside the town area; but it was a warning of how exposed we were to air reconnaissance. In bright sunlight the next morning, an experiment in camouflaging the white camels was greeted with shouts of delight by the Sudanese soldiers, as they plastered the roaring and protesting animals with mud.

In the late afternoon, too late for the bombing planes from Burye, a column of horsemen leading 700 camels and 150 horses and mules started off down the main arterial road to Burye, thirty miles away. Protected by a vanguard platoon of Bill Harris's company with anti-tank rifles, Boyle's Ethiopian Refugee Battalion led this irregular procession into the fading twilight. Slowly the column stretched out to a length of four miles as the Ethiopians' camels, worn out after their journey to Belaya, continually blocked the passage of the rear companies.

Gideon Force, as we were called, was to move first on to the fort of Matakal, some six miles east of Burye on the arterial road. Wingate's object was to stand astride the main Italian lines of communication between Burye and Debra Marcos, and to harass and weaken the subsidiary forts that lined this auto-strada. His strategy, and the psychological concept of this move, was typically imaginative; and it was decisive in its effect on the mind of the Italian commander.

But the tactical execution of the first night marches and the day perambulations that succeeded them were 'the blunderings of a Military Ape', to use Wingate's favourite expression of that period about the high command set over him.

Wingate's concentration of his force at Engibara achieved its purpose of alarming the enemy with enormously exaggerated reports of its size: but to keep it concentrated ran counter to all he wanted to accomplish. We were a guerilla army whose set policy was to rely on movement, on night operations carried out by small, mobile parties. Only in this way could we maintain the air conceal-ment which would protect the force and ensure that its real size was not assessed by the enemy. On this policy both security and surprise depended, and surprise was our main offensive weapon.

But in the event Gideon Force moved down the Burye road with the Ethiopian Battalion leading, for political reasons, with no estimate of how far this four-mile camel column could march before daylight, with no plan for a day camp, no reconnaissance for cover from the air, or defence on the ground, over open downland where no near cover was available for a force of this size. Moving as a military force, suffering all the risks and disadvantages of the most unwieldy form of mass transport imaginable, we outraged every military principle. Chance led our going; chance found our night camp; chance covered our day move, and some tolerant Deity protected us. In retrospect those first days and nights remain the nightmare that they were at the time. They wore down men and animals at the beginning of a campaign characterized by its ardours and endurances. They aroused in me a fury at the military in-competence which would expose men to wanton and useless fatigue which would hinder rather than help the operations.

The blocks, halts and telescoping continued throughout the night. It was already past midnight when the force was held up by a blown bridge. Steep double banks led down to a rushing stream, bordered by a strip of fringing forest which appeared to afford cover. The ramping of this crossing and the slow process of leading 700 camels over singly in the black darkness was clearly impracticable.

The sorting of this inconceivable tangle of Ethiopian camels, who were by now distributed throughout the column, was a long and exasperating performance. It was bright daylight before the last lagging camels were in and the companies concealed in tiny groups, when the familiar hum of Caproni bombers rose and swelled in the morning air. They flew low over the tree-tops searching the flanks of the main road. They circled round for ten minutes while the whole force froze into stillness.

We had covered some fifteen miles from Engibara and were camped on the banks of the Zingini river fifteen miles north of Burye. That day no Italian patrol, no banda cavalry, no armoured car approached the expectant camp.

The sun was setting behind a bank of crimson cloud when the column wound up the open down south of the Zingini River. Wingate had conceived the idea of himself moving ahead of the column with a team of thirty Ethiopians, who were to light fires on the successive ridges, as beacons for the winding columns. In contrast to the flaming beacons, the intervening darkness loomed black as Egypt's night, filled with small gullies so steep that the camels slipped down them on all four legs, or stumbled and fell with their loads. The beacons led to an even greater confusion than the previous night's march; part of the column lost touch and wandered off. The Ethiopian soldiers left by Wingate to make the call sign by whistling were quite unable to make a sound through their pursed lips. They stood in frozen stupidity, making a sibilant hiss which would be heard five yards away with difficulty. The scene culminated in one enthusiastic fire tender spreading a grass fire that lit a huge area of downland on the hills north of Burye, effectively obliterating all beacon lights.

The column resorted to the more practical method of officers flashing torches back from the successive ridges with the call sign. After a wait of three hours, the lost party came in, while the fire burnt its way over the great downs, terrifying the camels.

The false dawn had come when we slid on all fours down a steep grassy cliff into a wooded ravine, and it was daylight before the unwieldy confusion was set in any sort of order. Now only five miles from the Burye garrison, we once more escaped the notice of the circling bombers and enemy patrols. But our position was precarious.

In the late afternoon I rode out with Wingate and two protective platoons for a reconnaissance of the Burye forts and the country to the east. Viewed from a hilltop above our camp, the circle of low hills on which the forts were set presented a formidable appearance. A large cone-shaped hill surmounted by a fort formed the main feature, dominating a circle of four satellite hills whose sloping open glacis offered no cover from fire. Wire defences could be seen around the lower forts, a circle of low stone walls set in grassy mounds marked the crest of the positions. They were each manned by a battalion.

It was already evening, and the low mists sweeping up over the plain, when Wingate decided that he wanted to attack the same night. It was obvious, however, that we were still a concentrated force, most vulnerable to enemy bombers and within easy striking range of the main enemy forts. If we lost our ill-protected transport, our fighting role would be crippled. In short, we were breaking every principle upon which we had agreed for the conduct of the campaign. Wingate finally agreed.

He detailed Boyle's Refugee Battalion the same night, in an independent role, to harass the enemy communications between Burye and Debra Marcos to the east. The Frontier Battalion would pursue its original course of moving by night to a point south of Matakal. There we would leave all our camel transport to harbour in forest land at a safe distance, while the two companies with only their mule and horse transport would operate in a mobile striking role.

Boyle left at midnight leaving a M.G. section with us under one of his company commanders, Captain Beard. But at daylight the Frontier Battalion plunged forward out of the cover of the forests, over the steep and broken hillsides, heading for the main artery of the enemy communications – the Burye–Dembecha–Debra Marcos road.

Wingate had ridden ahead with one platoon of the Frontier Battalion, ostensibly to do a reconnaissance of the route to Mankousa. In the meanwhile news came in of two Italian battalions scouring the countryside in the valley below us. I warned Wingate that the Sudanese soldiers, eager for battle, would almost inevitably become prematurely involved in broad daylight if he sent them on an independent reconnaissance of the enemy positions.

Painfully and slowly the battalion, hindered by led camels, crawled over the steep slopes north-east of Burye and very close to the main Burye–Debra Marcos motor road, down which a column of armoured cars might appear at any time. By one o'clock the animals were exhausted after seven hours' marching, so we camped for two hours where there was both cover and a field of fire.

Shortly afterwards heavy firing started to the south, and I guessed what had happened. This was presently confirmed by a note from Wingate urging the column to press on and join him, as the platoon under Shawish Tumbal which he had sent off to reconnoitre, had become involved in action with the Eastern Burye fortifications. A spate of urgent notes followed. This precipitate and rash act might have involved the destruction or capture of the whole of the camel transport. The daylight move was in itself against all our agreed principles, and the decision of the previous evening. Two more violent notes followed, urging extreme haste.

I went on with Bill Harris and a part of his company on foot leaving the slow winding column to follow under the command of Peter Acland. Bill's riverain Arabs, excited by the sound of firing walked like trains.

Just north of the Burye–Debra Marcos road, I found Wingate now in full realization of the implications of his action, agitated and apprehensive. One Sudanese soldier had been killed and several wounded.

Desultory firing was coming from the eastern forts, but the immediate risk was the sudden appearance of a motorized column from the main Burye garrison, three miles away up this metalled road onto which the camel column had been drawn in broad daylight.

Wingate was violently reproachful at the slow progress of the column behind him. In turn, I taxed him with having pointlessly precipitated a daylight action which might well jeopardize the whole success of the campaign. However, the rapidly failing light and the need for immediate action curtailed further exchanges.

There was no time to be wasted. Wingate now headed east with the camel column under Peter Acland's command. An anti-tank section led the column to prevent an ambush on the main road. In the meanwhile I put Bill into a demonstration attack on the eastern fort to keep the enemy's attention engaged.

Covering his forward move with the Ethiopian mortars, under Sergeant Body, our fire brought down a heavy response. Every machine gun and mortar in the fort let go at once, and the wood where the mortars were concealed was a mass of flying twigs and branches as bullets whined and ricochetted through the trees. The Sudanese grinned, undisturbed. This was a comforting reflection; the rending tear of the Italian mortar shells, the whining crack of the bullets, skidding off the bark of the trees, left these young soldiers quite undisturbed in this, their first baptism of fire.

Ahead of this small wood, Bill Harris worked forward in the cover of long grass. We badly needed the dusk; there could be no question of close action against this position in broad daylight, and once night fell our task was accomplished – to cover the withdrawal of the camel column. Presently a cloud of dust rose from the long grass ahead of Harris's position. I heard a sound of galloping hoofs, and the long drawn out 'Lu-Lu' of rushing horsemen in the heat of a cavalry charge. The next few minutes were critical. Bill Harris and Hassan Musaad, acting with great coolness and firing their Bren guns from the hip in the long grass, drove off the mounted men, only twenty yards from their front and flank. The enemy left both men and horses dead and wounded. I managed to get the mortar away in the nick of time, the reserve platoon saving the situation by being in position to cover its retirement.

A cheerful, light-skinned, good-looking riverain Arab of the Shaigieh tribe from the Northern Sudan, Hassan Musaad fought with distinction throughout this campaign. He and Shawish Mohammed Abdel Rahim, another Shaigieh, were the two outstanding natural leaders in their company. Hassan Musaad won the British D.C.M. before Debra Marcos, and Mohammed Abdel Rahim the Sudanese D.S.M. They were both inspiring, fearless and utterly reliable day or night.

I had sent Johnson with a platoon down to the main road the previous morning to try and ambush any Italian column, but he had seen nothing. It was already dusk when, marching to the sound of the guns, he appeared with his platoon. This diversion under cover of the failing light had clearly disturbed the Italian fort commander; the threat of a night attack would add to his anxious state of mind. So Johnson, in spite of three sleepless days and nights, was left to keep the Italians apprehensive throughout the hours of darkness by desultory bursts of Bren gun and rifle fire, from positions widely dispersed along their fronts, and then to withdraw before daylight.

Carrying our wounded on horseback, we marched down the road to join the camel column. Poor lads, they suffered in this campaign what is probably the greatest trial of guerilla warfare, the lack of any possibility of an evacuation to hospital or of rest. The uncomplaining fortitude of the Sudanese soldier under these conditions of pain and suffering, of improperly attended wounds, of a splintered shoulder or a shattered leg, agonizingly painful at every movement of the horse, aroused the lasting admiration of their British officers. We did what we could for them, but God knows it was little enough. Even in the worst pain they would reply, *Malesh Genabak, mafish tab al ragil istahamill el taab* (It is of no consequence, your honour, there is no pain, a man bears pain).

It was near midnight when I saw Wingate and the camel column coming towards us. They had marched down the road, overshot their distance and were about to off-load the column in the forest at the side of the road when the machine guns of Mankousa Fort opened up on them at point-blank range. There followed one more of those interminable night marches, this time through a forest of scrub and thorn, blackened by a recent fire. The camels rubbed their loads against the trees, the progress was slow and the blackness of the night impenetrable. We cracked our knees against the forest trees and scratched our legs and tore our clothes in the blackened thorn scrub. At intervals the column got separated by a man or an animal getting hung up in the thick trees, and unable to see the camel ahead of him. The flashing of torches saved the situation. To the west, all night long, we could hear the roar and rumble of the Italian guns in the Burye fort, and see their flares lighting the sky: Johnson was keeping up a successful deception.

Wingate had gone ahead to select a night camp. At 2 a.m. we came upon him. Heavy with fatigue, men and animals camped in the black darkness somewhere on the forest edge. Daylight revealed our fresh blunderings, this time it caught us lying in a shallow narrow valley by a village exposed to the full view of the eastern Burye forts. Swiftly, stupefied with sleep, we loaded and turned back into the soot-stained sheltering forest as the mist lifted. As we were moving, Johnson's stout lads came marching in, cheerful and delighted with the night's performance. They had drawn artillery, mortar, machine gun and rifle fire about their imperturbable heads. We had not at this time realized how illimitable were the stocks of small arms ammunition held in all these Italian forts. Johnson's men suffered no single casualty from the hundreds of thousands of rounds that swept the air above and around them.

Filing through the forest south of Mankousa Fort, we suddenly glimpsed its outlines through the trees some two thousand yards away. The swish of machine gun bullets ricochetting through the branches quickly diverted the long line to the south. At last we camped near a watered village which offered concealment and rest and grazing for the animals.

Now we put into effect the one essential move which would enable us to carry out the guerilla war we planned, unhampered by this mass of lumbering camels. Protected by a platoon from Johnson's company, the whole of the camel transport moved out with its armed drivers, under the command of Yuzbashi el Hag Effendi Musa, to form a camel camp in the thick forested ravines of Damot, some five miles south of the Mankousa forts.

Left with mobile horse and mule transport, and with five days' supplies, we obtained the freedom of movement which alone could render our operations effective or our force secure. The camel column was directed by runners, and supplies were brought up by pack horses and mules sent down to the column to bring them. We carried a minimum and lived light. The horses suffered most from the cut rations, and were a continual source of anxiety to us. Sometimes supplies were available in the villages, and we could buy with Maria Theresa dollars *injara* (Abyssinian pancake) for the men, and wheat for the horses. More often at this stage of constant and continual moves we went without.

It was on this day, the 1st March, we stumbled suddenly on Clifford Drew of the Sudan Medical Service, the doctor of Sandford's mission, camped with a posse of mules in the forest. His arrival at this time was singularly opportune; his skill and kindness and practical ability did much to relieve some of the intense pain and suffering of our wounded. Only a week later he carried out a major operation in a forest glade on Bill Harris, which saved his life, though it was a year before he properly recovered from his shattering wound.

Chapter Twelve

DEFEAT OF THE ITALIANS

In all the endless road you tread
There's nothing but the night.
A. E. HOUSMAN

WE took up a concealed position on Mankousa Church Hill, and for the next two days harassed the fort with mortar fire, successfully burning most of the buildings. The Italians' efforts to put out the fires gave us a fine opportunity to strafe them with the Vickers guns of the Ethiopian Battalion. There were a number of desertions as a direct result of this.

Late in the afternoon of the 3rd March we had reliable information that the Burye garrison were going to march out in force and withdraw a hundred miles east or so on to Debra Marcos. After discussions with Wingate we agreed that the Frontier Battalion should move to a covered position some five miles to the north overlooking Mankousa, leaving Wingate with three platoons in observation of the fort. He agreed to withdraw on to the main body immediately the move of the Burye garrison to Mankousa was confirmed. There could be no question of trying to fight the enemy in daylight, and the agreed policy of night attacks on their camps must be the only sane role for our force. I moved the battalion after dark; an hour after daylight, as Wingate had not appeared and all seemed quiet, I moved the force slowly towards Mankousa in order to get better observation. About 7.30 a.m. three Caproni bombers appeared and circled low, obviously looking for us. I refused all appeals to shoot at them and kept the force concealed whilst taking up a position to observe Mankousa. The ensuing half-hour was startling. The road westward in the direction of Burye was black with enemy troops, in all some 10,000, preceded by four light armoured cars. As I watched, with Bill Harris alongside me, a large detachment broke away from the main body and surged up the hill to Mankousa Fort. Mortar shells were falling thick and fast on Church Hill, which I sincerely hoped and prayed had been evacuated by Wingate and my platoons. Presently the relieving detachment was joined by the garrison and together they closed up on the main body. Bill wanted me to stir them up with long-range Bren gun fire, but this would have brought the Caproni bombers on us and quite probably the large force of cavalry which accompanied the column.

After some time Wingate appeared looking particularly scruffy and rather shaken, having been caught by the mortar fire on Church Hill. I was angry that the platoons with him should have been uselessly exposed in this way and said so. It was clear that the enemy force was now well on its way to an afternoon camp site, which proved to be some ten miles ahead. I set off at once with Acland acting as my staff officer, and with Harris's company in the lead. Johnson was instructed to collect stragglers and investigate the remains of Mankousa Fort and to follow me up as quickly as possible. Wingate had to get back to Burye to tie up the administrative arrangements.

Moving at speed along the road after the enemy, we caught up with them at three o'clock making camp on a hillside where they were proposing to spend the night. I turned the force off into a wood some thousand yards from the enemy and waited for dusk to fall. That night Hassan Musaad and Mohammed Abdel Rahim spent an exciting and rewarding evening shooting up the enemy groups around their camp fires, beautifully silhouetted in the flames. Pandemonium broke out in the camp, and their firing in response was incessant. In the early morning at about 4 a.m. I decided to put the force in a position round their rear from which we could harass them with fire as they moved out of camp. The subsequent three hours spent shooting up their daylight move were exciting in the extreme. We broke into two parties, Peter Acland and myself moving well beyond their position to where we could get some really good shooting on to their lorries as they drove out down the main road. Bill Harris with his force moved in close to the exit of their night camp and after a very successful shoot was again very nearly taken by their cavalry. He had to run for it with his troops. Eventually Peter Acland and I were outflanked by a party of tough Eritreans and they nearly caught us.

When the Italian column eventually got away they left their casualties strewn along the road. At about ten o'clock Johnson arrived from Mankousa with his company, and together we continued the pursuit, leaving Bill Harris and his company, who had had a very tough night, to rest and follow us. He eventually joined me about nightfall and I repeated the operations of the previous evening with Johnson's company, shooting up the enemy all night. The next morning at 4 a.m. I moved Harris on again after his night's rest to an abandoned Italian fort, Fort Jigga, which I had reconnoitred the previous afternoon; it afforded an unequalled view of the enemy withdrawal down the main road.

We had caught up with Bill Harris in the hills when we heard a violent rattle of musketry to the north. It swelled to a roar and was punctuated by the short sharp sound of mortars and the deeper rumble of exploding aircraft bombs. A major engagement was in progress and since we had caught up with Bill Harris, it could only be Boyle with his Ethiopian battalion who had been sent on an independent mission some days earlier. We marched towards the battle when the gunfire fell ominously silent and after another half-hour we came on the debris. It had been quite a chance affair. Boyle had been carrying out night operations against Dembecha Fort the previous evening and, having withdrawn, had camped for the night by the roadside, quite unaware that the enemy were marching headlong for Dembecha. Fortunately he had two Vickers guns commanding the road which did considerable execution among the closely packed ranks of the enemy mass. The enemy Eritrean infantry, acting with great gallantry, overran his position, killed all the camels and looted all the kit. The force itself had managed to slip away into the woods, with a company commander missing and thirteen killed and wounded. With no transport, the battalion would be temporarily useless for future operations. A gallant N.C.O. of Boyle's had wrecked two armoured cars with Boyle's rifle. The Eritrean dead were lying over the road and hillside.

We were all of us extremely tired and very hungry, having fed mainly on dry biscuits for the past three days. Pressing on through the woods towards Dembecha with Bill Harris's advance guard, we came on some seven-pound tins of strawberry jam and the four of us each had a mug full and gave the rest to the troops. However, we suffered from extreme thirst all that afternoon as a result.

I remember we were marching up hill through forests at the time and came over a rise to be greeted by a sudden burst of firing. After surveying the position it was clear that we had come up to Dembecha Fort and that the enemy were holding a ridge in force on our front. It was now late afternoon and I called up Bill Harris and told him to try and establish posts well up on the enemy right flank. Bill went off and established a position from which he could clearly see the enemy making camp in the fort. He stirred up the hive with Bren gun fire and was thoroughly enjoying the enemy movements and watching Johnson on his right who had joined in the fun, when he was bumped by an enemy outflanking party. Unfortunately in a rash moment he stood up while giving instructions to withdraw, and a machine gun bullet knocked him flat on his back. He was in excruciating agony and began to crawl back on his knees with his left arm dangling. After passing out for some minutes he was brought down to where I was standing. I sent Bill back to our medical orderly whilst we disposed ourselves with the remainder of the force for the night. Bill looked ghastly. He was as white as a ghost, streaming with blood and obviously in frightful pain and looked as if he might not last the night. He told me afterwards that I had told him to get back at once and 'stop making a bloody row'. He said it had had a miraculous effect on him. He was a great personal friend and with his quick tactical perception had been invaluable to me throughout the operation. He was later to command a parachute battalion on 'D' Day and his regiment, the Royal Fusiliers, after the war. With his skill and gallantry he richly earned the Military Cross which he was awarded for his campaign in Ethiopia. He was very lucky to have come out alive. If Clifford Drew had not been present that evening I do not think he could have survived.

We spent two nights probing for a position from which to harass and attack Dembecha Fort, but the enemy saved us the trouble by abandoning it and continuing their withdrawal to Debra Marcos, a provincial city of considerable importance protected by a complex of forts, with forward positions in what was known as the Gulit area. We came up with them here on 13th March, and camped in a wooded area while we reconnoitred.

Wingate and I had another disagreement here: I told him I wanted to operate against the enemy from the high ground to the north, and not from the low bush country south of the road, where the troops would be plagued with flies, and where he would get no observation by day for our operations by night. He disagreed: but when we rode forward to a copse on a high hill, with a fine view of Debra Marcos itself and the Gulit positions, the issue settled itself. We might well have been in the Perthshire Highlands, with moorland grassy slopes running down to a wooded river, and with the purple heights of the Chokey Mountains behind us to the north.

Active patrolling produced accurate information about the enemy positions, but the Italians did not wait passively for us and counter-attacked vigorously. As a result of all this, I was able to plan with Peter Acland the series of attacks which were to end in the fall of Debra Marcos on 3rd April, nearly a fortnight later.

That fortnight was, I suppose, one of the most strenuous and exacting I have ever experienced. It consisted of a series of night attacks carried out on enemy positions night after night, each from a different angle and on to a different fort, made with bomb and bayonet, combined with mortars when practicable. We would withdraw before daylight to rest for the day in the uplands, only to return to attack another fort. Each night attack was preceded by an afternoon reconnaissance which I made with the officers and the senior N.C.O.s of the company, from High Hill camp. We would move out at 3 p.m. or so and go down under cover to a position from which we could survey the glacis of the fort or earthwork which was the object of the night's attack. There I would point out the particular targets. We usually rode down with horse holders to hold the horses well out of sight. Then I sent back to bring up the force to a rendezvous under cover where they spent the early part of the night. They would be fed before they left and came down on foot quietly; no fires were allowed.

Each successive night attack was launched between midnight and 3 a.m. I myself would remain at a vantage point with Very pistols and give the signal for the withdrawal. In the meantime I would wait there with a small escort suffering gruelling anxiety as to what was happening. The Sudanese troops were instructed to attack and then when firing was opened to lie down and move on again as firing stopped. This required tremendous discipline and courage; it was so easy once lying down to remain like that. The orders were to assault the trenches up to the point of bayonet and bomb and then to withdraw. It was essential that the withdrawal should be carried out and the forces well cleared before daylight, when they could be caught by the enemy machine guns or ridden down on the open hillsides by enemy cavalry.

Nearly all these forts were equipped with long sweeping glacis in front of them. Lying in position I would see and hear the firing going on, a tremendous crackle which would last perhaps ten minutes, and I wondered how these chaps could live on the open slopes. But it was all high, being fired at night without sights, and then the Sudanese soldiers would move forward until the next burst opened. Later there would come a crash of the bombs and one or two shots from the trenches.

It was always an immense relief when the first parties appeared, but one's anxieties would be prolonged when men were delayed or if they had not all turned up. As they came in I would send them back to High Hill camp and then wait for each succeeding party. Frequently it would be nearly daylight when the last party emerged having been held up by over-enthusiasm or by a man wounded.

These incessant night attacks cost us some casualties, though very few in comparison with what daylight assaults would have involved. The sheer difficulty of moving across such broken country in the dark led to accidents; in one night, three soldiers went over a cliff and broke their necks. Peter Acland was wounded by a bomb, and in the hand-to-hand fighting other officers and men were hurt. The most grievous blow was Colin MacDonald's death on 31st

March, from an almost random shot fired at very close range by an enemy sentry. We buried him near our camp, in a countryside that looked like his own Highlands; we had no prayer book for the service, so I read the usual verses from Ecclesiastes and Julian Grenfell's *Into Battle*, before we fired volleys over his grave.

We had heard rumours through my interpreter and liaison officer, Lij Makonnen Desta, that the Italians were about to abandon the Gulit positions and fall back on Debra Marcos itself, and then that they were about to withdraw completely from the province, down to the Abbai River (the Blue Nile). Probing patrols were still met by heavy machine gun fire from Debra Marcos, though one of the outlying forts was abandoned. We continued our night attacks, reinforced by some vigorous patriots led by Ajaz Kabada; he had struck me as a leader of great determination and intelligence, and I had rubbed into him the need for his chaps to get really busy.

During these last evenings I was camped out on a high down, overlooking Debra Marcos, and it was with enormous satisfaction that I saw on the morning of 3rd April the Ethiopian flag flying from the Citadel. At the same time it was reported that Ras Hailu had taken over from the Italians (hence the flag) but that he intended to resist to the last with several thousand Colonial troops placed under his command. I dictated a letter to him which was translated by Lij Makonnen telling him to hand over the town and surrender. I sent this in with Peter Hayes of No. 1 Company. Ras Hailu received him under a white flag with a small escort of troops, and plied him with great quantities of tej, and sent back a somewhat vague answer. The same evening I sent him another letter telling him peremptorily that he must surrender or air and land action would be taken against him and the troops in the town of Debra Marcos. At the same time I pushed in patrols to occupy the Abima Fort and I moved forward to the Citadel with a few men. Ras Hailu met me at the gates, dressed in the uniform of an Italian General with three or four rows of ribbons. He was a tall commanding figure with a most aristocratic face and jet black hair despite his age, and with a most disarming smile. He took me in and his daughter served us with coffee and cakes. He asked me straightaway, 'Will you make me responsible for public security?' He appeared by now to have taken for granted that he would hand over, but added, 'I would wish to live inside the Citadel in a style consonant with my dignity and my position.' I replied, 'I am afraid you can't. It would not be permissible under these conditions. I will make you responsible for security and for stopping any looting.' He pressed again, but I would not give way; he finally agreed and said he would move out the same evening, and handed over the keys of the Citadel. Jock Maxwell spent the rest of the day with me setting guards on the hospital, stores, etc.

At that time I had only three platoons with which to ensure the surrender, whereas Ras Hailu had some several thousand Colonial troops. Looting started the same night and I woke the next morning to peer out of the window of the Citadel when shots were fired. I saw that our guards were already shooting looters from the walls; three looters had fallen by the side of the hospital while walking away with blankets and the soldiers who picked them out from the Citadel walls were looking very pleased with themselves. The remainder had fled and we suffered very little further trouble.

The next day the Dejazmatch Nagash arrived with a large retinue of some hundred patriots and asked to interview me. He was pompous and bombastic. He said, 'The Emperor has made me the Governor of Gojjam and instructed me to take over the Citadel and stores.' I replied, 'Well, you are a part of the Emperor's forces as a patriot leader and you will take your orders from the Commander of the British and Ethiopian Forces whom I am representing here at the present time. You can keep the Forts of Wanke, Delaga and Makud, but you can't come into the town until the Emperor has arrived.' He said, 'This is most shameful.' I said, 'It is an order.' Later two more patriot chiefs came in to see me. Again I had to stop their forces entering the town but made them personally responsible for the Abima and Enda Metta Forts, and I hopefully prayed that the Emperor would arrive as soon as possible as we appeared to be getting too politically involved for my liking.

In the meanwhile I received splendid news from Henry Johnson whom I had sent forward some days earlier with three platoons of No. 1 Company and a mortar section to intercept enemy columns withdrawing from Debra Marcos to the Abbai River crossing. With the skill that he showed throughout the campaign he had successfully ambushed twenty-eight enemy lorries escorted by two armoured cars on the main road fifteen miles east of Debra Marcos. The surprise was almost complete and only three lorries escaped. Ajaz Kabada had co-operated both courageously and intelligently and Henry Johnson, as instructed, had moved forward highly elated to ambush the Abbai crossing.

On 6th April the Emperor arrived at the Citadel. He was accompanied by Chapman Andrews, political representative from the Foreign Office (and later Ambassador in the Sudan, and now Sir Edwin Chapman Andrews) and Wingate. I had the troops on parade, the Ethiopian Battalion on the one side and the Frontier Battalion on the other. After hoisting the Ethiopian flag the Emperor made a speech congratulating the assembled troops. He looked a tinier figure than ever. Whilst he was standing below the flagstaff, Ras Hailu, dressed now in a superb white robe and with bared head, walked slowly between the lines of soldiers to the Emperor, his nephew. Before reaching him he prostrated himself three times full length on the ground, the third time at the Emperor's feet which he kissed.

The Emperor looked on the ground without a motion of acknowledgement as the old man moved into the background. The Emperor then withdrew and the troops dismissed. As soon as the Ethiopian Battalion had taken over I moved the Frontier Battalion out of Debra Marcos into the field with all speed to try and reorganize them and also to get them away from the chianti bottles strewn about the Citadel stores.

I now had a breathing space to visit Henry Johnson's company. On the morning of 7th April I set off to find out how successful Johnson had been and where he had got to. To my surprise I found him, not at the Abbai crossing, but in a village two miles west of the Fort of Usata which was in enemy hands and which commands the Blue Nile approaches. With him were Lieutenant Rowe of the Operational Centre and Wilfred Thesiger, who had been sent ahead by Wingate to co-operate with Bilai Zalika and to encourage him to attack the Italians crossing the river.

Johnson, looking extremely disturbed, asked to see me alone. He said, 'You sent me to cut off the Italians crossing the river gorge and I am afraid I have been badly let down. Wilfred Thesiger in all good faith was prevailed upon by Bilai Zalika to ask me to hold hard, as the Italians were still in forts where we could not attack them successfully with our small force. But he said that he would give us word as soon as they started to move out. Only now have I heard that most of their forces have got across.' Johnson was terribly upset. I said, 'Well, never mind, you have been let down by Wilfred Thesiger's belief in Bilai Zalika and his patriots. The only thing is for us to catch the rearguard in first light before they get across.' I was furious but felt it was no time to say any more.

I then saw Thesiger, who was deeply mortified by what had happened; he had put his faith utterly in Bilai Zalika who had fought with great skill and bravery for years against the Italians. We learnt afterwards that he had been bribed with some enormous sum to let the Italian forces through. Thesiger had a very worried expression and I was almost too furious to say much. I felt that Johnson on his own would have been so effective that I could almost have cried at the opportunity which had been missed.

We moved forward to the edge of the Abbai which presented

an astonishing spectacle, a huge deep gorge cut like a miniature Grand Canyon into the Abyssinian plateau, with extremely precipitous sides covered in bush and scrub down which a road had been cut. I could faintly see a somewhat frail-looking bridge across the river at the bottom. I pushed Johnson on at top speed with his chaps and followed down to see what I could of his action.

When I was about half-way down the escarpment I could see the enemy blowing up the road on the far side of the river, and as Johnson's forces were reaching the river bed the rearguard could be seen along the cliff overlooking the bridge. The trestles of the bridge had been burnt. Since it was clear that the enemy was covering the crossing in force and Johnson would merely suffer casualties uselessly, I sent down a runner with a note telling him to delay his crossing till nightfall and then put in a surprise attack. Firing from the Italians across the river continued all that day both by mortars and automatics. Johnson had his chaps well under cover and there was only one casualty. In the meanwhile the road behind us was untenable, being in full view of the enemy who were shelling it at intervals.

On 9th April at a quarter past three in the morning, the Force crossed the Abbai River by wading, carrying the kit and guns on their heads, since the river was too deep for loaded animals. On 21st May, forty-three days later, the Italian force asked for terms of surrender. In the intervening period Johnson with a small force of determined Sudanese had kept pressing on the enemy in wet and in fine weather, in daytime and at night, though he and his men were for periods short of rations, in torn clothing and with worn out sandals. Italian demoralization was completed when Thesiger moved round by forced marches with a cloud of patriots led by Ras Kassa and his son to attack them from the north at Debra Sina.

Wilfred Thesiger, who inspired the patriot moves across the river, had now by his actions repaired all the damage done by Bilai Zalika and contributed enormously by his personal leadership to the complete defeat of the Italian army. He was awarded a very well-deserved D.S.O. for this oustanding action with the patriots.

On 23rd May Johnson, with twenty-five men covered by three Bren guns, began to disarm the enemy. The white nationals in the Carabinieri were allowed to keep their arms as honours of war and for self-protection. The total bag was 1,100 whites, 7,000 Colonial troops, 200 native women and one white woman. And it rained all day. For Johnson's force the campaign was over.

Having seen Johnson safely across the Abbai, I returned to Debra Marcos and moved off the following day to visit Jarvis, still pinning down Torelli's force at Bahar Dar. This expedition took me a week over tremendously rough country. I found Jarvis's soldiers suffering badly from Jigga fleas which embed themselves between the nails and toes and are very painful. I found Brown a bit short of mortar ammunition which we ordered up with all speed. I said, 'It is essential to try and get Torelli out of this and to operate on him as we have been doing at Debra Marcos every night, and to attack bombs, rifle and bayonet.' Jarvis was clearly delighted at the prospect, and got going at once. Only a fortnight later after eleven night attacks had been carried out during which some six Italian officers and 268 other ranks were killed and wounded, including Torelli himself, the main enemy force was evacuated by dhow to Gondar.

I got back to Debra Marcos camp on 16th April to find that Jock Maxwell had re-equipped the whole force and everyone was ready and alert for the next operation. Bill Allen of the Life Guards, who was my Transport Officer, had arrived with the camel transport column and dined with me that night in camp. It was at the end of dinner, about midnight while we were exchanging some really good talk, that an emergency operation order came over from Wingate instructing the Frontier Battalion to move with all speed on to Mota Fort carrying the minimum weight. I set off at four o'clock on the afternoon of 18th April with two platoons of No. 1 Company. The main column followed under Jock Maxwell. The road north led over the Chaigul Pass, a 14,000-foot pass through the Chokey Mountains. As we went up and up the cold became intense and it was clear that the men from the Sudan plains were suffering from mountain sickness. A high wind rose and was followed by snow which then worked up into a blizzard. The men only had one blanket for covering and we spent a miserable night below the pass shivering with cold and suffering from the mountain sickness.

It was remarkable how quickly the soldiers began to recover when we crossed the pass and came down to a lower altitude and the clouds began to clear and the sun to break through. Allen brought the camel transport along with few casualties – a remarkable feat for animals brought up in the Sudan plains.

Everyone was in tremendous heart after the tough and successful trek through the mountains and it was a crashing blow to my plans and most perplexing suddenly to receive a signal from Wingate saying that Nos. 2 and 4 Companies would be withdrawn forthwith leaving only two platoons of No. 1 Company, Brown's Operational Centre, and the Mortar Platoon for operations. We all cursed heartily. This entailed increased hardships for the two companies who had only just arrived and recovered from their mountain sickness; the men were desperately disappointed at not being in on the attack on Mota.

The Fort was a strong one, and the commander refused to surrender when summoned. This time, I did not fancy a night attack with bomb and bayonet: instead, our platoon kept up harassing fire all night while the mortars were well dug in. All next day the mortars maintained a steady fire, despite enemy counter fire, and after most of the buildings within the perimeter had been set ablaze, the Italians had had enough and surrendered. All the Eritrean troops in the garrison and their N.C.O.s agreed to enlist in the Emperor's army, and the Italians, nineteen officers and W.O.s, marched back with us to captivity.

The capture of Mota Fort on 24th April was the scene of my last Ethiopian operation; in April the Eritrean campaign was closed by the capture of Massawa on the Red Sea, and in May official resistance in Ethiopia ended in the Duke of Aosta's capitulation at Amba Alagi.

On 1st June in Addis Ababa I was invited by the Emperor to dine with him in the little palace with all my officers to celebrate the successful campaign. He received us with his usual dignity and charm and we had a most enjoyable evening, made the more so by excellent champagne and the finest tej which I had yet drunk. The Emperor was extremely friendly. We talked of his time in England, of the original Italian campaign and of the difficulties and endurance of the past campaign.

After dinner he spoke for some time personally to Johnson, who had greatly distinguished himself during the whole campaign and had been awarded a D.S.O. and bar, immediate awards. On no previous occasion had I heard the Emperor speak in English to anyone and I always spoke to him in French. He both spoke and understood English but was shy of making mistakes. On this occasion he broke his rule and went out of his way to tell Johnson personally how much he appreciated his gallantry, since he knew that Johnson spoke no French. The dinner party left a very happy impression on all the officers. Subsequently the Emperor awarded me with the Abyssinian Order of St George for the conduct of the campaign. In January I was awarded the D.S.O. by His Majesty King George VI for the operations leading up to the capture of Debra Marcos.

In early June the Frontier Battalion left Ethiopia for Asmara en route to Khartoum. At Asmara General Platt saw the whole Battalion on an informal parade to thank them personally for their part in the successful campaign in East Africa. He told the officers and men that the Eritrean campaign itself could never have been carried out successfully without the knowledge that a vast body of Italian and Eritrean troops were being contained by the Frontier

Battalion attacks on the Gojjam forts, and said that he could not thank the men enough for what they had done and the hardships and dangers that they had undergone. He then went round the whole Battalion and shook hands with every man personally. This was enormously appreciated by the Sudanese soldiers who were now all sweating to get back to the Sudan to see their families after a very long break.

Jock Maxwell and I had jumped an Alfa Romeo in Addis and had driven it down through Adowa, the scene of Italy's first great defeat by King John of Abyssinia, and Adi Ugri to Asmara. We entrained the troops at Asmara and then drove on through Eritrea and across the Butana desert from Kassala to Khartoum to prepare for the reorganization of the Battalion. It was now mid-June, 1941.

Chapter Thirteen

RETURN TO DARFUR

Wide is the world, to rest or roam,
And early 'tis for turning home:
Plant your heel on earth and stand,
And let's forget our native land.

A. E. HOUSMAN

I PAID a visit to Cairo, and was sent for by General Arthur Smith, whom I had last seen when he introduced me to Wavell on the evening the Italians declared war. He wanted me to take command of a mechanized brigade of the Arab Legion, then form-ing. I spent a few weeks in Jordan, and although I decided that I preferred to stay with my Sudanese soldiers, the time was not wasted since it gave me an opportunity of meeting Glubb Pasha, the com-mander of the Arab Legion. This was invaluable to me ten years later when I found myself Resident Adviser in the Hadhramaut, and depended on Glubb's help in finding officers for the Hadhrami Bedouin Legion.

I had several other offers of appointments before the war was over. One was as liaison officer to Tito in Yugoslavia; since I should have been only an adviser I turned this down in favour of an active command, that of an Ethiopian Brigade to be trained in Cyrenaica for the projected landing in Sicily. But this fell through because the Emperor needed all his regular forces at home to suppress a serious rebellion which broke out in the Tigre province of Ethiopia.

The third occasion was in May 1944, when I was suddenly ordered to report to Cairo to take command, in conjunction with a Brigadier Zervas, of all Greek irregular forces. These consisted of two rival groups, Eoka and Elas, who had at last agreed to sink their differences and fight the Germans under one command. No sooner had I got to Cairo than the two sides quarrelled again and refused to co-operate: so to my intense disappointment the command was off.

Instead of soldiering in Yugoslavia or Jordan or Sicily or the Levant, I was kept fully occupied on security duties in Eritrea, commanding the Border Force which grew to a brigade group, with a regular Camel Company and a Mounted Infantry Company under command in addition to three battalions of the Sudan Defence Force, including my old Frontier Battalion. It was brigandage on a large scale which kept us so busy. It had always been more or less endemic along the border between Eritrea and the Sudan, among the Beni Amer, but was given an enormous stimulus by the huge quantities of arms and ammunition made available by the Italian surrender, and also by the reinforcement of numbers of well-trained Eritrean soldiers who had fought well for their Italian masters and had no intention of settling down to a pastoral life.

Here, as on the North West Frontier of India, nature has contributed to lawlessness by withholding from the tribesmen the means of leading a peaceful existence – if anything, the Frontier is a little more hospitable. Both areas consist of savage hills, whose only vegetation is thorn scrub; in the rains, the wadis that cut the hills are in spate, and for the rest of the year the only water for man or beast comes from holes dug in their dried up beds. The lack of any road system increases the isolation of the Eritrean hills. The frontier brigands had about 27,000 square miles to operate in, so they were hardly squeezed for elbow room; the terrain ranges from the Basso Piano by the Sudan border to the Northern Hills, rising between 4,000 and 7,000 feet above the plain.

Your brigand may be a professional or an amateur. The former is well armed and probably has relatives in the area on whom he can rely for food and a hide-out when the necessity arises. The amateurs were far smaller fry. They were found amongst the Beni Amer herdsmen who joined up with their more notorious brethren now and again to help in driving captured cattle back into the hills and in the disposal of the dead and wounded. For arms they probably carried nothing more lethal than a spear, and as a reward for their services received a few stolen cattle or camels.

In Eritrea, as in Ethiopia, a band of brigands is known as a 'shifta'. In the summer of 1942 it became evident that punitive measures would have to be taken against them, so a company of the Frontier Battalion was sent to Aicota on the main road between Tessenei and Barentu. There the men were mounted on camels, since infantry operating as such stood no chance against the fast-moving brigands mounted on camels. The company quickly made its presence felt; they were selected men who had served in the Camel Corps in the past.

The winter of 1942–43 was spent in training the Frontier Battalion on the plateau of Asmara and in limited operations against the shifta whose activities were now increasing. The scale of counter-operations had to be stepped up, and I shifted my base to Keren. Fortunately wireless sets were plentiful, with trained Sudanese operators, so the companies could be dispersed and given areas of mountain and desert country to patrol and secure.

The infantry battalions produced six camel columns with eighty riders up and twenty spare camels each for baggage and spares. These were perpetually on patrol in the company areas throughout the Eritrean Hills. In the bush country to the south between the Gash and Setit Rivers I organized similar mule columns as mounted infantry from the Sudan Service Mule Company. A mounted infantry company on horses from Darfur also covered this area. We tried a jeep column as well, but the north Eritrean country was too mountainous for it to be effective, and the bush too thick in the south, so its main work was done in the western plains.

Keren has a wonderful climate. It is some 6,000 feet up, catches the cool winds from the east, and its gardens are full of citrus, pomegranates, melons and grapes. The Italians are great gardeners and the Commandant's house was surrounded with flower beds tended by Italian prisoners of war.

Keren itself, which has attractive white buildings and fruit and grain farms lying to the north and west, is surrounded by a circle of great peaks to the west and south which were the objectives of the British forces in the Battle of Keren. Looking at these towering hills it seemed incredible that any force could have captured them from the east. During a visit to the battlefield I came on the grave of General Lorenzini; on it were his boots and spurs and his sword. I had last seen him at Sarra Well when I was with Bagnold in 1932. He was a fine soldier.

The shifta were led by men of considerable personality. They were cruel, daring and intelligent; they knew the country inside out, and they made sure of help from the local nomads and peasants by ruthless oppression. The operations against them developed a keen hunting spirit in the units. The outstanding master of hunting the shifta was Mulazim Musa, a Beni Amer Arab, late Bashawish of Johnson's company, who had earned a D.S.M. for great gallantry in Ethiopia. He was put on to chasing the principal brigand Ali Mumtaz, a late corporal of the Italian Army and a fellow tribesman of Musa's. He followed Ali Mumtaz's band relentlessly, on one occasion covering 330 miles of mountainous country in fifteen days whilst engaged in running fights with the shifta. One night he came on Ali Mumtaz and his personal escort in a wadi bed. He captured Ali's camel, his boots and his sword but Ali Mumtaz himself slipped off in the darkness and got away.

By the spring of 1945, the job was done and the shifta had been broken up. It would be too much to claim that all brigandage could ever be suppressed in that wild countryside, but no longer did large armed bands terrorize the people; the civil administration could cope, and the troops could go back to normal routine in the Sudan.

I took some leave in England, first going to Khartoum to stay en route with Douglas Newbold. I was sitting at the airport waiting for his car to pick me up when I heard a young R.A.F. officer say, 'What time is the funeral?' I asked him whose funeral he was talking about; he looked surprised and asked, 'Didn't you know, sir, that Sir Douglas Newbold died yesterday?' This was a grave shock to the whole Sudan, and a blow I felt very painfully; he had been my close friend in Kordofan when I commanded the Camel Corps, and ever since. He was much loved, and it was striking to see the great numbers of Sudanese who came to the service and to the cemetery.

In July 1945 I was on my way back. Soldiering was over, and the Sudan Government had been pressing for my early return to take over my old district at Zalingei.

Dudley Lampen, whom I had last met as Deputy Governor in Kassala Province, was now Governor of Darfur, and gave me a warm welcome when I arrived at El Fasher. We spent two days discussing future policy before I set off in a lorry for the Azum River and my district.

At the Azum I was met by a crowd of a hundred and fifty Fur chiefs and their followers. This was their pleasant custom: whenever in the past I had left Zalingei on leave, and again on my return, a band of horsemen would escort me to and from a certain wadi, about four hours' ride away. On this occasion it was a special welcome, and we rode along with singing and cheering and volleys of shots, the chiefs curvetting their horses. *Chefalhal, Inshallah Kheir, Murhabha, El Hamdalillah* (How are you? Pray God you are well, Welcome, Praise be to God). It was indeed a homecoming: all that week the welcome and the feasting continued.

During my absence at the war the district had been temporarily amalgamated with Southern Darfur, and had been held on a sort of caretaker basis under the Dimingawi with the British District Commissioner in Nyala, who was far too taken up with the huge Southern District to give much time to the West. The administration had been in cold storage during the interval. As soon as I had time to get the courts straight I turned my whole attention to the Green Hats – the chiefs' sons whose education I had started ten years ago, and who were now young men ready to be trained to hold their fathers' areas. I found this a stimulating task. They were a most promising lot of young lads, keen to learn and to help. With them I was able during the succeeding five years to set up sub-grade schools, to increase the dispensaries and improve village hygiene throughout the whole district, and to improve the road system.

The Fur when trained proved to be remarkable builders and were adept in putting up red brick pillars with beautiful rain-proof thatched roofs which lasted for years. In order to establish the dignity of the Courts, Beaton and I at an early stage worked out the best type of open court building where all could come and go, and all could see what was going on while at the same time they were sheltered from sun and rain. These were put up throughout the district in every chief's dar and eventually by the time I left Zalingei after my second five-year tour most of the chiefs' headquarters had, in addition to a court house, a school, a dispensary and small administration building with a resthouse for the D.C.

There were in addition a hundred and one other demands: checking court books, setting up dispensaries, stamping out the forest fires, poisoning baboons and hyenas, tree culture – all of absorbing interest to the District Commissioner. For a year or more these lads trekked with me in my lorry around the district on tour. We were out in camp or in district resthouses from twenty to twenty-five days a month. Within two years, the original boys had all been posted to executive jobs in the administration of their fathers' dar, and I took on a set of new lads.

There were some difficulties in individual cases in persuading the brighter lads to go in for higher education, which would in the long run enable them to take up important positions in the Sudan Government. A particular case which stands in my mind was that of the son of the Shartai of Tebella, Ahmed Ibrahim, who had lately returned from his intermediate school with special reports as the most intelligent boy in the school and clearly suitable for higher training. He was known everywhere as Grigg because one night fourteen years previously Colonel Grigg, then District Commissioner of Zalingei, rode into the village of Kergulla on a visit. That same night Ahmed Ibrahim was born and his father called him Grigg after the Colonel.

During my absence from Zalingei, Grigg's father had died and the Shartai's position was empty. But fortunately I had at this stage a trained Green Hat, a nephew of the Shartai's, and the obvious person to take on the appointment and to release young Grigg for higher things. There were great protestations from the boy Grigg, who told me I was oppressing him dreadfully. I said, 'One day you may become a Minister and you will then remember this.'

In the winter of 1966, nineteen years later, I stayed for two months in Khartoum revisiting many old friends among the Sudanese. One of the first to visit me was Ahmed Ibrahim, now Minister of Labour in the Sudan Government. He was the youngest Minister by some years, was looked on as outstandingly intelligent, spoke perfect English, and had studied in England and Germany, from whence he had returned with a quite charming young German wife who was devoted to him.

During the rainy season and after, the wadi beds were rife with mosquitoes, and although the houses were built on the high ground, the peasants who were working all hours by the river suffered enormously from malaria. In 1946 I had spent twenty-one years in the Sudan with only one go of malaria and then in the twenty-second year I went down with cerebral malaria and was delirious in Fasher Hospital for some ten days. There was no doctor in Zalingei and the Health Assistant, who was unable to find the malarial bacteria on the slide, treated me for undulating fever. The malaria got steadily worse and I never remember in all my life such headaches, which seemed to stay with me day and night. It was at the end of the rains and the roads were only just passable. I left Zalingei with a temperature of 104 for Fasher Hospital. I had made some plans that winter to visit French Equatorial Africa, and in my delirium I thought that I was in a French hospital. I started to talk French to the Sudanese orderlies who were of course extremely puzzled. Eventually, having lost over a stone in weight, I was flown down to Khartoum, where the fever was properly diagnosed in the laboratory, but it took me weeks to recover my strength.

It was not long afterwards, when I was thinking about leave, that I had a letter from Charles Arden-Clarke, my old friend whom I first met at Novocherkask in 1919. In the years that followed we met at infrequent intervals, but, as one does with someone who is a fast friend from youth, it was always to take up where we left off. By now, after a distinguished career in Nigeria and then Basutoland, he had been appointed the first Governor of Sarawak in succession to the Brooke family. His letter ended, 'Your time in the Sudan must now be coming to an end. Why not come out this year and see whether you would like to serve with me in Sarawak?'

I shaped my leave accordingly, and in June 1948 found myself in Aden cursing the heat and the delay of four days waiting for the *Himalaya* to take me to Borneo. Little did I realize that for the second time in my career fate had stepped in to produce a plan which far exceeded my expectation of service in the Far East. The Military Secretary to the Governor of Aden was Ken Nichols, an officer whom I had met previously. He asked me to dine in the Club with him the night I arrived, and over dinner told me that the Governor, Sir Reginald Champion, who had been my guest one night when I had been commanding the Sudan Brigade in Eritrea, had asked me to dine *en famille* at Government House.

M

After a quiet dinner in the terrace dining room of the old Govern ment House which now no longer exists, Sir Reginald Champio called me aside to sit and talk, looking across the bay at the shar hills of Little Aden silhouetted in the moonlight. He began b saying that my visit was very fortunate as he had only yesterda learnt from Ken Nichols that my time in the Sudan was due t finish early next year. He said, 'I am looking for a man with you experience and knowledge of Arabs and the Middle East to fill th tricky and difficult post of Resident Adviser to the Hadhramau States and British Agent to the East Aden Protectorate, based o Mukalla.' I laughed and asked, 'where is Mukalla and what is th East Aden Protectorate?' Champion explained briefly and said 'I'll show you the whole area on the map tomorrow. But in cas you should not care to take it, I would offer you as an alternative the Command of the Aden Protectorate Levies.' I then explaine to him that I was in fact on my way to Borneo with a view t deciding whether to take up an administrative post there. At th same time it became as clear as daylight to me that here to han lay a chance of using my past experience in a country so similar t parts of the Sudan. I explained this to H.E. and said, 'If I can ge Charles Arden-Clarke to agree, without letting him down, I wil accept your offer of the East Aden Protectorate but not the Levies I've already commanded the Sudan Camel Corps and a brigad in the war, and I'd like to switch to the constructive work of adminis tration in an under-developed country.' Champion was very please and said, 'Wire to me when you are clear with Charles Arden Clarke.'

I had a splendid leave in Borneo with Charles and his wife Gina I went with him on tour, travelling up the great rivers, stopping a Dyak long houses and enjoying the heavily forested country although I realized that for me the desert beat the jungle hand down. When we got back to the Istana, the Brooke palace whic was now Government House, I told Charles about Champion' offer, without giving him my reaction to it. After some thought h said, 'I had planned for you to take over as Resident in Brune which is an important post here, but I should be a dishonest knav if I didn't point out that your transfer here will mean a new lan guage, a new religion, new customs, new thought, and a totall different background. It would not be right of me to hold you t coming here.' I interrupted and told him what I had said t Champion. Charles then said, 'If this doesn't come off I will b delighted to have you here. You will presumably know in a mont or two.' I stepped out of his office very relieved and found a peo waiting with a telegram from Champion which read, 'Are you sti free?' I showed this to Charles who laughed, and I wired back, 'I am free and do accept your offer.'

A year later Charles was transferred to Ghana, where after seven distinguished years as Governor he became the first Governor General. When he retired from the Colonial Service (one of the most distinguished Governors the Service has known), it was to continue his work for the British Commonwealth. He became Chairman of the Commonwealth Society and the African Society, he lectured on colonial administration; and when he died in 1961 he had just returned from Pakistan, where he had been organizing educational development. He represented the very best that the Empire had to offer to the underdeveloped peoples of Africa.

My return journey took me back through Cairo and up the Nile to Khartoum. The train at Cairo was filled with twenty or more young Sudanese who were studying law and political economy in the Universities at Cairo and Alexandria. They were without exception communists and talked communism day and night. They were obviously sold to the Moscow radio and I listened with amusement to their ingenuous chat. Eventually at dinner in the restaurant car I got into conversation with them with a view to pulling their legs. One of them asked me what I was doing in the Sudan. When I told him I was a D.C. he said, 'Where?' The reply, 'Zalingei, in Western Darfur,' immediately evoked a scornful remark that 'You must be one of the Christian D.C.s stopping Islamic Northerners from visiting the South.' I asked him where he thought Zalingei was, to which he replied, 'Of course, in the Southern Sudan.' I asked him how long he had been in Egypt, which he obviously knew better than his own country, since Zalingei and Western Darfur are both in Northern Sudan, and I was the only Christian in a Moslem community.

This incident was followed by an interesting sequel only two years later when I had come over from the Hadhramaut with the Director of Education, a Sudanese, to collect staff. I was greeted by a young lad who said in good English, 'Colonel Boustead, don't you remember me, I was on that Nile steamer and train with a team of young communists. I've had my lesson. I have spent over a year in an Egyptian prison and my father has been ruined getting me out.' I asked him what he was going to do, and when he said, 'I want a job in the Hadhramaut,' I laughed and said that communists were not acceptable. He foreswore communism there and then and the Minister selected him. Later he married the Minister's daughter and has never looked back. He is now headmaster of a secondary school in Khartoum.

On my return from leave I found that my Western District in

Darfur had been selected for Sudanization during the New Year, 1949. The new D.C. who would take over from me was Ali Abu Sinn; I had known him as a Marmur (Junior Administrative Officer) in the Nuba Mountains during my command of the Camel Corps. He was a man of fine character and personality, greatly respected by the British D.C.s and Governors with whom he had worked. His tribal position as the son of the paramount Sheikh of the Shukria tribe gave him a somewhat special position.

It was March 1949 when he eventually arrived some five weeks before I was due to leave. I was greatly struck by his quiet, unassuming manner and his dignity and intelligence; his sympathy and understanding of the peasant and the nomad tribesmen were most marked and it was clear to me that he would be an understanding ruler. I could not have wished for anyone else to have taken over from me. Later he became the Governor of Darfur Province, succeeding the last British Governor. Unfortunately he had to retire due to ill-health within a year or two and died shortly afterwards of heart trouble. His loss was mourned by all in Darfur.

Now came the time for farewell celebrations in Zalingei. Said Fadil Abdel Shafie, a charming and distinguished Sudanese who had now been my Marmur for a year, told the assembled Fur chiefs that I had been appointed Governor General of Southern Arabia – this with the idea of impressing them with the importance of my position on leaving the Sudan. For me these were sad occasions: I felt like Kipling's Roman Centurion when the legions were leaving Britain:

> *Legate, I come to you in tears – my cohort's ordered home!*
> *I've served in Britain forty years. What should I do in Rome?*
> *Here is my heart, my soul, my mind – the only life I know.*
> *I cannot leave it all behind. Command me not to go!*

After fifteen years' knowledge of Western District, I could see and judge the tempo of its development. It was very slow indeed. There were few of the pressures that confront, say, oil states in the Gulf or in Arabia, and the impetus for improvement and for development had to come from the District Commissioner himself. Progress depended on his impact on the chiefs and on their sons, and the reaction that he could get from them.

It was with great reluctance when the time came that I rode out for the last time on the road to Fasher with the one hundred and fifty chiefs and followers who had come to greet me on my return after the war. They rode out with me much further than the normal point, and our goodbyes and good wishes were fervent. Western Darfur still remains about the most distant and most isolated of all the districts in the Northern Sudan, lying as it does on the far Western border, beyond the great range of the Marra Mountains. I hope that the people still retain as much of their happiness as ever, such happiness as I was able to share with them during the period of British rule.

Chapter Fourteen

RESIDENT ADVISER, MUKALLA

I ARRIVED in the Hadhramaut in August 1949, after three intensive days of homework in Aden. Flying along the southern coast of Arabia, I had my first sight of the country in which I was to work for the next nine years; forbidding, impressive and on the grand scale – tumbled mountains, deep wadis, high and desolate plateaux. We landed at Ryan, the nearest airfield to Mukalla, and seventeen miles east of it, where I was warmly welcomed by the Heir Apparent, the State Secretary and members of the Sultan's State Council.

I drove to Mukalla in the Resident's official car flying the Union Jack, accompanied by the State Secretary. As we reached a small fort on the top of a pinnacle rock beside the main road, a soldier fired a rifle which was apparently a signal for a thirteen-gun salute. The saluting guns were drawn up just above the road and fired across it, so my driver took good care to speed ahead between guns as we passed their position. I felt distinctly nervous, although it was very pleasant to be considered sufficiently important to carry thirteen guns. We drove in through the large honey-coloured gate which is barred nightly, and turned into the Residency yard.

There no less than three guards of honour were drawn up, as well as the Mukalla band. The guards were chosen from the Mukalla Regular Army, the Hadhrami Bedouin Legion (the Resident's own force) and the Qu'aiti Armed Constabulary, all in distinctive uniforms. I was greeted by the Acting Resident, who accompanied me round the subsequent inspection.

I paid my official call on Sultan Salih that afternoon; he had arranged a tea party for the principal members of the State Council, a group of men headed by the State Secretary who met from time to time in order to discuss with the Sultan matters of policy and administration. I was placed on the left of the Sultan with the Council drawn up in early Victorian chairs, facing each other, with early Victorian tea tables in front of them. The Sultan presided on an acutely uncomfortable sofa. After he had introduced me as the new Resident, and we had had tea, I felt I really must try to make a speech of thanks to him and to the Council.

I stood up in my white uniform and addressed the whole party in what to me was the easy Arabic of the Sudan which I had spoken for twenty-five years. I thanked the Sultan and told him how honoured I was to have the opportunity of helping the administration of his state, and that he could be assured at all times of my devoted service. It suddenly became clear to me, as the speech closed, that only one person apart from Sheikh Qadal, a Sudanese, had understood it; this was the Assistant Political Officer, a Hadhrami. So I asked him to stand up and said that I was very sorry that, owing to my inability to speak the Arabic of the Hadhramaut, nothing I had said was clear to anybody but that I would put this right within the next three months, provided the members of the Council would do the same by me and make a determined effort to understand my gradually ripening Arabic. He repeated this and the Sultan smiled and the members nudged and grinned to each other and the party broke up happily.

Officially, the area loosely called the Hadhramaut was the East Aden Protectorate, as opposed to the West Aden Protectorate and the Trucial States on the Persian Gulf. The population was about 380,000. It takes its name from the great Wadi Hadhramaut in the interior, an enormous watercourse which only flows after the occasional rains, but is adequately watered by wells. The resulting irrigation supports a considerable agriculture, both grain and dates. It boasts a number of cities, Shibam, Tarim, Seiyun and others, with towering mud buildings eight and twelve stories high. To the north of the Wadi, and to the south cutting it off from the coast, lie savage peaks and a high, rocky plateau rising to 6,000 feet. This is the jol, almost waterless, burning hot in the sun and bitterly cold at night. For generations the Bedouin have been the carriers between the townsmen of the Wadi and the traders on the coast, in particular in Mukalla.

In ancient days the famous spice trade traversed this part of Arabia, but it can never have been a rich land. For a century or more, the Hadhramis have gone overseas to seek their fortunes, in particular to East Africa and Zanzibar, and to Java and Singapore, remitting money to their families at home, and eventually retiring – often as very wealthy men – to their homeland. The Japanese conquests of Malaya and Indonesia hit the Hadhramaut economy hard.

But even in my years, the invisible export of the Hadhramaut was mainly the Hadhrami boy between the ages of ten and sixteen. These people appeared to be born with an Elizabethan sense of adventure and enterprise, and an astonishing ability in trade. From the East Indies to Cardiff, Hadhramis will be found, usually as traders, engineers and builders. There were in those years some 300,000 in the Indonesian Archipelago. They were mercenaries in

Southern India, particularly in Hyderabad, and they traded from Zanzibar to Port Sudan on the East African coast. Hadhramis could be found in every conceivable trade on the coast and in the interior.

After the dhows with their red sails had come coasting into Mukalla with the sunset, a quite unforgettable sight of beauty, the quay would be filled for several days with youngsters waiting to leave for some chosen port on the African coast or for Malabar in India. I used to get much pleasure sitting on the quay, asking their origins and their destination. The sort of replies I had were 'I am Ahmed Yussef, an Amari from Tariba in the Wadi Hadhramaut, and I am bound in that dhow for Zanzibar where my uncle has a bicycle shop.' Ibrahim Omar, on the other hand, came from Hureidha in the Wadi Duan, is now twelve years old, and is off in the other dhow to join his cousin in Addis Ababa in a leather shop.

These lads quickly succeed in their chosen occupations and soon are sending back large sums of money to their relations through merchants in Mukalla. The relations are able to buy goods and the import duty on the goods provides revenue for the Hadhramaut.

The curse of the Hadhramaut for 150 years had been tribal warfare. The Qu'aiti Sultanate, pushing in from the coast, had gradually dominated the Kathiri sultans; a shifting system of alliances between sub-tribes led to constant unrest, and warfare between the towns led to the destruction of date groves and crops, and interruption of trade. The British Government had been in treaty relations with the Qu'aiti Sultan since 1888, primarily over suppression of the slave trade; and in 1918 an agreement was patched up between Qu'aiti and Kathiri. But internal disorder was nothing to do with Britain, and indeed was scarcely appreciated until Harold Ingrams visited the Hadhramaut in 1934. He returned as a semi-official peacemaker, spending arduous months persuading the factions to sign a three-year truce. When the truce was concluded in April 1937 it had over 1,300 signatories, an indication of the multitude of chiefs and leaders involved in the perpetual warfare.

In consequence of this great achievement, recorded in his *Arabia and the Isles*, Harold Ingrams became the first Resident Adviser to the Qu'aiti Sultan, and also to the Kathiri Sultan, under a treaty of 1937. Based at Mukalla, he had helped the Sultan in his plans for schools, medical care, irrigation and agricultural improvement; and had encouraged the formation of the State Council, with officials appointed to run the various departments of the state. The first Resident Adviser had set a tremendously high standard for his successors.

*

I was enchanted by Mukalla, and the spell was as strong when I left as on my first sight of it. It is a white-walled city, the houses fringing the shore round the little harbour. The dhows ride under the wide dome of the Arabian sky, the surf beats on the golden shore, and behind stand the great ramparts of the jol. It is a great fishing port, huge quantities of dried fish being exported or sent up country; and fish is the smell of Mukalla.

The Residency was an impressively large building, originally a previous Sultan's palace. It had its own extensive courtyard, with offices and houses for my two Assistant Advisers and the Health Adviser. The Residency was built as two wings, joined by a large reception room (I suppose originally a hall of audience) where thirty or so people could be seated. This room was rarely empty, for there was a perpetual flow all day long of traders, Bedouin, fishermen and visiting Arabs from the interior who would look in for advice or help, and would sit drinking tea until I could see them. The policy of keeping ever-open house I found an enormous help to my work, and in my relations with the people.

A small office jutted into the courtyard, with splendid views of the town on the east side and the bay to the west, fringed with mountains running up to 4,000 feet. In the other wing was a dining-room where normally I had a large round table for eight. Here I would sit in conference with the Ministers and heads of departments or Province Governors; next to the kitchen, it was a convenient place to hold these meetings, since Arabs enjoy an informal atmosphere, and tea and coffee could be brought in at intervals. In the nature of the work, four or five mornings a week would be taken up in conferences at the round table. Mani, my secretary, kept notes of all our meetings, which were typed and sent out in English and Arabic the same day to all those present. The British Advisory Staff would only come in over matters concerning their own branch. Occasionally matters would be referred to the Sultan and a Minister would be able to see him personally or with me. I made it a practice at Council meetings to intervene as little as possible but, often had to do a good deal of lobbying beforehand, or between sessions. Before long I could tell pretty accurately how the different members would think on most issues, as I came to know them well.

The dominating influence was that of the State Secretary. When Harold Ingrams had obtained an agreement with the Sultan to set up a Government he looked round for a State Secretary. One of the preconditions of the appointment was that the State Secretary should have a white beard, because Arabs of the period respected age and considered that wisdom could only come with years and experience. As the older generation then were usually bearded, a

long white beard had a cachet of its own. Sheikh Seif had been the
Chief Clerk in the Survey Department of the Tanganyikan Government, before his appointment as state secretary. He had an extremely pale face and was in fact an Omani Arab of the Bin Aloui
family from the interior of Oman. Though a small man, he was an
imposing figure, always immaculately dressed. He gave me the impression of being extremely cunning and very power conscious. In
his years of authority, he had tended to centralize the government
more and more into his own hands and to weaken the position of the
Governors (Naibs) and District Commissioners (Quaims) on whom
the administration of the country depended. After some months it
became clear to me that one could not teach an old dog new tricks,
and that so long as power remained in his hands this paralysing
centralization would continue.

— Arabs are very prescient and are apt to apprehend what is in your
mind long before you have spoken. Sheikh Seif was no exception.
He had strengthened his position by proposing to the Sultan that the
arrival of a new Resident was a suitable moment to increase his Civil
List, in this case by some £15,000 a year. It was clearly difficult for
a new R.A., to whom it was most important to be on cordial terms
with the Sultan, not to back the proposal. I backed it and it went
through, and Sheikh Seif of course got more marks. When the Mukalla riots exploded in the Palace yard at the end of 1950, it was
really Sheikh Seif's last despairing effort to re-establish himself.

I found the position of Resident Adviser a very delicate one, in comparison with the straightforward role of a District Commissioner in
the Sudan. There the D.C. was himself the executive, and his
effectiveness could be measured by the results which he, and only he,
could achieve in his district. The Adviser and his staff are there to
advise the existing Executive and not to usurp its authority. This
may mean slow progress when new ideas and approaches have to be
put across tactfully to provincial governors and heads of departments, but it means that when new developments are finally under
way, they are not 'gimmicks' enforced by an outsider, but flow
naturally from the local administration. In the last resort, under the
terms of the Treaty of 1937, the Sultan had agreed to accept the
R.A.'s advice; but it would have destroyed our whole relationship,
and stopped the development of an independent state authority if
this clause had ever been invoked. We never did, and in spite of Suez
and all that episode meant to the Arab world, the Sultan and I remained on the most friendly terms.

In the Eastern Aden Protectorate, the Naibs of the provinces were

in effect District Commissioners, with the Quaims as their subordinate assistants. They had no very clear notion of their responsibilities, and I tried to put this right, laying great stress on the value of
moving round their districts, and of gettings their priorities right.
For instance, the Naibs of Shibam and Kathiri had to be led to
devote all their energies to irrigation work, for where a shortage of
rain meant famine, water was more immediately important than,
say, road building or education.

I found the Naibs and Quaims to be very conscientious, on the
whole, and remarkably responsive to suggestions. The latter, for the
most part, came from my 'travelling team', Fadil Abdel Shafie and
Mohammed bin Mutraf. Fadil had been my Administrative Inspector in Zalingei in the Sudan. He was a man of great charm, and
one of the most intelligent Sudanese I had met, with enormous tact
and an ability to bind people to him. The Sudanese in general are
looked down on as blacks by the very fair-skinned Hadhramis, but
Fadil was as light as they.

Mohammed bin Mutraf was an Hadhrami whom I had arranged
should attend an administrative course in the Sudan. The two of
them spent two years touring the Qu'aiti and Kathiri States, setting
up town and village councils, and helping to educate the Naibs and
Quaims by their example. They were both intensely keen, and saved
from being tiresomely so by an irrepressible sense of humour.

Once a year I used to collect the whole of the state officials from
these two states and from the Wahidi in the west, who were at that
time something of a Cinderella, for a ten-day course in Mukalla.
Talks and official discussions were interlarded by some junketting –
bands and dinners, football matches and military shows – which
kept them all both interested and amused. Here again, both in
framing the programmes and in their execution, Fadil and Mohammed were invaluable.

Life in Mukalla soon took on a fairly regular pattern, at least when
I was there and not travelling up country. The day would be spent
in desk work for an hour or two, before a Council meeting, or an
ad hoc discussion group on some particular problem, in my dining-
room. One problem in Mukalla itself was that of exercise (on tour,
one had plenty), and I would sometimes take the car four or five
miles along the coast road and walk briskly back along the shore,
revelling in the superlative colouring of the sunset over the sea,
the golden sands, the white walled town and the amber cliffs rising
in the background.

One of my frequent evening entertainments was a visit to the
camel park, just west of the honey-coloured gate that guards
the back door to Mukalla from the interior. It was forbidden

to keep camels in the town itself; and so, after unloading, convoys from the mountain areas would barrack their camels here, in separate groups. The whole convoy would wait at the camel park until they had obtained fresh loads for the Wadi – rice, sugar, cloth and tea – and then set out again on their two-hundred-mile march into the interior. I got much amusement walking around their encampments and sitting talking to them by their fires. Their Arabic was difficult for a European; in fact the Hamum from the East talked a different dialect from the tribes on the Western Jol known as the Seiban Zei (tribal confederation). The Johi, of whom my escort sergeant was a member, had a peculiarly affected accent and I used to rag them by taking off their precious intonation, which to an Englishman sounded pansy to a degree.

The same Bedou with their cheerful, laughing, indolent ways while sitting at ease waiting for loads, could be seen screaming, shouting, furious, when aroused by what would to us appear some trifling matter but which they considered in some way affected their face or their economy. The everlasting thorn in the Bedou flesh whilst I was in Mukalla was the threat from lorry owners, whom they considered were depriving them of their livelihood.

Occasionally a cruiser or a frigate would put into Mukalla harbour for a day or two, an excuse for much gaiety. A cricket match would be arranged with the Residency staff which contained a number of Indians who were ardent cricketers. The Hadhramis favoured football, which they played in their bare feet on the hard mud grounds with astonishing agility. Huge crowds watched them and cheered madly whenever any one fell down, or jumped up and down like jack-in-the-boxes if a goal were scored. The naval team after the match would be taken off to have tea in one of the numerous youth clubs in the town. The cricketers repaired to the Residency Club to be entertained by the Indians and such British as played; in the early days there were only three or four of us in the station. The officers would come out on shooting expeditions after wild duck in the season along the coastal pools, or partridge and guinea fowl behind the mountains. In the evening I used to have a formal dinner party for the captain and for as many officers as we could fit in to a table of fourteen.

The Mukalla band was always an asset on these occasions. The band presented a remarkable sight in their blue, red and yellow Ruritanian uniform, selected by the Sultan himself; they were excelled only by the bandmaster who was some six feet four inches tall and had a foot of turban on top. Swandzi Khan was a born musician,

the son of the bandmaster of the 12th Rajputs who had been killed
in France in 1915. He himself became bandmaster of the same regiment until Sultan Saleh acquired him for the Mukalla band. He
was an astonishing musician and had an enormous hold over the
band, who could play anything from Arab and Egyptian music to
current musicals. Just before I left England I had attended the second
night of *Oklahoma* and came away with the long playing record of
the show but without the music. I played it to the bandmaster, who
took it down by ear, put it into parts and within two months the
band were playing it with great skill. He did the same with *The
King and I*. The technique of this huge figure, almost throwing his
baton at the band boys, kept the visitors enormously amused.

They included a choral party of eight, playing on clarionets, cello,
two violins, an oboe and cymbals, who would both sing and play
Indian and Arabic music at parties. Lilting songs such as the Egyptian Harvest Song and other favourites went down enormously well
with the locals, and whenever I had a big dinner party of some 150
or more guests at an Arab floor dinner, this singing band entertained the guests; they were listened to with such enthusiasm that it
was difficult to end the party. Their songs were recorded and played
in Egypt and all over the Middle East.

In the 1920s and earlier, the Hadhrami population was practically
self-sufficient, growing their own crops. It was an agrarian society,
though it is true that the Saids and the tribal leaders depended on a
class of serfs who were the drawers of water from the wells, either by
their own labour or in conjunction with camels and donkeys. The
water level lay between fifty and forty feet below the surface and
over a large part of the valley the soil was suitable for grain crops
and date palms. With the increase in emigration abroad and with
the introduction of rice from the East Indies, the economy of the
Hadramaut greatly altered and the eastern valley, with a population of probably some 80,000 or more, took to rice. It was easier
for the women to cook and there was no grinding, and they
welcomed it. The men found it most palatable, particularly with the
Javanese curries and side dishes which make the most enchanting
flavour for western or eastern palates. The agriculture gradually
fell away, wells fell into disuse and the series of drop-weirs which
held up the water level down the main wadi of the Hadramaut and
which were maintained by water boards, became more and more
ragged and ineffective.

Then came the war, the entry of the Japanese submarines into the
Indian Ocean, and the cutting off of both rice and money from the

very extensive population in Singapore and the Indies where several hundred thousand Hadramis supported their relations in the homeland. Harold Ingrams, the first Adviser, was suddenly faced with a disastrous famine. There were no lorries in those days to transport supplies from the coast and indeed there were no supplies to transport. Money was useless. In the middle of the life and death struggle of the war, the R.A.F. were called on to fly supplies into the country, but despite immense efforts some ten thousand people died. When I reached Mukalla in 1949 a somewhat similar situation had arisen in the western valleys. Here wheat was still grown to a certain extent, but owing to poor floods and bad rainfull on the jol, the crops had failed and the people were starving. Again grain was flown in but on a lesser scale then in 1943. On my arrival the situation was somewhat restored, but it was clear that we must take action to avoid another famine at all costs.

The agriculturists and irrigation engineers were called in from Aden and as a result of a conference with them it was agreed that immediate steps must be taken by the Government of the Qu'aiti State, which had very considerable reserves, and of the Kathiri with far less reserves, to re-build the dams and drop-weirs in the Hadhramaut Valley in order to maintain the water level. At the same time I was advised that an irrigation scheme for small pumps should be put into operation with all speed to make the whole Wadi self-supporting in its principal staple crop, wheat. At the same time the date palms in the valley would benefit enormously by increased water. The next four years of my stewardship were devoted to this task as one of the priorities of the many and urgent calls for the country. The beginnings, as one could have imagined, were exasperating. The Hadhramis are very quick in the uptake, but having once learnt the start of something they know everything, and will not get down to seeing it through. We introduced the first hundred odd pumps and unfortunately they were unsuitable for so dusty a climate, and the frames were very light, so they were sensitive to illtreatment or lack of skill. We got in engineers, some good and some bad. Eventually a German engineer called Kaltenbach saved the day. We set up a huge pump spares organization and used a tougher type of engine, and gradually confidence was restored.

It had required from me great persuasion to get the Qu'aiti State to put up £180,000 from their reserves to capitalize the pump scheme and the building of the dams. Day and night I and my Political Officer were up and down the Wadi in the burning summer of 1950, watching the progress of those two projects, directing and encouraging. I used to travel from village to village, collecting all the population of the surrounding district, and address them in the late

afternoon when their day's work was done. Gradually they became more responsive, and as we learnt more ourselves and the pump owners thus became better at overcoming their difficulties, results began to show. From that year on, the pumps increased in the Wadi by roughly a hundred to a hundred and thirty engines a year, and there were nearly 1,200 when I left nine years later. The danger of famine had completely passed and the pump owners were actually exporting wheat to the West Aden Protectorate, a thing never known in the history of the Hadramaut. Reflecting on these matters afterwards, I was enormously struck at the people's willingness to accept advice in a way which I have never found in the Gulf States of Arabia.

In the Protectorate there were three separate armed forces; the Qu'aiti Armed Constabulary, the Mukalla Regular Army (the Sultan's standing defence force) and the Bedouin Legion which had been formed in Ingram's day to patrol the desert areas, and which still came under the orders of the Resident Adviser.

The Qu'aiti State had been founded by invaders from the western part of South Arabia, the Yaf'ai tribe. As they set up an organized government, they policed the newly conquered territory with their own tribesmen; and when I arrived, the constabulary, some 600 men, was still largely Yaf'ai. On the other hand, the Sultans in the past had recruited the Mukalla Regular Army from the local tribes. Originally officered by Indians, who were not popular, the M.R.A. was at this time commanded by Kaid Bin Zamaida, a well-educated and extremely intelligent Bedouin. It seemed to me that the composition of the two forces should be reversed. The Constabulary, who were only armed because everybody in the Hadhramaut bore arms, were really village policemen, and ought to be of the same stock as the people among whom they lived and worked, while the striking force of the M.R.A. – should it ever be required to act against the local Bedou – had better be composed of Yaf'ai, with less compunction about shooting at Hadhramis. The Sultan agreed with me, and we gradually reversed the mixture.

The Bedouin Legion was partly a means of keeping the peace between nomad tribes, and partly an educational task force. Ingrams had started a Bedouin Boys School, and took some years to overcome a natural fear of confinement within walls and under a roof. I did all I could to help the school, which contained over a hundred boys, and we soon had the muqadams (chiefs) clamouring to get their sons in. Although it was essentially a cadet school for the Legion, with much emphasis on games and swimming and drill, it was possible to put across to these bright, quick lads ideas on hygiene and husbandry and administration which bore fruit when in due course

Wayside gossip on the jol

13. The Hadhramaut

Peace talks with the Manahil

14a. Mukalla: S
Council assembl
greet Harold In
Sheikh Qadal is
second from rig
front row

14b. Muscat: a
village meeting
discuss irrigation

14c. Abu
Dhabi: inspect-
ing the Trucial
Oman Scouts

they succeeded to positions of authority in their tribes. The school of course was run by a Bedouin officer.

In the not-so-distant past, the Yaf'ai by various acts of brutality had earned the distrust of the tribesmen they had conquered. On my first visit to Shihr, about thirty miles west of Mukalla, I was startled to be told by Ahmed Ba Surra, the Naib, 'This is where the Hamum muqadams are buried' – we were standing under the arch of the West Gate. Apparently one of the first Governors of Shihr, the original capital of the newly-founded Qu'aiti State, had invited some forty of the leaders of the Hamum tribe to dine with him, to discuss their role in the government. When the party were drinking coffee at ease after the meal, a body of Yaf'ai soldiers walked out of the darkness, tied them up and cut their throats. It was still, in my day, a job to reconcile the Hamum to the Qu'aiti Government.

The Hamum inhabit the jol, and always seemed to me a more thickset people than the other Bedouin of the jol who are by descent Dravidians from Southern India. They were said to be great fornicators and very casual about Islam.

Sheikh Seif's age and maladministration clearly indicated that the Sultan's government could not be efficient until a new Secretary of State had been appointed, but I could tell that he would do all in his power to retain his position and the excellent salary that went with it. My candidate for the post was Sheikh Qadal, a Sudanese of towering personality and extremely honest. In particular he had shown his abilities when bringing the Kathiri and Qu'aiti States together. To get them to co-operate with each other was one of my early objectives. We met, I remember, in Tarim, the ancient capital of the Kathiri, and Qadal that night had both the Kathiri and Qu'aiti councils in his hands. I was deeply impressed by the force of his character, the clarity of his ideas, and his influence both on the Sultan and on the prominent citizens in the councils. However, when it came to the point the Sultan, who was 76, was reluctant to remove Sheikh Seif and I had to press the matter hard with him.

Eventually he agreed, in June 1950; and I suggested that the change should be kept secret since Sultan Salih was about to go to India to visit the Nizam of Hyderabad, where he was still a nominal commander of the Nizam's bodyguard. This ancient appointment had been bestowed on the Qu'aiti Sultans for their faithfulness in supporting the Nizam as his mercenaries. The Ruler left in early July after agreeing with my proposal; he intended to return, he told me, in November. His son Awad, the heir apparent, was a man of no personality or character, given to drink, addicted to drugs and to

N

some strange habits. The people had no respect for him at all. It was useless to consult him or discuss anything of a confidential nature, so I confined my contacts to formal calls. He was always polite but could not sustain any intelligent conversation.

In August and September 1950 I was on tour in the Hadhramaut busily engaged with my main preoccupation of that period, the appalling difficulties over the irrigation pumps.

It was in the Wadi that I first heard rumours of a great deal of talk in Mukalla against the appointment of Sheikh Qadal. It then occurred to me that the Ruler must have leaked this information to his son, who had divulged it to the people. It obviously had got back to Sheikh Seif himself, who was putting it about that they could not possibly have a Sudanese as State Secretary. Taken up as I was with the pump scheme in the fiercely hot weather of a Hadhramaut summer, I tried to push these things to one side of my mind. My deputy, Ernest Kennedy, became uneasy over the general movement in Mukalla against Sheikh Qadal's appointment and urged me to come down, but I told him that I must carry on to the Wadi Duan and could not leave. With this spectre in the background I worked my way west into the steep gorges of the Duan Valley, where I was trying to get money from the wealthier merchants and sheikhs to build dams which were a complementary part of the pump scheme, to maintain the water level.

I had reached the capital of the Wadi Duan and was lodged for the night, I remember, in the village of Masna. I was sleeping in the Naib's house, about a third of the way up the 1,500 foot cliff which formed the wall of the Wadi. About one o'clock in the morning I heard continuous banging on the door down below. I called one of my servants and told him to go down and find out what it was. He came back with an officer of the Hadhramaut Bedouin Legion carrying a letter marked urgent in red in Arabic on the envelope. The officer said, 'I have come from Sultan Awad, and there is great disturbance in Mukalla.' I deciphered the letter slowly by lantern light; it was written in Arabic, in Awad's own hand. It began, 'The matter is very serious. You must please come at once to Mukalla. There is great opposition to Sheikh Qadal's appointment as State Secretary and there is a meeting of four thousand people in front of my house this afternoon at four o'clock. If you do not come there may be bloodshed. The situation is very dangerous and I am preparing the troops.' I told the officer to wait outside and lay back thinking on the best course to take. Kennedy, who knew Mukalla, had already left for the Wadi on a mission, and the young officer who was in the town had only just arrived. Sultan Awad's house was in the Residency grounds. I thought at first that perhaps it would be better to let the matter settle itself. Then I thought, 'The young-ster will not know what to do. He may well think that he must help Awad and call out the army; so I must go down and deal with this personally.'

The Naib was awake and was giving coffee to the officer. I told my sergeant to get all the kit together and the Naib to get porters immediately. We left his house and scrambled down to the wadi bed and then had a stiff climb by lantern light up the other side of the Wadi Duan. It was now four o'clock in the morning, and a full moon was riding in the sky. My Ford V8 tourer was waiting at the top of the cliff with the lorry, and we set out at once on the 150 mile drive to Mukalla across the rolling rocky steppeland of the jol. We drove over the 7,000 foot range that separates the main plateau from Mukalla without stopping, reaching the town at 9 a.m. I was greeted by my young officer who said, 'I've been anxiously waiting for you. I have got the army to stand by.' I had done a good deal of thinking during the drive and was clearly determined that at all costs there must be no crisis which could lead to any sort of disturb-ances during the Sultan's absence, particularly not in the Residency courtyard. Should that happen, the Crown Prince would undoubt-edly throw the blame onto the Resident, and probably the Residency would be burned down as happened in Cyprus. So I told this young lad not to worry but to tell the army to stand down since I would not use it at any cost. I said, 'I will see Sheikh Seif at ten o'clock so please arrange to bring him along and be present yourself.'

Sheikh Seif appeared on time, a very smooth and very suspicious man with his long white beard, his white sheet of a face and his one wall eye. In quiet tones he said, 'The situation is very serious. There is great opposition to the appointment of a Sudanese as State Secre-tary and there will be a meeting of the people in front of your house this afternoon to demand that this appointment should be cancelled.' I asked, 'But who said that Sheikh Qadal is appointed State Secretary?' He replied, 'The Sultan.' At this moment Sultan Awad, the Crown Prince, appeared and after salaams said he cabled his father and that he was proposing to tell the people that the appointment of Sheikh Qadal was his father's decision. I said to Sheikh Seif, 'You go on leave in December, but the actual appoint-ment itself ends in April next year. How can we have two State Secretaries?' Sultan Awad then butted in, 'Ah, but my father said so.' I said, 'The decision on the State Secretary will have to wait until your father's return. It is not for you or me or Sheikh Seif to tell the crowd anything at this time.'

Sultan Awad then pressed me to see the representatives of the people who would come forward in front of the crowd. I said, 'No.

I am the Adviser. I am not the ruler or his representative.' He asked, 'What shall I say to them?' I replied, 'I will put on paper what you should say to them. There is no crisis. There is no problem. You cannot give this decision, nor can I.' They both looked very puzzled and went off.

At about four o'clock I heard the shouts of a large crowd advancing down the Mukalla main street. They were carrying banners and they streamed in columns about eight abreast into the Residency courtyard. The banners were to the effect, 'We want no foreign State Secretary.' They gave that sinister growl which one hears from a great crowd of angry people. The shutters of the Residency were closed against the afternoon sun, but I watched them from a small opening. It took about half an hour before all of them assembled in the Residency square facing Sultan Awad's house which lay to the flank; a delegation of some six prominent Arabs went forward to Awad's house. In the meantime I had sent a note over to him: 'The answer to any delegation you receive is, "All decisions lie with my father. The present State Secretary's appointment does not finish till April next year, and my father will name his successor when he returns from India." '

There was a pause of some five or ten minutes while the delegation, it seemed, were drinking coffee in Awad's house. Then they appeared and one of them read out the statement. Tension was removed and the crowd clapped and slowly moved out of the courtyard.

This was October 1950. I have no doubt that Sheikh Seif's intention was to precipitate a riot in which the Resident would be involved. He was undoubtedly deeply disappointed at my refusal to acknowledge that there was any crisis which required immediate settlement. However the troubles were not ended, and no doubt at his instigation the feeling against Sheikh Qadal continued to be stirred up. But on Boxing Day, after his return from India, the Sultan made the appointment. I drove down to the Customs Quay with Sheikh Qadal in my car and sat there in the open talking and rejoicing in the fact that the Sultan's fears had been overcome and the decision had been made in open council, and with their acclaim.

On the morning of 27th December at 5 a.m. I was awakened by the Mukalla Town Police Officer coming into my room. He said, 'There have been conferences going on all night among the people who are opposed to Sheikh Qadal's appointment. The position is pretty bad. At half-past eight this morning several thousand people will be assembling in the palace yard and the delegates are going to protest to the Sultan against the appointment.' I asked, 'Have you told Sheikh Qadal about this?' He said, 'Yes. I have just come from him and he sent me to you.' I said, 'Well, go back and tell him to go into the palace with the more prominent of the Council members including the Yaf'ai Sheikh Nassr and let them keep the Sultan firm.' Around about eight o'clock I could hear the sinister boom of the crowd filing up the Mukalla main street. I told Kennedy, my deputy, to ring up the Mukalla Regular Army to have lorries ready at the barracks to bring the troops immediately if required. They were not to move down without an order.

The crowd had assembled at the palace yard and some young hooligans tried to stop my car as we drove in. I told the driver to drive past them and they broke away, smashing the window as they went. I went upstairs and found the Sultan with the Yaf'ai Sheikh Nassr bin Batati, Sheikh Qadal and three others. Presently a delegation came up. The Sultan, his great height stooped with rheumatism and arthritis, was sitting looking extremely angered on his sofa, and when the delegation appeared he glared at them. He had never before been confronted with direct opposition to his orders. They sat on chairs opposite him and their spokesman said, 'We have come on behalf of the people to tell you we do not want a non-Arab as State Secretary.' The Sultan replied to them curtly that this appointment was one for him and was not one to be made by the common people, and it was not in their gift but his. Sheikh Qadal then stood up and made a magnificent speech, ending, 'I have known you all for fourteen years and I have educated your children, and you have known me as a member of your Council. Never before have I heard any of you speak against me.' They looked embarrassed and nervous and came forward to shake him by the hand, and then said, 'We will go down and tell the people that we wish to recognise you.'

But by this time loud shouts were coming from all over the palace yard and already the crowd was breaking flower-pots and windows down below. I heard a shot and saw that the guard had been over-powered by the crowd who had seized their rifles; there were only six soldiers on guard at the time. Sheikh Nassr, a huge man over six foot six, went down to argue with them, but was shouted down and met with a shower of stones. Hearing the noise, we hustled the Sultan upstairs to his room on the second floor of the palace and I sent someone to ring up Kennedy and tell him to get the M.R.A. in immediately. The delegation had gone down but were never able to open their mouths to the crowd. Down below I could hear the smashing of doors, and soon I saw some of the mob on the verandah outside. I went through the door and a tall Somali attacked me with a cudgel. As he did so I was pulled back and the door slammed from behind. This was Sheikh Nassr's doing, and the Somali's cudgel merely hammered on the door mantle and I was not harmed. Down

below there was more shouting and more breaking in of doors and
windows.

I then heard a volley in the yard and an answering howl, then a
second volley, followed by a much louder howl of pain. The M.R.A.
had come down under Kaid Bin Zamaida and found the iron gates
of the city locked against them; so Bin Zamaida, who was quick as
a cat, led a platoon over the Residency wall, into the Residency
courtyard, through the Residency gate into the palace yard. He
formed his soldiers up in line at the eastern end of the courtyard
and ordered them to lie down. He shouted to the crowd to stop or
he would open fire. The first volley was fired over their heads. They
yelled, 'Go for the soldiers. They only cost 20 rupees,' (this was their
monthly pay) and advanced on Bin Zamaida's troops. He fired again,
this time straight into the body of the crowd. Eighteen fell dead and
forty-seven were wounded. The crowd turned and fled for the gate
and those who were in the palace made good their escape as best
they could. The Sultan, whose only emotion was anger, kept saying,
'*Kilab*' (What dogs, what dogs).

We then had a conference with Sheikh Qadal. I said, 'We must
have a curfew immediately and the M.R.A. must come in and patrol
the streets.' The ringleaders were arrested and tried by a special
Court consisting of three Naibs and two members of the Council;
in all, some seventy people were convicted and sentenced to between
three and five years' imprisonment.

I sent a private wire to the Governor at Aden asking him to ensure
that only the bulletin that I sent him should get into the paper and
nothing more. Actually only three lines appeared in *The Times*.
Within three weeks of all this, Sheikh Qadal was installed as the new
State Secretary, and proved immensely successful in that capacity.
Once Sheikh Seif's influence was removed, the antipathy to Qadal's
Sudanese origin disappeared, and he became as popular as he had
been previously.

There is a long tradition in Southern Arabia of appointing
Moslems from outside to positions of authority; many of the best
administered States employed Indians and Sudanese as well as
Arabs from other localities. The feeling against Sheikh Qadal's
appointment was not genuine. However, as more boys are better
educated, there will clearly be pressure to appoint the state's own
citizens, and perhaps some of the clever lads will seek to make their
fortunes at home instead of abroad.

Until the Colonial Office took it over in the thirties, Aden and
the Protectorates were under the Indian Government and in consequence a large number of the clerical staff were Indians. The
Madrasis in particular excelled in accounts and book-keeping and

English appeared to be as natural a language to them as their native Tamil. On my arrival one of my first preoccupations was to find an adequate private secretary to deal with the mounting correspondence which administrative development produced.

Mani was then about twenty-seven, though he looked considerably younger. He had a wife and two children in Mukalla, and was working in the general office. His shorthand and his quick intelligence were so marked that I took him out within a week or two as my private secretary. He had been brought up in a Roman Catholic Secondary School in Madras where his father had been chief accountant of one of the biggest cloth firms, but had a nervous breakdown on the death of his eldest son; so Mani, who should have gone to the University, was forced to support the whole family.

He had a completely English sense of humour and an astonishing capacity for work. He had been captain of football and cricket at school and was a good tennis player. He remained a Hindu and practised Yoga regularly. During the nine years I was Resident in the Hadhramaut he became increasingly valuable, accepted more and more responsibility, and was a general favourite among all the British staff. In the summer of 1957 I took him home to England; he visited me in the country whenever I was staying with friends who had been with us in the Hadhramaut. We became great friends, and when I left Mukalla to take over as Development Officer of Muscat and Oman, he accompanied me as my Deputy.

Chapter Fifteen

THE HADHRAMAUT

But I will sit beside the fire
And put my hand before my eyes
And trace to fill my heart's desire
The last of all my Odysseys.
HILAIRE BELLOC

MUKALLA was the centre of government and the home of the Ruler, and much of my work kept me in the Residency office. But in any underdeveloped country it is essential to get out and about to find out the people's problems at first hand and learn how you can help them. Constant touring is the only method, but it must be planned, and not hurried. This part of my work was particularly important here, where the inter-tribal peace was still rather precarious, and where there was antagonism between the town dwellers of the coast and the Wadi, and the Bedouin of the wilderness.

As a D.C. in the Sudan it had always been a principle of mine to stop and talk to passing cars, to convoys, and to road parties *en route*, and I would make a point of allowing plenty of time to reach the area where I had my first definite appointments. I was struck on my first tour from Mukalla with the apparent haste with which my companion wished me to reach the main wadi centres. We passed long convoys of Bedouin carrying goods from the coast to the interior, on occasion other cars, prisoners being taken under escort; and my companion was astonished and irritated at my insistence on stopping to find out what it was all about. He said, 'You will be late.' I asked, 'What for?' 'For dinner.' I said, 'Where?' He replied, 'Wherever you dine.' I said, 'We will dine wherever we find ourselves after making camp this evening, which will be about half an hour before sunset.' I gathered that it had been his custom to tear at great speed through the countryside in order to reach some town or village where he could settle comfortably in a house; but what he saw or found out on a hundred-mile journey would be little.

We camped that night on the high jol and I asked my Javanese cook, who was quite new to me, to make dinner. He looked horrified. He pointed to the tents which were being put up and said, 'But you don't mean to dine here?' I replied, 'For twenty-five years in the Sudan I have fed like this in the open, and no Sudanese cook has ever refused me dinner.' After a delay a most excellent meal was produced.

On these treks we carried round on a lorry an escort of the Bedouin Hadhrami Legion who put up tents, collected wood, put down the water from the fantasses (water tins) for cooking and for baths while the servants put up the chairs and tables, canvas ground sheet, and made the camp beds. Drinks and a hot bath would be produced, while the Bedouin would sit round cooking their evening meal on the rocks, singing and playing on the 'chanter' and laughing and talking incessantly. Between ten and eleven o'clock the camp would lapse into silence until the dawn. Where there was enough wood we would have a large camp fire, but in the Hadhramaut there was usually only sufficient for cooking and making baths.

Touring had to be planned carefully to avoid wasting time. I would first list the enterprises and works and people to be covered by the tour, and advise those concerned in advance. On the spot, one had to be sure to deal with everything on the route before moving on to the next place. The items might comprise a visit to one or more schools, and getting to know the schoolmaster; a check on a dam being built under my own instructions; a check on the main wells and pumps to ensure that the land was being economically irrigated, and that the pump owners were having their difficulties solved by the visiting mechanics from the pump scheme H.Q.; a visit to dispensaries or a health centre, and a general survey *en route* of the agriculture and irrigation. In the larger villages, one would probably have a half day's discussion with the village council whose books would have to be checked.

I found that the Arab provincial Governors and their D.C.s were quick to follow my lead over touring their areas, and as a result, we were able to get to know the people and their needs in a remarkably short time and to maintain that friendly contact with them, whether tribesmen or peasants, which makes this sort of life so absolutely rewarding.

I had inherited from Harold Ingrams a Jordanian Bedouin Affairs Assistant, Abdullah Suleiman, from the Arab Legion: when I arrived in 1949 he had already served nine years advising on Bedouin affairs on the coast and in the interior. During the years of my stewardship in East Aden Protectorate I found his help invaluable.

I got very cross with him on one of our first tours together, in the winter of 1949; it was also my first experience of entertaining Bedouin muqadams or chieftains. We were camped on the Seiban Jol, well north of Mukalla; and I had asked to lunch about ten of the sheikhs of the Seiban – the 'blue warriors', naked except for a small loin cloth soaked in indigo, their skin dyed dark blue with a protective film of indigo and oil. Thinking that each sheikh would bring a couple of retainers, I had told my cook to prepare food for thirty. To my horror, when my guests turned up, each armed with a rifle, a jambiya or dagger, and a stabbing knife on his arm, there were about eighty of them. I rounded in a fury on Abdullah Sulei-man and asked, 'Where the hell is food for eighty people coming, and haven't you any control over the situation?' Abdullah laughed in his usual gay way, shrugged his shoulders and said, 'They will all have to wait.' I replied, 'Do you think I am carrying an emporium on trek, where's the rice coming from?' Abdullah shrugged and said nothing, and in due course and after a long wait there was food for about sixty for a full meal, eighty for a skimpy one. So they all ate and went off in a very cheerful mood. It turned out that Abdullah had brought a spare sack of rice for himself and we ate that. It served him right, and he then said, 'They will bring any number unless you give them a limit in advance.' So I was warned and for the future we were able to feed them without embarrassment.

In the summer of 1956 I was touring in the Wadi Hadhramaut with him. He left me at Shibam, a town with astonishingly high mud-built houses of many storeys, for work in one of the northern forts on the frontier. The following day I heard over the radio from Cairo and from England that I had been assassinated on the steps of Government House in Aden by an infuriated mob. This was actually quoted in *The Times* without comment and a number of my friends were extremely upset; one of them actually wrote an obituary which fortunately was not published. The Sudan Govern-ment sent a long telegram of condolence to the Governor in Aden which was almost an obituary in itself.

Abdullah Suleiman got the news over the radio at Zimakh Fort on the frontier and, knowing that he had only just left me, sent a telegram: 'We in Arabia have heard that you have visited the next world and have returned, so please report.' I replied in kind, 'It is true that I have visited the next world and found many Bedouin but no Bedouin Affairs Assistant to help me with all their difficulties, so I was forced to come back.' The next telegram was one from the Secretary of State for the Colonies, Alan Lennox-Boyd, congratulating me on being safe and well. The whole mischief had been falsely spread by Nasser's radio and was typical of this period. Throughout these years Cairo Radio remained responsible for a very large per-centage of the troubles, disorders, deaths and discontent in the Middle East generally and in the two Aden Protectorates in particular.

The greatest harm was done to the younger generation, the school-boys, the students and the schoolmasters, a number of whom (but not the Sudanese in the Hadhramaut) seemed to delight in Nasser's mischief, which had been responsible for the destruction of many years of solid achievement by the British, Sudanese, Pakistanis, Indians and educated Arabs in the two Protectorates. Looking back on this past scene of nine years' work and seeing all that was built then falling to pieces now, ought to make one cynical; but under-lying all the harm being done now, there is still, I believe, a residue of the good that was done in the past, and I have hopes that one day it will emerge.

I had completed a tour of the Hadhramaut Valley with Pat Booker who was at that time running the Wadi pump scheme. We had reached a palm oasis on the shore of the Indian Ocean, some twenty miles east of Mukalla, when I told my driver to stop. Awad, a young sergeant of the escort, came down from the lorry and I told him to put down the table and two camp chairs under a tree for myself and to put out a rug under another tree for the Governor of Shihr, who was travelling with me, to enable him to have some coffee with his staff. Awad protested that I must have the rug, and when I told him to shut up and do as he was told, looked very angry. I was sitting in shorts and a pair of sandals at the breakfast table when I was conscious of an intense tickling round the ankles, spreading quickly up the legs, and when we got to the fried egg stage, I was conscious of urticaria all over my body and a quite unbearable desire to scratch. We left the eggs and bolted for the car. It was clear that camel ticks under the tree had attacked me. Pat Booker was only mildly uncomfortable. I set off in great discomfort telling the lorry to follow with the Bedouin escort and servants and the Naib. I was presently conscious that the skyline was fading out, followed by the trees. I could then no longer see the side of the road, my driver became a blur, and I turned to Pat Booker and said, 'I am now completely blind and can't see you.' He said, 'Your eyes have got a film of red all over.' I rode on shaken and terrified. About half an hour later as we were approaching Mukalla I was suddenly aware that I was beginning to see the driver and slowly the world unfolded in the same order as it had disappeared; leaving me enormously relieved but shaken and rather sick.

The Naib turned up presently in the Residency and said that he had known many cases of Bedouin being blinded, sometimes up to forty-eight hours, by the bite of camel ticks. Awad came in and gave me a stern lecture for not listening to him and for not keeping the rug under my feet. He said, 'You wouldn't listen and this is very dangerous and now you've had it.' I have since been very careful about camel ticks. These loathsome grey insects are parasitic on camels, sucking their blood; the shade of trees where camels have been resting is notoriously dangerous. The ticks vary in size, though the average when full is about the size of a large thumb nail.

Anyone touring on the jol in those days when the camel convoys were plying continuously between the Wadi Hadhramaut and the coast would be enormously struck by the astonishing independence and toughness of the younger Bedouin children, anything from four upwards. When driving my car down from Duan in the Western Wadi, I was frequently stopped by a youngster shaking his fist furiously. About three foot tall with a huge mop of hair, wearing a stabbing knife on his arm and naked except for a wisp of loin cloth, a child like this would lead some thirty or forty camels, the other members of the party probably having dropped off to shoot something or buy sugar at a wayside stall. Once he had succeeded in stopping the car, the youngster would stalk past with a long silent column, tail tied to headrope, padding behind him.

My first years as Resident Adviser were haunted by the fear of another famine. When the pump schemes and intensive dam building so improved the irrigation of the wadis that the danger of famine receded, my main worry was trouble between the Bedouin tribes, and between them and the peasants and townsmen. Sometimes the trouble arose from a genuine grievance, which had to be remedied, sometimes from camel raiding, and sometimes from tribal power politics. It was the policy of the Protectorate to use force only as a last resort, since fighting could easily spread, and would prove a serious drain on the State's scanty revenues.

On occasion a show of force sufficed. In 1953 there was a severe threat of disturbances by the Manahil tribe in the Wadi Maseila which is that part of the Wadi Hadhramaut which runs south below the town of Tarim. After some discussion with the R.A.F., I decided to carry out a demonstration with a flight of Brigands with which I decided to fly at wadi level below the cliffs. This was a most tricky and exciting business, as the wadi bed is very narrow in this area with high steep cliffs on either side, and it was difficult to tell which was a re-entrant into the cliff and which was the open wadi bed.

I was the one officer who knew this area extremely well from my initial tours on the pump scheme, so I decided to fly in the leading plane as guide to the pilot. I have rarely been more terrified. The actual bed where the Hadhramaut River flows is a very long way below the cliffs, about 1,500 feet, and we flew just above the water, zigzagging in and out with the twists of the wadi. Furthermore I had ordered that the flight should be done both up and down wadi, so when we arrived in Tarim safely, sweating with fright, I felt it incumbent upon me to fly back again the same way. We could see the scared Manahil tribesmen making for the cliffs as we passed them; one astonishing sight I will never forget was a Mukalla Regular Army sentry presenting arms as the plane passed below him within a few feet of the fort on which he was standing, built on a rock in the centre of the wadi. I think it was one of the most exciting experiences I have had.

An example of what I suppose is the traditional form of Bedouin trouble – raiding – occurred on an international scale in 1953 and 1954. A huge number of camels had been stolen by the Dahm tribe of the Yemen, and almost as many in return by the Kurab and Seiar of the Qu'aiti State. During the accompanying raids there had been a considerable number of casualties on both sides. In order to arrange a settlement and mutual compensation a meeting was arranged at the El Abr Fort in November 1954. The Yemeni delegation was led by Qadhi Mohamed Abdullah el Shami, the Yemeni frontier Governor, with four local high officials under him. The Qu'aiti delegation were led by the massive figure of Sheikh Qadal with two very bright Province Governors of Shibam and Irma and a leading judge from the Qu'aiti Legal Department. The Yemeni delegation arrived in aeroplanes at Qatn landing ground and were accommodated in a large Arab house in the town. Jock Snell, who was at this time Assistant Adviser, Northern Deserts, accompanied me to the meeting. The first lunch party which was held on the floor of the host's house, the seat of the local Governor, was socially hardly a success. Both Shami and his delegation were coldly hostile in their manner, and during the meal addressed one or two quite rude remarks to the Qu'aiti delegation. Shami himself said in an acid voice, 'Do you talk at meals like these people?' indicating Jock Snell and me. The Qu'aiti Qadhi replied, 'Of course we do, we have been brought up to be polite to our guests.' Then no comment for a few minutes. The following day was a Friday and it was decided to move out in the late afternoon into tents at El Abr Fort some thirty miles to the west, after attendance at the mosque followed by another lunch together. The Qu'aiti Qadhi took the opportunity of giving the address or sermon at the mosque that day, and his subject was 'good manners', a very pointed commentary on our guests' behaviour. It had a remarkable effect, and from the lunch party that followed and during the succeeding week in tents out in the field, relations became increasingly more cordial.

At El Abr Fort the tribesmen from the Yemen and the Qu'aiti tribes came flowing in great numbers on their camels to the well-field below the fort with their lists of camel claims and persons wounded and killed in the raids. Some of the delegates were busy on these lists continuously while Shami and Sheikh Qadal sat in judgement with two other members.

Shami, who was already over seventy but a very alert wiry figure, looked like a cobra sitting on its tail (Sheikh Qadal's description). He never missed a trick, but Sheikh Qadal with his booming voice and quiet manner appeared to dominate the proceedings. The claims and arguments were interminable and I thought at one time that we should be there a month, but the proceedings were enlivened by a great deal of humour and laughter as well as by fierce talk. When the party eventually broke up everyone appeared satisfied and the Yemeni delegation returned to Marib in the cars of the H.B.L. mechanized patrol. The patrol's activities had largely contributed to the success of the negotiations, in that it had been the means by which six Yemeni raiders had been intercepted and lodged in Mukalla jail, an argument more compelling than much verbal reasoning. The patrol had by arrangement been much in evidence during the meeting. It was clear from his reactions that Qadhi Shami was quite astonished at the greater aplomb, education and intelligence of the Qu'aiti delegation than that of his own.

Our most serious difficulties with the tribes arose from their bitter resentment at competition from motor transport. Before the middle of 1947 the whole of the carrying trade from the coast to the interior was done by the camels of the Bedouin of the Seiban and the Hamum tribes; the roads into the interior were still new. During the famine of 1944 and again in 1948 the camel population diminished on the Western Road from about 7,000 to 2,000. In the Hamum area on the al-Kaf Road there was also a great falling off both as a result of famine and owing to subsequent bad years of drought.

Aviators in the thirties flying up from Aden to survey the Hadhramaut Valley two hundred miles from the coast would be astonished to find motor cars moving up and down roads that had been made between Tarim and Seiyun, the capital, and Shibam to the west. There were no roads between the Wadi and the coast, and the East Aden Protectorate at this time was known only to explorers like Colonel Van der Meulen. The wealthy Seiyids, with money pouring in from Singapore where their countrymen were running shops, hotels and clubs, had contrived to send motor cars from Singapore to Shihr on the coast where they were dismantled, carried two hundred miles on camel back and put together again in the Wadi. Subsequently in the forties Seiyid Bubakr al-Kaf contrived with Ingrams' inspiration to persuade the Bedouin to allow a road to be built from the coast to the interior across the eastern jol. By the time I came to the Hadhramaut the al-Kaf road had been going for some years.

In the years since the war, motor lorries had steadily increased in number, and in the 1950s there were nearly one hundred commercial lorries in the Qu'aiti and Kathiri States, many of them five-tonners. They were essential as a famine prevention measure. At the same time the demands of the people in the Wadi for perishable and consumer goods had greatly increased, and they were most averse to such goods being transported by camels because of the damage and losses, and the higher cost.

In order to prevent the Bedou from losing their livelihood, it was necessary to maintain the balance between camel and lorry traffic by restricting the goods to be carried by the latter. When there was a shortage of camels, the restrictions had to be relaxed, a proceeding which the Bedou invariably regarded as a direct threat. The matter had not been eased by the action of some of the merchants who tended to abuse this arrangement since they naturally preferred to send their goods by the faster, cheaper and often more reliable lorries. The improvement in the condition of the camels owing to the satisfactory rains during the year brought the matter to a head, and in the winter of 1953–54 a large number of animals remained in the coastal ports for long periods without loads. The resulting hardship to the Bedou produced incidents on the East and West Roads.

The Muqadam Banheim of the Hamai tribe of the Seiban confederation of Bedouin on the jol was the instigator of most of the disturbances in 1954 and all those that happened subsequently when the Mukalla Regular Army were trapped in the mountains. He was an extremely intelligent man, full of intrigue, very bold and outspoken and quite indifferent to any threat from Government. At all costs the States were anxious to avoid a clash with the Bedouin which would run them into a great expenditure and hold up essential convoys of supplies to the inhabitants of the Wadi Duan and the Wadi Hadhramaut.

We met on the jol at my rest-house on Mala Matar, 7,000 feet above Mukalla and only forty-five miles from it. For two days running we sat for hours on end, the State Secretary with his towering figure and booming voice talking slowly and ponderously while Abdullah Suleiman wheedled the muqadam in his best Bedouin style. Jock Snell was with me as a sort of indication to the Bedou (at that time he was my Military Adviser) that things would not be too well with them if they were recalcitrant. The muqadam was quite impervious to any sort of threat, but after two days we eventually avoided a direct clash and got him to agree to a Board of Muqadams who would sit in Mukalla with the representatives of the lorry drivers and the merchants. I had a feeling that this solution was bound to go wrong through the greed of one party or another, no matter how closely we watched it, and I had neither staff nor time to supervise the situation. But we were able to tide over any real troubles for the moment.

In March 1955 I decided to take advantage of the Moon Festival at Quaidan to talk to the tribal leaders. This celebration at the tomb of a pre-Islamic saint was always attended by seven or eight thousand Bedouin from the jol, the very people most concerned about the threat from the motor lorries. The Minister and the Financial Secretary and Abdullah Suleiman were all sitting in my large drawing-room ready to move off and the lorry down below was loaded with the Bedouin Legion escort, and my servants, tents, and bedding and food for the whole party, all as usual chattering sixteen to the dozen. I was just about clear, when I looked up to see an anxious-looking chap in white shorts and a white shirt, carrying a B.O.A.C. handbag. I asked, 'Can I help?' and he said, 'I am Hammond Innes and I sent you a wire asking you if I could visit you.' I replied, 'I'm very sorry, nothing has come here and I am just about to leave in the car waiting below to attend a major tribal gathering in the mountains of Duan. But first do tell me what you do.' He looked somewhat surprised and said, 'I write.' I then asked him whether he would like to accompany me on trek if he had the time. He jumped eagerly at this and I got my servants busy producing some warm clothes and a camp bed and bedding whilst I introduced him to the Ministers.

The interest of the journey that followed was enormously increased by Hammond Innes's lively and fascinating company. We camped that night in the mountains some 5,000 feet up beside a Bedou ferik. There were small camp fires everywhere; the Bedou were singing and talking and grilling goat meat on the red-hot rocks. We joined them and shared their meal. Hammond Innes was enchanted by the whole scene, with these almost naked warriors with long black oiled curls, glistening white teeth and shining eyes, their almost naked bodies covered in oil and indigo, their sole protection against both heat and cold. He remarked on their marvellous physique. We had our camp beds in the open. It was a cold, starlit night with no dew and before going off to sleep I

15. Sheikh Zaid bin Sultan el Nahiyan, Ruler of Abu Dhabi and Trucial States

16. The Author

asked him what sort of sales he had for his books. He replied, 'About fourteen million readers in America alone.' I turned over to sleep; it was now about eleven. At one o'clock I woke up and was surprised to see Hammond Innes lying on his tummy writing hard at what was evidently a diary. He was still writing at two. In the morning I asked him if he always put down the day's happenings on the same day and what would come of it eventually. He said, 'Yes, I invariably do, and enough to convey an absolute picture of what I saw if necessary five years later. For it may be as long as that before I'm able to turn to the particular scene and transform it into a novel or story.' The subsequent days which I spent with him are vividly described in a chapter of *A Harvest of Journeys* which was not published until six or seven years later.

After a few miles' journey in the main wadi we turned left into a side wadi at Quaidan, the home of the Sheikh of Budha, whose family were responsible for leading the tribesmen to the tombs of their saint. As each party of tribesmen entered the wadi, they had a 'zamil', when ten or more of the tribe would weave in and out of the advancing line firing their rifles into the air. The compliment was returned by the other tribesmen; if somebody important was present, he had the great honour of having the rifles fired as close as possible to him. I used to find this procedure singularly trying when walking hand in hand with the State Secretary or a prominent muqadam or the Sultan.

The valley we presently entered, between towering cliffs, was crowded with Bedouin and camels, goats and oxen, the latter mainly here to be slaughtered for the coming feasts. It was very hot in the middle of the day and the temporary markets were burning centres of heat and alive with flies. The chatter was indescribable. We were very warmly greeted by the Sheikhs, who made us extremely comfortable in their storied mud houses, cool and attractively designed.

The following days were spent in extended talks with the tribal leaders of the main tribes of the Seiban Zei. Tribal trouble was working up and this was the time and the place to try and stop it. Sheikh Qadal, the wise Jehan Khan, the Financial Secretary who could charm a bird out of its cage, and Abdullah Suleiman, all worked for long hours on the assembled tribal heads in the Sheikh's house to try and get an agreement. When the gathering broke up things looked much better and I sent Hammond Innes on with the Minister to see something of the Hadhramaut Valley. I myself had to return over the jol on the two-hundred-mile journey back to Mukalla to deal with tribal troubles that had arisen in the meantime in the neighbouring Wahidi State.

o

All the Qu'aiti trouble came to a head in a few months. The tribes had real reason for complaint, it appeared later, but unfortunately they would not produce any evidence of the undoubted evasion of the transport regulations by certain merchants and even government officials. As a consequence, they believed the State would never act on their complaints and so took the law into their own hands. On the East Road the Hamum federation began to inspect trucks, and turn back those which they thought were breaking the rules. The Qu'aiti Government decided to negotiate, and a new agreement was soon reached.

But on the West Road, the tribes decided to force a showdown, and on 14th–15th June, 1955, while I was on leave in England, they blocked the 7,000 foot pass between Mala Matar and Bein al Jibal. A force of the Mukalla Regular Army was sent to clear the road; but they themselves were cut off when the tribesmen blocked the road again below them. The road from the coast is ideal for ambushes and road blocks, climbing tortuously into the hills through narrow defiles. Several hundred 'blue warriors' could hold their positions almost indefinitely against infantry assaults from below. It was decided therefore to operate from the north, and the R.A.F. flew a small force of sixty-five men to Qatn. They were joined by Armed Constabulary from Shibam and Irma, making the total up to 100 all ranks.

The operation was, of course, under the control of the Qu'aiti Officer Commanding, Armed Forces, although the R.A.F. were asked for fighter support to help clear the position. It was entirely successful, and in a fortnight all the road blocks had been cleared, and the road was open to normal traffic, although lorries had to travel in convoy with armed guards.

When I got back from leave in early July, I was very uneasy since nothing had been permanently settled. We had to get into touch again with the tribal muqadams and persuade them to come to terms; this meant sitting in the Wadi Duan, at the hottest time of the year, while emissaries went to and fro. I went up there with Sheikh Qadal (who, being very fat, suffered enormously from the heat) and with the Bedouin Affairs Assistant, a small escort of the Bedouin Legion and with Jim Ellis, then my Military Assistant. We sat in the house of the Mansab of a side wadi which cut right up into the jol, where we felt that the Bedouin might possibly approach us without too much alarm. I knew the Bedouin were very short of food and were really rather anxious to get back to a peaceful life in their own camping areas.

Abdullah Suleiman and the local Naib, Hassan Ba Sura, himself a Bedouin of the Hamai tribe, and much loved by the people,

ould go up the valley and send people ahead to try to get in touch.
he muqadam of the Hamai, Banheim, would not come himself
ut would send down two or three representatives with proposals to
s. After interminable talks they would go back and carry our reply
ɔ the muqadam. After some three weeks of this process, sitting
ɔasting in a mud house, the muqadam appeared himself with his
wn sub-sheikhs and a hundred and fifty or two hundred Bedouin.
Ve were, I may say, most alarmed as I only had a handful of
Iadhrami Bedouin soldiers, but we walked up the valley with
ʌbdullah Suleiman and greeted them. Among the Bedouin on the
ɔl where conversation is carried on across the valley, all talk is in
. high-pitched voice and the greetings were loud and fierce. But
.fter we had sat down and coffee was produced and Abdullah
ɨuleiman had arranged the slaughtering of twenty goats, and rations
ɾf rice had been cooked, we sat down together to a large meal
pread under the trees in the valley bottom. Muqadam Banheim
ɨimself sat next to me and in his somewhat brusque way appeared
ɔ be trying to be friendly. Abdullah said when they had eaten,
All is well and we shall get sense out of them.' It was clear that
hey were terribly hungry and had been without adequate food for
nonths and were ready to come to a sensible agreement. Again they
ɨgreed to send their representatives to Mukalla, but never did we
ʒet the Muqadam Banheim himself to set foot there. He was like
ι wild animal and would not enter the town, afraid of being trapped
ɔr imprisoned for past offences against the Government. The sub-
ɨequent meetings with the representatives of the lorry owners and
:he merchants from the Wadi were successful and peace lasted until
ɨome years after I left the country, when I heard of a great slaughter
ɔn the West Road, when more than twenty of the Mukalla Regular
Army were killed in an ambush. In one sense the problem is
ιnsoluble until the Bedouin can be helped to find another livelihood:
the lorry is bound to oust the camel.

Owing to the increasing prosperity of Hadhramis in the Hedjaz,
the Persian Gulf and Aden, a steady stream of emigrants has continued to these places, including a large number of Bedouin from
tribes who have never been known to emigrate in large numbers
before. It is doubtful whether the full effects of this movement will
be seen for some years but some Bedouin are noticeably keener to
try their hand at work they previously considered beneath them,
though rather more rewarding than camel and goat herding. A
few Sei'ar and Manahil are known to be undergoing technical training in the Aramco centre of Dahran and others seem to have found
reasonable means of livelihood there. Some of the Hamum have
taken to the sea, notably Beit Ghorabh, Beit Ajil and Jimha, and

supply a fair proportion of the crews of the Halal Shipping Com
pany amongst others. Beit Ghorabh have procured three dhows of
their own.

In July 1957 I went to the Wadi Hajjar where we were building
a new road over some three hundred miles of very rough country
down to one of the richest river valleys in the East Aden Protectorate
It was late in the evening when a car arrived with a note from the
Naib of Duan Province to say that a terrible disaster had struck
the Wadi Duan and that thousands of pounds' worth of palms had
been washed down by floods such as had never been seen in the
history of the Wadi. I drove all night up the mountain pass which
we had only just completed and thence over the jol to reach the
cliff above Masna at dawn. Here I left the tourer and my lorry and
went over to the cliff edge. Fifteen hundred feet below was an
appalling scene of destruction.

The Wadi presented a picture which I could not recognize. The
palm forests which rise high up, and the irrigation works above the
Wadi, had been swept away on the cliff side, and I could see towns
which were never before visible through the trees. More than eighty
thousand palms were swept away by a flood which stretched from
side to side of the Wadi, and which came down in a relentless wall
of water some thirty feet high sweeping everything before it. This
particular area was regarded as one of the finest palm areas in the
Hadhramaut and the trees themselves had a high capital value,
and a status value far beyond their value in dates. The owners had
lost literally thousands and thousands of pounds with their destruction. I went down the cliff to the Naib's house but found he was out
trying to do what he could do for the people. I met him with a party
of villagers in the valley. They were absolutely overcome, stunned,
in tears, and in despair. Never had they known a tragedy such as
this. I sent a telegram down immediately to Aden asking for a
very large sum for relief and stating that at least eighty thousand
pounds' worth of damage had been done. The Government found
it hard to believe and insisted on sending up the Director of Agriculture to check. When he came, I took care that he saw everything,
and we toured from village to village and saw the extent of the
destruction and heard from the lips of the villagers the losses they
had suffered. I am glad to say that the compensation was paid as
a result. The Naib was terrific. He and his assistants worked with
my own assistant advisers to try to re-root the smaller palms which
had been turned up. Two years later when I left the Wadi for
the last time the Duan valley was well on its way to recovery,

though it would be many years before they would see a forest ich as they had known; it takes some seven years for a palm to ructify.

The Wadi Hadhramaut was not, of course, entirely Qu'aiti: mbedded in it was the Kathiri Sultanate, sadly reduced over the enturies by the invading and colonising Qu'aiti. By now, the total opulation of the state was only about 150,000, ruled by a very oung Sultan, Hussein bin Ali. He lived in an enormous white alace, eight storeys high and with a round tower at each corner. t looked like a gigantic iced cake, sitting on a rock above the town f Seiyun.

Sultan Hussein bin Ali was a small man, quiet and reserved, and vith very agreeable manners. His brothers were not distinguished, ut his cousin Abdullah was a very lively and promising lad of ighteen. His burning wish, encouraged by the Sultan, was to ecome a doctor: at this time all the doctors in the Protectorate were ndians apart from the Health Adviser, who was British. So we ent him to England to learn English as a first step, and when I vent on leave I visited him at his digs in Norwich. He asked me, vhen I arrived, whether I knew the cathedral. When I said no, ie said eagerly, 'I must show it to you before lunch, it is too remark- ble,' and so I had the great pleasure of being shown round one of he masterpieces of our Christian heritage by a charming and ntelligent young Moslem.

I went back to London determined to get him into a university omehow, and was subsequently able to introduce him to Alan Lennox-Boyd, who was enormously impressed by him. He helped iim with introductions to relations in Dublin, where he took a good degree. After a period as a house surgeon in England, Abdullah returned to the Kathiri State, where ever since he has been Medical Officer to his people.

To the west, the Wadi Irma was very unsettled, with constant tribal fighting. After several tours of the area, I persuaded the Qu'aiti Sultan and his Council to turn it into a separate province, the Western Province, and equip the Governor with some men of the Hadhrami Bedouin Legion and the Qu'aiti Armed Constabulary to maintain order. This they did: but I believe the character of the first Governor, Seiyid Mohammed Kharusi, did more to en- force peace than the garrison. Kharusi was an Omani Arab of very good family whose father had been Agricultural Officer to the Sultan of Zanzibar; he was a superb boxer, one of his victims being the British Fleet Champion who remained unconscious for twenty-four hours. He proved a very tough but fair governor; he was quite incorruptible and fearless in any situation.

Alas, he drank enormously, which naturally upset the Seiyids. Once when he was very tight he chased a British Locust Officer down the Seir Valley in his Land Rover, taking pot shots at him with his rifle. Luckily he kept missing. He had some curious fantasy that the Locust Officer was a Yemeni invading his province.

Not all invasions were fantasy; the frontier of the Protectorate lay for a thousand miles mainly along the great Empty Quarter of the Rubh 'al Khali, with the Yemen and Saudi Arabia as neighbours. A very powerful Yemeni tribe, the Daham, frequently raided over into the Protectorate, killing the Seiar Awamir and Manahil who opposed them and carrying off their camels and sheep. The efficacy of their raids depended on access to well-heads where they could replenish their water supplies before returning home with their booty. One of my first jobs was to build forts to control these well-heads, and we soon had four at Zimakh, Minwakah, Thamad and Sanau. They were the proper 'Beau Geste' kind of fort, each manned by twenty-five or thirty men of the H.B.L. mounted on camels, but with a Land Rover patrol in addition. Later we built four more to give security to oil exploration parties.

All this meant a big expansion in the H.B.L., from 300 to some 1,200, but it achieved security for the people of the East Aden Protectorate. The force was a highly efficient one under its commander, Kaid Naif, a very solid-looking, red-faced man with, I should think, Turkish blood. The second-in-command, Taibel Hodi, was a man of magnificent appearance and of great prestige with the girls at the well-heads and known to us as Clarke Gable.

We had no more trouble with the Daham, but some years later a party of Americans from Aramco, with Saudi guards, penetrated the frontier and started to drill for oil some thirty miles inside Qu'aiti territory. My Assistant Adviser in the northern desert at that time was Captain Ellis, and with him I planned their ejection, which was neatly executed. The Americans called up the Aramco H.Q. at Dahran on their R.T., and the manager there gave Ellis ten solid minutes of expostulation and recrimination. Ellis's reply must have maddened the manager beyond measure; all he replied, with real Scots terseness, was 'Noted.' The Americans withdrew, saying they were quite careless of equipment which the Saudis paid for anyway. We promised to guard their caravans and equipment, a million pounds' worth, for ten days, by which time Ellis estimated the water in their tanks would have run out; after that we accepted no further responsibility.

The Saudi guards were told that they were under arrest, but could go back to Saudi Arabia across the border. They pleaded that they would have their heads cut off if they returned. Ellis said, 'All right,

ome with me in my cars, but you must hand over your arms.'
he guards wept and said this was a cut at their honour. Ellis,
who was extremely soft-hearted though a formidable-looking man,
wired me to ask if he could bring the guards down armed. I
answered, 'Don't be a bloody fool.' A reply came back, 'Sorry.' The
guards eventually turned up without their arms and were flown
back to Saudi Arabia via Jeddah, where I believe they lived happily
ever afterwards.

Within a month the Aramco stores and equipment had been
completely sacked by the Seiar, Manahil and Kurab tribes in the
neighbourhood.

The life of an officer in these vast desert areas is fraught with
risks, in particular of mechanical breakdown. Jim Ellis was skilful
in maintaining the transport, a lot of it long overdue for renewal,
and in finding his way about in the maze of vast dunes with lanes
running between them which might run you into a cul-de-sac. In
the early hours of the morning when the sand is hard, the Land
Rovers could run at great speed along the dune ridges, but the
visibility is most deceptive and there is a continual risk of suddenly
shooting over a fifty-foot cliff and turning over and over. We lost
a number of drivers killed in this way.

Apart from stopping the raiding, the Bedouin Legion in the
northern forts were the means of maintaining contact with the
nomad tribes, and securing their allegiance and their friendliness
to the Qu'aiti and Kathiri Government. They also gave a sense of
security to the oil companies' personnel operating in these regions,
who would otherwise have been in the power of the Bedouin. In the
event, by 1958, the northern Mahra desert country and the area
of the Beit Sumada tribes became perfectly peaceful.

The Wahidi Sultanate was a very troublesome part of the East
Aden Protectorate, and developments there demonstrated, in a
concentrated form, what could and could not be accomplished by
foreign advisers. Potentially it was the richest of the Sultanates from
an agricultural point of view, but its inhabitants were wild tribesmen with little interest in their well-watered and fertile country.
Sultan Nassir was a lively young man, but real power lay in the
hands of his dictatorial uncle, Mohammed Bin Said, who made
little or no attempt to prevent his people raiding their neighbours.

The first step was to ensure local security and peace; Jock Snell
spent some time in building up the Wahidi tribal guards with the
help of the Hadhrami Bedouin Legion. After a year or so, we agreed
with the Sultan on a plan for his administration and for the introduction of a court of law, schools and dispensaries. An Agricultural
Officer was appointed who directed farming experiments and began

to train agricultural advisers and pump mechanics; but we went
very slowly, since the Wahidi people were largely semi-Bedouin
and there was no administrative class to build on.

I visited the Sultanate several times, and gradually was able to
persuade the young ruler that his first priorities should be the health
and well-being of his people, and not quarrelling with his neighbours.
On my latter tours with him and his officials it was heartening to see
the progress that was being made, and the warmth and affection
showed for him by his people. They were heavily armed, and like
the Bedouin of the Hadhramaut Jol were covered with indigo and oil.

It was a curious experience to sit in a three- or four-storey mud
house with these magnificent-looking people, and to notice among
them a few lads dressed in elegant silk shirts and coloured sarongs.
They wore no indigo or oil and with their wrist watches appeared
as civilized as any Seiyid in the Hadhramaut. When I asked them
whence they had come, and why this dress, the answer was nearly
invariably, 'From a two-year visit to Jeddah,' where they were in
some trade or shop. They had returned with some money and would
return to the indigo standard again when they had married, which
would be within a month or so. The astonishing thing was that
they all declared that the indigo and oil were much warmer than
their clothes, so much so that in the hot weather the oil was reduced
considerably. In the jol the Bedouin use oil partly for warmth and
partly to prevent the dry air from cracking their skins and causing
intense irritation.

Our other main trouble spot in the E.A.P. lay to the east, the
twenty thousand square miles of mountain and desert that formed
the Mahra Sultanate. Its coastline had no harbour, only a few open
roadsteads pounded by the Indian Ocean. The inhabitants were
barely civilized Bedouin, with a few oppressed fishermen living by
the shore; and it had no government at all. The hereditary ruler
of this wilderness was the Sultan of Socotra, who lived on his
island, two hundred miles away from his mainland subjects.

The first step in bringing order and progress to any community
was to get the ruler to appoint administrators, and to agree to
setting up some form of police to stop feuding and raiding. But in
the case of Mahra it proved impossible to take this step for a long
time because the Sultan resolutely refused to go to the mainland.
The island of Socotra is most uninviting, and ridden with malaria,
but the Sultan preferred it to the dangers of visiting his unruly
tribesmen in Mahra. Much diplomacy and a good deal of pressure
was needed to persuade him to accompany me to the mainland

where I spent a very disagreeable time at Gheidha among a people who clearly were unenthusiastic about their Sultan and absolutely opposed to any form of control on their anarchic and brutally oppressive society.

The Sultan decided to stay until a landing ground had been prepared, so that he could be flown home, but I had to get back to report to Aden and the Colonial Office. So I took passage with Abdullah Suleiman, my Bedouin Affairs Assistant, in a sailing dhow which turned out to have a cargo of sardines, rotting and infested with fly worms. The smell was appalling, the weather bad, and every swing of the boom brought another cascade of worms down on us from the sail. The dhow was so ill-found that I thought we should sink, and I was relieved when we finally made port and could leave the smell of sardine manure.

Clearly the Sultan could impose no authority, and the only immediate course appeared to be the use of troops. I was strongly opposed to this, both because it would look like colonial adventurism and also on the practical ground that it would be impossible to maintain any force in a harbourless, roadless country. It was eventually agreed to postpone any direct action, but to try to civilize the Mahra tribes from the north, where the H.B.L. were manning Sanau and Habarut Forts. Their patrols made friends with the Beit Samada tribesmen, and then extended their influence to the south; and three years after I had left Mukalla, Gheidha and the coastal areas were quietly controlled by the H.B.L., and an administration could at last be set up.

I had originally been appointed to Mukalla in 1949 on a two-year contract as Resident Adviser, which had been renewed several times; after nine years I felt that it was time to make a change, and that a change would be good for the Protectorate. Julian Amery, who was then Under-Secretary of State for War, visited the Sultan of Oman in the winter of 1957–58 to discuss security matters in his territory, and in addition had talked over the advisability of setting up a Development Department. Its purpose would be, with financial assistance from H.M.G., to set up schools, health centres, agricultural and fishery improvement schemes. The Sultan agreed, and Julian Amery asked if I could take on the job of Development Secretary. I had no wish to sit back farming or gardening in England, so I agreed. The Governor in Aden, now Sir William Luce, recommended that my name should go forward to the Sultan, and after an interview with him the matter was settled.

But it was with rather a sad heart that I spent my final three months touring in the Duan and Hadhramaut valleys and along the coast. Wherever I went there were huge farewell parties and dinners where a hundred or more people would assemble over goat meat and rice, or over exquisitely cooked Hadhrami meals in the Wadi, which the Sultans and the Seiyids knew so well how to serve with all the tastes of Java and the Indies in the food.

In Mukalla the forces were all present for a final parade, with most of the townspeople watching. After the State band had played 'The Queen', I was presented by the Sultan with a superb sword inlaid in gold; then Jehan Khan, the new Minister of State, delivered a speech. Then on to the Kathiri State, where there was another presentation in front of the army and police with crowds and bands. It was extremely exacting, at the same time very warming, to leave such friends behind.

In my farewell speech to the people at Mukalla, I said:

'I thank you all for the friendliness, kindness, courtesy and patience you have shown me and my officers over these years and I wish you all and your States the peace, progress and prosperity that you deserve. I am sure that, if and when oil is found, your Rulers will use its wealth with the wisdom and interest that you have shown in running your Governments. It has been my privilege to serve you through the happiest years of my life. I leave with thankfulness for having had these years, but with the inevitable distress at leaving such friends.

'There is one end, our works live after us and by their fruits we should be judged in days to come. If we have worked well and faithfully, then it is well.'

Chapter Sixteen

DEVELOPMENT SECRETARY, OMAN

THE three years I spent working in Muscat and Oman were intensely frustrating, although the Sultan himself was always charming and considerate to me. He was a quiet, soft-spoken man whom I had met in his palace at Salala on several occasions on my way to Socotra. Muscat, his capital, is unbearably hot and surrounded by forbidding black volcanic peaks, whereas Salala, a thousand miles away, has a good climate and a lovely setting between green, wooded hills and the sandy shore of the Indian Ocean.

Muscat was in a deplorable condition. This could only in part be blamed on local unrest which amounted to rebellion against the Sultan's rule. I had seen what could be done in the Hadhramaut and in Qu'aiti State in particular, with a revenue about one half of what the Sultan of Muscat drew in customs duties; yet here there were no medical services in the whole country. I made a tour soon after my arrival with an economic expert and a representative from the Development Division at the British Embassy in Beirut. The latter told the Sultan after the tour that, in twenty years' experience of most of the countries in the Middle East, he had never seen a people so poverty-stricken or so debilitated with diseases capable of treatment and cure. This report led to the building of some twenty health centres and dispensaries throughout the Sultanate.

Although the rebel forces had been driven into the Jebel Akdar, a 10,000 foot mountain massif, irregular bands still penetrated the plain and shot up convoys. But their principal activity at this time was planting mines along the roads. The large plastic mines caused many casualties.

It wasn't the most auspicious moment to inaugurate a brand new Development Department, the more so since the Sultan was, I felt, very half-hearted about plans for health, education, agriculture and so on. My first job was a road, something the Sultan really was keen about: but before I could start on anything, I had to organize the Department and find trained staff.

Fortunately I was able to arrange for Mani, the Madrasi who had been my private secretary at Mukalla, to come to Muscat as my Deputy. He soon had a proper accounting system going, which was vital since I was responsible for the Development Budget both to the Sultan and to the Foreign Office. Through Mani, I found a first-rate confidential clerk, so I was able to go out on tour knowing that the office work would be kept going.

The Sultan wanted a road into the interior of the Shargia, the wild south-eastern province of Oman. It was planned to run up the Wadi Auq, so in early September I set off. The weather was harsh at this time of the year in the Wadi, and the presiding Sheikh who was responsible for producing road coolies was as greedy as anyone I had encountered in the whole Arab world. His demands for the road work were quite beyond belief and he protested vigorously that he could not get coolies at the exorbitant rates he was asking. I discovered that the coolies were paying him two-thirds of the wages they were getting. The Ruler's representative who had been allocated to me appeared to be of very little assistance in checking the inordinate appetite of this Sheikh.

Working in the burning heat of the Wadi in the roasting sun was a severe strain on the temper, and at one time I returned to Muscat to report the whole matter to the Minister of the Interior, Seiyid Ahmed bin Ibrahim, a white-bearded Omani Arab. Dressed in a cream *aba* with a golden edge and a beautifully coloured Omani turban, and always carrying a silver jambiya at his waist, he was a most impressive and dignified figure.

He was probably the most conscientious and hard-working official that the Sultan ever was likely to have, and he appeared, like a sergeant-major, to be on duty all day and night. He was never in a hurry, but never lazy and always as helpful to me as he could be. I have always felt that the Sultan, who never went near the country during the whole period that I was Development Secretary, and has never been near it since, now ten years ago, was singularly lucky to have a man of such outstanding qualities. Seiyid Ahmed virtually ruled the interior.

The first burning month was spent carrying out a road trace which filled me with doubts and anxieties as to whether the Wadi Auq would come down in flood when the rains came, and sweep it all away and destroy my reputation as a road-builder. Fortunately during the three years I was there this never happened, and the main difficulties were overcame after the first three months of really hard work.

Living in a small forty-pounder tent with practically no camp kit, my cook and servants camping under the rocks in burning heat, bitter cold, high winds, among the scorpions and hornets, was not a comfortable experience. Travelling was a strain because of the ubiquitous mines. We had Land Rovers armoured against these horrors, but motoring all day in the sun did not encourage one to take off the steel roof, though there was little doubt that with a

lastic mine a roof meant a broken neck. I used to have the wind-
screen removed; it is in any case much cooler without it in the hot
weather. The Development Department were attacked on two
occasions, when mines were put down at the entrance to our com-
pound and the road foreman was blown up, though fortunately
undamaged.

During the first year of my service in Oman the Sultan had
agreed to the introduction of a travelling ambulance to move in the
Bedouin areas with a suitable British Medical Officer in charge, if
he could be found; and suggested that I should explore the reactions
of the Bedouin to this.

I had gone up to Mudeibi in the Shargia and was sitting discussing this matter with the Wali (Governor) and his staff when a large
tribesman came stalking up with his rifle in his hand, and said,
'What is that kaffir (infidel) doing among you? We do not want
him here.' The party around the Wali, with whom I had been
drinking tea, looked extremely uncomfortable and embarrassed, and
tried to turn the conversation. When he had gone they said, 'Well,
he is a Waheibi from the Waheibi Sands at Sanau and they are very
fanatical and wild.' However, I laughed and said to the Wali,
'I'm proposing to go to Sanau tomorrow and will talk to them.'

Next morning I drove into the well-field at Sanau and parked
under the trees, where I found a number of elders sitting consulting.
After passing the normal Arab greetings we sat down near them
and they asked the representative who I was. He explained but they
continued to look at me coldly and suspiciously. However, I quietly
approached the question of diseases among them and the possibility
of the travelling ambulance with the doctor. They asked somewhat
pointedly, 'Have you got a letter from the Sultan?' I said, 'No.'
They said, 'Well, we cannot discuss this with you unless you have
a letter from the Sultan.' I see, 'I see,' and told my boys to open
the Abyssinian table under another tree nearby and took out my
camp chair and started to read the *Sunday Times*. In the meantime
I told the boys to open the medicine chest and to put the whole of
its contents on the camp table. They did so and I went on reading.
Presently I was conscious of some of the Waheibis under the trees,
about thirty yards away, saying, 'Oh – he has got medicines'; then
one said, 'Oh, I have bad eyes,' and another, 'I have dysentery,'
and another said, 'I am suffering from a cold in the chest.' Presently
two or three came over furtively. I sat reading paying not the
slightest attention to them when one asked me, 'What is that on the
table? Is that not medicine?' I pretended not to hear him until he
repeated the question and plucked my sleeve. Then I said, 'Yes.
Why? How does that concern you?' He said, 'My eyes are bad with

the dust and the wind, and they are hurting. Have you no medicine?' Another said, 'My stomach is very sore. I have been running all night. Have you no medicine?' I said, 'Yes. I have, but firstly,' (in a hard tone) 'have you got a letter from the Sultan?' At this they all laughed and the ice was broken. I treated those that were there and they took me over to their camp where I stayed with them. During the next twenty-four hours, I treated about a hundred and sixty people, mainly for eye trouble from which the Bedouin suffered continuously in these areas.

One of the earliest health centres, at Musna, had to wait for over a year and a half while the Sultan and the Treasury discussed who was to pay for the builder. The Sultan, of course, won and the Treasury paid. The Development Department had in its initial stages been based on the idea that the buildings should be produced by the Sultan and the staff and medicines by H.M.G. I used to wonder greatly over all these matters, since I knew that only recently the State of Gwadar in Pakistan, which had belonged to Oman, had been sold by the Sultan to the Pakistan Government for three million pounds, the interest of which accumulated in Swiss and American banks. Over and above this of course was the income from the customs duties which was very considerably more than that of the Qu'aiti State when I first joined it as Resident Adviser.

During the following year, 1962, doctors and health assistants gradually began to arrive from Pakistan. I was also able to obtain a first-class Indian Moslem agriculturalist from Madras called Wazir. He became one of our key people with his skill in agriculture and his ability in spreading a pumping scheme, as we had done in the Wadi Hadhramaut.

It was the Sultan's habit to call me down to Salala periodically to discuss plans which were in hand. We would sit on the sofa together in his very charmingly appointed drawing-room in front of a low table, and I would go through all our points with him. It shook me to find that letters sent to him asking for an early decision had not even been opened, so I resorted to an old ruse, and thereafter wrote to tell him I was proposing to do so-and-so, and would go ahead unless I heard to the contrary within the next ten days. He was normally extremely courteous, but I always felt he was not really interested in development.

The general programme was supposed to include schools, but the Sultan allowed me to build only one school in Mattrah, the commercial capital, which is practically entirely inhabited by Baluchis and Scinde Pakistanis, all merchants or small artisans with no Arab connections. The existing primary school in Muscat had a few Arab pupils but was largely filled with the sons of Indian merchants. At an early stage I put up to the Ruler a scheme to get primary schools established in each Province H.Q., mainly to instruct the sons of the leading Sheikhs and Province Governors, who in the future would be able to play an active part in the Administration.

The Sultan would have none of this. He said to me cynically one day, 'That is why you lost India, because you educated the people.' In the meantime, of course, a large number of lads were moving out to schools in Kuwait or Bahrain or other more advanced places in the Gulf, to become an active body of young Omanis who were determined to work against their own Ruler and his retrograde policies.

I enjoyed these visits to him, and our discussions. I called the Sultan 'Your Highness' on my early visits, but I was informed later by his Financial Adviser, a Pakistani, that he wished to be called 'Your Jalalath', which means 'Your Majesty', and so we kept to this singular form of address. He would call me Boustead in the most friendly way.

Forty minutes' drive from the palace, the Sultan had a huge garden filled with palms and flowering trees, which I found gloomy in the extreme. He had a curious habit of half finishing a building, and there were traces of them all over the garden. In consequence the place always had a *triste* look about it, like a deserted home which had become a haunt of ghosts. It was forbidden for visitors to go about without one or two armed retainers from the Sultan's bodyguard.

The Sultan's army had the task of driving the rebels from their stronghold in the Jebel Akdar, and H.M.G. provided help. Two squadrons of the Special Air Service were flown in from Malaya; a heavy air bombardment was carried out and at the same time the S.A.S. troops and the Sultan's Armed Forces stormed the Jebel Akdar heights. The operation was successfully carried out and the whole of the area occupied, but the ringleaders and many of their followers managed to extricate themselves and slipped away to Saudi Arabia, where they prepared to fight another day.

At the end of this operation, a fort and an airstrip were made some 8,000 feet up on the mountain and the succeeding months were spent in trying to rehabilitate the tribesmen in the Jebel. Their fruit gardens, fields, irrigation system and dwellings had been destroyed by the air bombardment.

This meant further demands on the Development Department. I was mainly occupied with irrigation development in this beautiful highland country where we found a better supply of water both in the mountain rivers, Persian springs and wells than I had seen anywhere else in all southern Arabia. Much of the land was of a high agricultural standard and it was clear from an early stage that we must push ahead with pumps for the interior as we had done in the Hadhramaut. The Indian Agricultural Officer was enormously successful; he had green fingers and was very quiet and persuasive with the people. He gained their confidence increasingly and the standard of farming improved steadily. In three years nearly a hundred and fifty pumps were installed in the interior.

Here again the diseases which debilitated the people and the shocking state of the communications contributed greatly to our difficulties, which were added to by the mining of the roads. It was essential to help these people by giving them assistance with our government agricultural lorries. Always there was a danger of their being blown up. In three years more than a hundred lorries and Land Rovers were blown up on the roads by mines.

Raids were made, too: the new dispensary at Bahla was blown up, and the Health Assistant badly wounded and blinded. As no compensation was given by the Sultanate to anybody other than the armed forces, this kind of thing was not much encouragement to doctors and Health Assistants doing their duty to the interior.

Roads were essential to the development of the territory, not only for the encouragement of commerce but also to help the search for oil, vitally important in any Arab state. I could see that trouble would arise, as in the Hadhramaut, between the lorry owners and the camel convoys. I was struck by the immense columns of Omani camels, the most renowned in Arabia. They were led by people of the Habus tribe, distinguished like one or two others of the Shargia tribes by their orange turbans. The convoys were laden with dates, limes and oranges from the interior.

Another point of interest for the traveller were the herds of donkeys driven up from Mattrah on the coast, carrying salted fish. This is a great delicacy in Oman as in the Hadhramaut, where the Bedouin look on salt fish, and in particular dried shark, as a staple food and an aphrodisiac. It was certainly a strongly scented one.

I have already mentioned the almost total lack of medical facilities in Oman before the establishment of the Development Department Health Centres. But the American Mission had been operating under Dr Thoms and his father before him for twenty-five years in the town of Mattrah. They were devoted people, and an enormous solace to the populace. They cost the Sultan nothing and they would willingly have worked in the interior had they been so allowed.

Later I met in Buraimi on the Muscat border the parallel Missionary Hospital with doctors as devoted as Thoms and his wife, and who had won the affection and gratitude of the tribesmen of the Buraimi area for their work among them. Such people were Dr and Mrs Kennedy of the Evangelical Mission. Although they did no actual preaching among the Moslems, the Bedouin and pastoral tribesmen and their wives have become utterly devoted to the best of the missionaries. The thing that struck me in particular about them is their astonishing capacity to work at full pressure continuously, and the obvious feeling of happiness which they obtain from their work.

It was towards the end of spring 1961, when my second contract with the Sultan was drawing to a close, that the Political Resident in the Gulf, then Sir George Middleton, asked me whether I would like to consider taking over the Political Agency at Abu Dhabi which was now blossoming into a rapidly developing oil state. He added that the Sheikh there was extremely difficult and was known for his unpredictability, and that it would not be easy. As the P.A. at Abu Dhabi was then subordinate to Dubai, I declined but said that provided it was to be an independent command I would welcome the experience.

About this time Sir George Middleton left. During an urgent visit to London to my dentist, I saw Sir William Luce, an old friend from the Sudan and Aden who was now taking over as Political Resident in the Gulf. He had already been primed by Sir George Middleton and said that provided I was agreeable he would welcome my coming and would certainly arrange with the Foreign Office that Abu Dhabi should be an independent command. The idea of working with Sir William Luce was an enormous attraction to me, since I had known him since he was Private Secretary to General Huddleston in the early forties, and had worked under Luce's general command in Aden, when he was Governor, for two and a half years.

There was still an enormous lot to do in Muscat to complete the agreed programme. To my great loss, Mani had left me to take up the position of Assistant Adviser on finance to the Aden Federation. I spent practically the whole of the burning summer of 1961 touring in the field, completing health centres and dispensaries, building roads and spreading the agricultural and pump gospel through the interior. Physically it was probably the most trying experience I have had in the Middle East. The heat in the interior was intense. Living out in a tent as I was, I found most trying of all the burning dry winds known as the Gharbi which seems to sear right through one, and left me with a perpetual thirst and with skin desiccated by the heat.

In Sohar on the coast where I had a Health Centre it was not the heat but the intense humidity which put down both spirits and enthusiasm. Nightly I drove out five miles into the interior to sleep in the open away from the coastal damp which made sleep almost impossible. Muscat itself when I returned was insufferably hot and I realized the full force of a Persian saying that 'the sinner who goes to Muscat has a foretaste of what is coming to him in the after world'. When October came round I had completed three years and I left for a month's leave in Kenya before taking up the post in Abu Dhabi. I was not sorry to say goodbye to Muscat and Oman, nor in the slightest surprised that in July 1970 the Sultan was deposed and replaced by his son, Sultan Qabas.

Chapter Seventeen

POLITICAL AGENT, ABU DHABI

That is the land of lost content,
I see it shining plain,
The happy highways where I went
And cannot come again.

A. E. HOUSMAN

ABU Dhabi Sheikhdom lies between the states of Qatar and Dubai on the Trucial Coast, and comprises about 40,000 square miles, mostly rolling dune country rising in the south-west to the Liwa, a sand sea of high dunes running up to 700 and 800 feet, vividly described in Wilfred Thesiger's *Arabian Sands*. About one hundred miles to the south lies the oasis of Buraimi, which for many years has been amicably shared by the rulers of Abu Dhabi and the Sultans of Muscat and Oman.

Abu Dhabi Island, the capital, was first settled in 1761 when some Bani Yas bedu discovered drinkable water there. In consequence, the ruling family moved from the Liwa to the new settlement, and the Bani Yas became pearl fishers and, no doubt, pirates in the summer, harvesting their dates in the Liwa in the autumn and grazing their flocks in the winter. It was the maritime activities of the Arabs along the shore of the Persian Gulf which first brought Britain into contact with them; their attacks on shipping, and the continual tribal fighting along the pearl banks, made the Gulf unsafe for trading vessels. By a long series of treaties and maritime truces, culminating in the Treaty of Perpetual Peace of 4th May 1853, the British Government gradually succeeded in establishing peace and order along what came to be known as the Trucial Coast, or Trucial Oman, rather than the Pirate Coast.

The Ruler of Abu Dhabi, the westernmost of the Trucial sheikhs, was a signatory to all the maritime treaties, and was thus in a special treaty relationship with H.M.G. This meant very little until after the last war; until then, British interest was limited to peace at sea, and the sheikhdoms were free to feud and fight as much as they liked. In Abu Dhabi, for instance, there was twenty years of near civil war between rival factions of the ruling family before Sheikh Shakhbut came to power in 1928 after three successive Rulers had been killed. Inter-tribal fighting went on, the last major war taking place as recently as 1945–48, when Abu Dhabi and its neighbour Dubai fought one another up and down the coast.

The first British Political Agent for all the Trucial states was appointed in 1948 and stationed in Dubai. Abu Dhabi's development can really be said to have started then. In 1951 the Trucial Oman Levies were formed and, like the Hadhramaut Bedouin Legion in the East Aden Protectorate, had an immediate effect on tribal feuding, and in suppressing the flourishing market in slaves for Saudi Arabia through the Buraimi market. The Saudis invaded and occupied Buraimi in 1952, but very few of the inhabitants sided with them. Most of the local tribes rallied to the Ruler's representative at the oasis, his brother Sheikh Zaid (now himself the Ruler), and with the aid of the Levies the Saudis were expelled.

Basically, life for the people of Abu Dhabi had changed not at all in the two hundred years since the Bani Yas had settled there, until the discovery of oil. This will of course have an immeasurable effect; no one can predict the outcome of a population of about 15,000 people, brought up in the simplest bedouin traditions, suddenly – via the Ruler – disposing of an income of some £80 million a year, rising to £100 million in the near future. The Abu Dhabi Marine Areas (A.D.M.A) is owned two-thirds by B.P. and one-third by Compagnie Française des Petroles; its main operation is centred on Das Island, about eighty-five miles north-west of Abu Dhabi, where production started in 1962. On the mainland the Petroleum Development (Trucial Coast) Ltd (P.D.T.C.) have a number of oil-bearing wells in their field at Murban, some seventy miles west of Abu Dhabi.

It is a state which in a decade has to jump two centuries. It was this which made my assignment to it so absorbingly interesting. My first impression of Abu Dhabi was of the pleasing openness of sea, land and bay after the closed volcanic circuit of black hills round Muscat. Here the house which Sir George Middleton had promised me was all that I had hoped, with wide double verandahs overlooking the sea and the dhows lying behind the coral reef of the Gulf, and white sands stretching behind the house to high dunes covered with palms in the interior. There was a freshness which, added to the best climate I had known in the Middle East, made the days here delightful. The comparatively small English population, then never more than fifty, were friendly and ready to work together and play together, sailing, swimming and riding on the Sheikh's horses.

The morning before I paid my first ceremonial call on Sheikh Shakhbut, the Ruler, I received a letter from Mr Edward Heath, the Lord Privy Seal, as he then was, the Foreign Secretary's representative in the House of Commons: 'Since I had a chance of seeing something of your devoted work in the Sultanate last winter,

I have been all the better able to appreciate how much you have done in getting the whole development programme under way in the face of great difficulties. I should like you to know how much we have appreciated your work in the Sultanate and I take your success there to be earnest of great things in your next uphill job.'

I realized that although I had been for the past three years the Sultan of Muscat's humble and obedient servant – years more arduous and exacting than any during the whole of my service in the Sudan and the Hadhramaut – I had received not one single word of acknowledgement, let alone thanks, from His Jalalath. It was something of a commentary on his attitude to receive this gracious recognition of service through the Head of the Foreign Office to whom I was half responsible for the budget.

Shakhbut greeted me most warmly. He had, I already gathered, been told that in deference to his position (his state had an enormous oil potential) an officer of considerable seniority and experience was being appointed to him as Political Agent, and that the Agency would be entirely independent and not as hitherto under Dubai. He was extremely pleased at this recognition of his rising influence and position in the Gulf.

During the early days tycoons of all sorts from every company under the sun came crowding to the Ruler to exhort him to accept their wares. He had been brought up in thrift and poverty till nearing sixty, and of no apparent importance to the world until oil was discovered. It must have been an astonishing experience for a Bedouin, with a certain innate shrewdness and an inbred suspicion of everyone he met, to be surrounded by men of high importance in the commercial world coming as suppliants to his throne.

One of the scenes still vivid in my mind is of the manager of one of the largest banks attempting to make an entry for his bank into Abu Dhabi. He spoke in laudatory terms of his Chairman who was a Lord, and Shakhbut quickly wanted to know what degree of Lord he was, how many Lords preceded him. He seemed satisfied with the answer and asked me if I had any relations in the peerage. The bank manager was accompanied as interpreter by a Lebanese of distinction who was on his knees before the Ruler praising him, his wisdom, generosity and charm. It really would have been difficult for the Ruler not to accede, and it was only when the bank manager put his hand to his inside pocket and started to extract a paper which was obviously intended for the Ruler to sign that Shakhbut drew back with the look of a trapped animal.

The Lebanese was forward on his knees like a praying mantis, hands raised in supplication. The Ruler sat terrified on the back of the sofa and I shook my head to the bank manager signalling him to put the paper away quickly. So keen was he on his object that he was a bit tense and tried to press on, resulting of course in the Ruler's even greater apprehensions and more solid resolution not to sign the paper.

Shakhbut did not appear to have any dreams of a large palace or ostentatious wealth. His attitude towards religion was always one of great tolerance. He attended officially with all his family the inauguration of the only Roman Catholic church in Abu Dhabi, following the service with interest. He was tolerant towards, and allowed, the use of alcohol by Europeans. He had an inherent dislike of Egyptians. Many years of poverty and a natural inborn reverence for money for its own sake made him permanently unwilling to show any of the generosity which is a part of his brother Zaid's nature.

From the start Shakhbut was obsessed with the idea of obtaining water from the interior. It was about the same time as the episode with the bank manager that a representative of a most distinguished American firm who had been very successful in Kuwait called on the Ruler and asked for my help to assist them to obtain permission for an overall survey for water. Shakhbut was, however, horrified at their estimate and said he would not dream of it. Instead he suggested that they should carry out a water scheme without a survey, as he said he knew where there was water enough, and it was therefore useless to waste money on a survey. All the arguments in the world for carrying out a survey and ensuring a supply before spending a million pounds or so on a pipe line of some sixty or seventy miles were of no avail.

I remember this company lost face at an early stage when the Ruler was visited in the Majlis by the director to obtain his signature to a letter of intent. He too, like the bank manager, had not realized Shakhbut's horror of appending his signature to anything that might commit him to spend, and when the letter was read out in detail the Ruler tore it up and handed it back to the director saying, 'You are trying to trap me.' The pipe line was eventually put through, fortunately by a most able and effective company, and the water supply seems to be assured. In this field the Ruler's prescience was proved correct.

On looking around Abu Dhabi it was clear to me that if development up to the forecast wealth of the country was going to take place, covering schools, health service and agriculture, it must be based on a port and town which would act as an adequate base. I was accordingly anxious at this early stage to get out a development plan which would be brought into operation as soon as possible.

I was helped by the arrival among the tycoons of one Spencer of the firm of Scott Wilson and Kirkpatrick, who were anxious to be taken on as Consulting Engineers. We worked out together the terms of reference for the development plan for his firm to put up, and then put this forward to the Ruler.

Here in the 'honeymoon' stage soon after my arrival, the Ruler was full of easy optimism and appeared enthusiastic about the plan. He turned a bit pale when confronted with the actual cost of planning, some £10,000, and said purely for planning this was ridiculous. We talked and persuaded him, while all the time he was playing for a direct deal with the contractors. I tried to point out how the contractors would do him down and he would not know how to check on them. Eventually he agreed and signed for the development plan. There was much surprise in Bahrain at this astonishing conquest and Spencer, delighted, went ahead with his plans, in combination with the firm of Sir William Halcrow and Partners.

The Ruler was all smiles. In the meanwhile he was keen to have a Director of Education and to take on two accountants and staff for a government. Peter Tripp, who had been Political Agent in Dubai and dealing direct with Shakhbut for years, and was now in Bahrain Residency, wrote to me of his astonishment at this incredible success with Shakhbut, and Sir William Luce could hardly believe it. I was unaware of what was to come.

In March 1962, four months after the honeymoon had started, the blow fell. Shakhbut loathed with deadly hatred the ruler of Qatar. The island of Halul had been in dispute between them, and had been the subject of a Board detailed to enquire into the rights of ownership. Having first read all the correspondence at home, the members of the Board left England with the opinion that Halul belonged to Shakhbut but were convinced that they ought to obtain personal evidence on the ground from the two Rulers before giving a decision. The Ruler of Qatar employed an Egyptian lawyer to put up his case to the Board and he neglected no single piece of evidence in his favour. When they visited Shakhbut, however, he merely flew into one of his rages and said that this was not a matter for evidence, it was a matter of facts; Halul was his island and he would not demean himself by discussing it. The Board and the Political Agent tried to persuade him to obtain the services of a lawyer, but he said he would not waste his money on lawyers. On the evidence, the Board became convinced of Qatar's rights, and awarded ownership of Halul to Qatar. The infuriating thing was that I myself was on tour in the Liwa when it was decided that the decision must be divulged immediately, and a telegram reached my Assistant telling him that if I was absent he should inform the

Ruler personally. I had left the Ruler smiling, warm and co-opera-
tive, and I returned to find a black face and a look of loathing.
He said to me when he greeted me, 'What sort of a friend are you
to give away my lands without even telling me?' I did not have
the least idea of what he was talking about. He talked on and on
in a shrill rising voice like a child. I then realized that the land was
Halul and told him this was something that had happened long
before I came on the scene and over which neither I nor the Political
Resident had any control.

The effect was devastating. Shakhbut's confidence fell away. The
development plan was due in two months' time and he declared
himself uninterested in it and completely averse to forming a government or obtaining officials or anything else. During the subsequent
months all plans were held up, and for the first time since my arrival
I had time to read up the past files on Halul and discover what I
have recounted above. I reproached Shakhbut later with this and
told him that it appeared to me that it was largely his fault for not
having attempted to put up a case. I said, 'We have been on
excellent terms until now and this all happened before I came, and
you have no right to take it out of me, and I won't stand this treatment from you.' He asked me to lunch and relationships were
better, but no further real progress was made.

I am not altogether sure that it was entirely Shakhbut's fury
over the Halul decision which put a stopper on all development
plans; to a considerable extent he simply could not bring himself
to spend money, perhaps because he could not believe that his oil
revenue would continue to pour in.

During the three and a half years of my appointment here the
only scheme that was ever allowed to be carried right through,
as I have mentioned, was the water supply by Paulings. The opening
situation of employing them was comic to a degree. Having heard
of the firm the Ruler said that he would not deal with a common
person as General Manager but that he must have a Lord to deal
with. Paulings, who were pressing for the contract of approximately
a million pounds, had to get a peer as Chairman *ad hoc*. Eventually
Lord Brentford was appointed. He came out and we sat together
with the extremely able Resident Engineer, to whom Lord Brentford
obviously had to defer to answer the Ruler's more technical questions.

Lord Brentford stayed with me for some three weeks and we
became friends. The company found satisfaction in the eyes of the
Ruler, and all their work was deemed good. They certainly worked
magnificently and their contracts were finished long before the
appointed period. The Lord appeared once again and then withdrew into the background.

During this period I called in the assistance of the Agricultural Adviser from the Development Division in Beirut, Jack Eyre, a man who had been the Director of Agriculture in two colonies, was experienced in the Middle East, and whose advice has been invaluable to the countries with whom he worked. We visited Buraimi together, the finest agricultural area in the State with many square miles of excellent soil and water.

The Ruler of Buraimi, Shakhbut's brother Zaid, was delighted and welcomed Jack Eyre's budgetary schemes and assistance, and asked for supervisors to help him.

I went down with the Adviser to Abu Dhabi and we told the Ruler of his experience and schemes in the Middle East and of how they had been welcomed from the Sudan to Pakistan, in Saudi Arabia and in Jordan. All this fell on deaf ears. Shakhbut said to him, 'My people know more about agriculture in their own land than you can tell them. The budget is a pure waste of money. We do not want it and we will not have it. What can you tell us that we do not know?' To say that the Adviser was disappointed would be to put it mildly. Sheikh Zaid was very disappointed. He took on a very able Pakistani Agricultural Officer, Mr A. H. Khan, and paid him from his own funds, but there was no supporting budget, and as a result agricultural development has been held up completely where it could have flourished as in Nizwa and in Sohar in Oman, where a proper budget and proper staff had been organized.

The most disheartening feature of all was not that the Ruler had not put in hand great buildings or public works or engineering schemes, but his simple refusal to give his own people, a pastoral, agricultural and fishing society, the easy assistance which his growing wealth could provide.

I will not easily forget my first visit to Buraimi and my first meeting with Sheikh Zaid. It is impossible to meet him without immediately being taken by him. He is a most ebullient character, always laughing, cheerful, and popular, easy to talk to. He is a great sportsman, keen on horses and camel racing, and was brought up to the nomadic life of the desert.

I was always astonished at the crowds who gathered around him wherever he went in Buraimi, and who treated him with the sort of reverence and attention due to a minor saint. He invariably had a kind word for everybody, and was most generous with his money. I was immediately struck by all that had been done in Al 'Ain, his home town, and in the Buraimi area, for the benefit of the people. The Persian springs had been dug out to increase the water supply to the gardens, wells dug and pumps supplied and cemented baths for men and women had been built in the fallujahs. Everyone who visited Buraimi noticed the happiness of the people in the area.

I spent various periods with Zaid hawking on the dunes to the north-east of Buraimi during the bustard season. This indeed is one of the sports practised by the Sheikhs on which they are keenest. It is a most expensive pastime, as a hawk costs anything from £70 to £200; Zaid usually keeps thirty or forty.

Hawking, riding and camping with Zaid formed the most pleasant interludes during my years in Abu Dhabi. After hawking all the morning and a delicious lunch of bustard baked in the sand, the afternoons would be spent with his followers in foot races, wrestling and competing in the long jump. My first day of this was marked by an amusing incident when a very tough young tribal retainer came up to me and asked me whether I knew how to wrestle. I was sitting on the sand at the time and the others looked at me to see my response. I jumped up quickly and before Mohammed bin Amri had time to think I had thrown him on his back with a cross buttock and fell sharply on top of him. All the followers were vastly amused and pulled his leg for being thrown by the Political Agent. I may say I did not experiment again with him, ready and prepared to wrestle. The evenings would be spent sitting in a circle around big log fires talking over coffee or singing, with the lute players and drummers setting the music.

Like all other Arabs, Sheikh Zaid's followers would talk endlessly, and conversation is one of the Arab's strongest points. Good talk round the leaping fire, against the soft sound of the lute, with the great dunes – golden or amber or red – in the background, epitomizes for me the essence of Buraimi. It is now known as Al 'Ain since the actual town of Buraimi lies in the Sultan of Muscat's territory.

It was in the middle of July 1965 that I reached England on retirement from Abu Dhabi. I had served for twenty-five years in the Sudan and sixteen years in Arabia. I had no particular place to settle, for I had sold my house at Effingham, which looked over farm land to the Surrey hills. It had been my mother's home since 1934; while I was abroad a building like an aeroplane hangar had been put up at the foot of the garden, ruining the view. It was clear that life at home on a small pension would be very restricted, and that the capital which formed my private means would soon disappear.

I spent some time in lecturing, both to the Central Asia Society and, at the invitation of the English Speaking Union, in the United

States. This was a fascinating month, covering the continent from coast to coast. In the meantime an opportunity occurred, which I jumped at, of returning to temporary service in my old district of the Sudan as an adviser to the Food and Administrative Organization of the United Nations.

So I bought a Volkswagen Dormobile and set out with a friend, Donald Kilgour, and my Arabian driver Bakri who had been my head boy for ten years, for a leisurely tour of Southern Europe and North Africa before going on to the Sudan. I was entranced by Morocco and the country round Tangier, and I decided to make it my place of retirement. I bought a house on what is called the New Mountain, with splendid views of the Riff ranges to the east.

At this point in the journey I received a letter from the Emperor of Ethiopia asking me to be his guest at the celebrations to mark the twenty-fifth anniversary of the reconquest of his country from the Italians. I welcomed the invitation, which was followed, very thoughtfully, by a return air ticket. The following ten days as the Emperor's guest in Addis Ababa were memorable; the celebrations were most impressive, and the hospitality unsurpassed. In Addis I found a number of old friends who were also enjoying the Emperor's generosity, among them Laurens van der Post, Wilfred Thesiger, Chapman Andrews, Ringrose and Dan Sandford and his wife. The Emperor's endurance amazed us all. After taking the salute, standing for six hours in a fiercely hot sun, at a march past of the armed forces and representatives of the patriots and civilian groups, he graciously shook hands for another hour with every single one of his personal guests. When the time came to say goodbye, he gave each of us who had served him in the Gojjam campaign a silver cigarette case emblazoned with the imperial arms in gold.

On my return to Morocco, we resumed our tour. While we were in Tunis, I heard from Zaid Bin Sultan, who had been governor of Buraimi and my good friend throughout my time as Political Agent in Abu Dhabi and who had now succeeded his brother Shakhbut as Sheikh. He invited me to spend the winter with him, and I gladly agreed to join him in Abu Dhabi after Ramadan in the following January (1968) when the work in the Sudan would be finished.

I had re-visited the Sudan regularly since I left in 1949, and once more I found the people as welcoming and hospitable as I had always known them. After attending a F.A.O. seminar in Khartoum, I flew out to Western Darfur to advise on a project in Zalingei. Outwardly it had altered little, but the work which had been done in building dams and irrigation works, and the sight of large areas of newly planted citrus, were impressive. The only worry was over markets and the cost of transport from this remote land behind the great Marra Mountains.

The Dimingawi held a large party for me, where I met old friends, and then I visited many of the villages I had known well as a D.C. The people were enormously welcoming, and all remembered and called me by my Fur name, Dongol.

I returned by Land Rover, and passing through Kas village, I called in on the shartai's Court, which was in session. The open Court House which Beaton and I had designed in 1936 was still in use; the young shartai, who had been one of my 'Green Hats' and had now succeeded his father, was trying a case, sitting with his back to me. As soon as I stepped out of the Land Rover, the accused, witnesses, the Court Elders and peons came rushing out without a word to the President and started to hug me in the usual Sudani fashion when greeting an old friend. Basi Deldum, the young shartai, turned round in bewilderment at the sudden disappearance of the entire courtroom, and then followed them. It was some time before we could re-assemble the Court, when I suggested that I should sit and have tea with them. The incident was a fitting climax to a heart-warming visit.

After a trip to Kassala to see Sheikh Qadal, who had retired there after his service as Minister of the Qu'aiti State, I eventually found my way to Abu Dhabi, and at Buraimi, his spiritual home in the Sheikhdom, I was given a hospitable welcome by Sheikh Zaid. I spent two happy months there, which happened to include a state visit by King Hussein, and it was late March 1968 when I left to return to Tangier.

I settled down in my new house, and set about writing down these memories. This looked like genuine retirement at last, but fate worked out differently. I received a summons from Sheikh Zaid to come back to Abu Dhabi and take charge of his stud of ninety or so mares, foals and stallions, on a farm below the Oman Mountains, where the broken violet ranges border on the red-gold sands of the Rub-al-Khali.

On my return I found an Arabian Klondyke in being. Al 'Ain, the Inner Capital, was crowded with every tribe and race from the Middle East. At every turn I found welcoming laughing faces of Arabs from the Hadhramaut, from Muscat, from Aden and all the Trucial States, from the Sudan and from Jordan – men whom I had known or met during the past forty-five years' service in these countries. It was indeed a cheerful atmosphere to return to. I was happy to be serving once more a people among whom I had worked for most of my life.

To those of my generation who fought in the First World War as we were stepping into life at eighteen or nineteen, the experience was indelible. The war stands like a great peak on the horizon of one's life; the lengthening perspective of the intervening years never seems to have taken one much further from it. To be still alive at the end of it was almost unbelievable, and the fact of survival gave me an even greater zest for life. I have never ceased to be thankful for the gift of life, and in turn life has been good to me.

I learned, too, the worth of comradeship in shared danger, and the astonishing resources of the human spirit. That spirit can be the same, I found, in Cossack or Sherpa, in a Sudanese farmer, or an Ethiopian patriot, in an Arabian seiyid or a Bedouin nomad. Honour, courage, unselfishness and a good heart stamp the true man whatever his land or race. These are not just military qualities, though no good soldier lacks them. I found them just as frequently in ordinary life when fortune led me from soldiering to administration.

There can be few deeper satisfactions than to have played a part in helping a country or a people forward – to a life of peace, with agriculture and commerce prospering, under an honest government with justice administered under the rule of law, with education for the young, with medical care for the sick. We can never accomplish all that we hope to do, but to have left something better than we found it is our due return for the gift of life. As I said to the people of Mukalla when I bade them farewell, 'There is one end, our works live after us and by their fruits we should be judged in days to come. If we have worked well and faithfully, then it is well.'

INDEX